Orly

you made a wise choice

D Bubalce

4/22/23

PSYCHOSOCIAL POLITICAL DYSFUNCTION OF THE REPUBLICAN PARTY

Dr. Daniel Brubaker

Copyright © 2022 Dr. Daniel Brubaker.

All rights reserved. No part of this book may be used or reproduced by any means, graphic, electronic, or mechanical, including photocopying, recording, taping or by any information storage retrieval system without the written permission of the author except in the case of brief quotations embodied in critical articles and reviews.

Any diagnoses made in this book are made strictly on the obvious observable behavior of a person. No medical history, physical, or psychologic testing was completed to validate these observations. Nevertheless, facts, not fiction, are presented.

Archway Publishing books may be ordered through booksellers or by contacting:

Archway Publishing
1663 Liberty Drive
Bloomington, IN 47403
www.archwaypublishing.com
844-669-3957

Because of the dynamic nature of the Internet, any web addresses or links contained in this book may have changed since publication and may no longer be valid. The views expressed in this work are solely those of the author and do not necessarily reflect the views of the publisher, and the publisher hereby disclaims any responsibility for them.

Any people depicted in stock imagery provided by Getty Images are models, and such images are being used for illustrative purposes only. Certain stock imagery © Getty Images.

ISBN: 978-1-6657-2755-6 (sc)
ISBN: 978-1-6657-2754-9 (hc)
ISBN: 978-1-6657-2756-3 (e)

Library of Congress Control Number: 2022913985

Print information available on the last page.

Archway Publishing rev. date: 08/05/2022

CONTENTS

About the Author ix
Introduction xi

Chapter 1   Republican Confusion in Differentiating Fact versus
            Fiction 1
Chapter 2   Republicans Behave Like Toddlers 47
Chapter 3   Psychology of Represented Personality Disorder
            Associated with Republicans 59
Chapter 4   Why Republicans Call Democrats Socialists:
            Understanding Socialism versus Utilitarianism 77
Chapter 5   Understanding Crowd and Herd Psychology 111
Chapter 6   Fascism and the Republican Party 159
Chapter 7   Psychosocial Analysis of the Republican Party 181
Chapter 8   Psychology of President Donald Trump 221
Chapter 9   Summation of the Psychosocial Dysfunction of the
            Republican Party 237
Chapter 10 Recommendations to Reform the Republican Party... 267

"This book is dedicated to the preservation of Democracy"
–Dr. Daniel Brubaker.

ABOUT THE AUTHOR

Dr. Daniel B. Brubaker has spent half his career in academic medicine, including the University of Pittsburgh Health Science Center, Oklahoma University Health Science Center, the University of California, Los Angeles (UCLA), and the University of California, San Francisco (UCSF) Departments of Pathology. He has spent the past twenty years in medicine. A lifelong registered Republican, he is deeply concerned about the direction of the party.

INTRODUCTION

The Grand Old Party (GOP) is no longer the party of Lincoln, even though they refer to Abraham Lincoln continuously. It is apparent that the party has lost its way with increasing speed in the past two decades. Why?

Republicans have had difficulty distinguishing fact from fiction. Facts have become blurred with nonfacts. Some Republicans in Congress spin conspiracy theories and lies, all the while claiming to Americans that theirs is the voice of truth. Chapter 1 discusses facts, untruths, and beliefs.

Republicans also often act like five-year-olds. Chapter 2 provides context about the neuropsychological development of two- to five-year-olds.

Observation tells us that at least some of the leadership in the Republican Party have antisocial personality disorders. Chapter 3 provides an understanding of antisocial personality disorders.

The Republicans frequently direct their fear toward Democrats by calling the other side socialists. This is fearmongering. Today's Republicans do not understand socialism or utilitarianism; they are simply buzzwords used to invoke fear. Chapter 4 provides further context and understanding.

The Republican Party has developed a Far Right nationalist agenda. Chapter 5 addresses this troubling issue.

Chapters 6 and 7 analyze how the Republican Party has moved to the far, Far Right, led by a clinically psychopathic president.

Chapter 8 reviews crowd psychology to understand why the Republican Party has evolved into the dysfunctional crowd it is today.

Finally, chapter 9 summarizes all the facts of the preceding chapters for a better understanding of the psychosocial political dysfunction of the Republican Party, and chapter 10 presents ideas for how to change them.

Words are linguistic facts. Definitions of words used in morality, politics, religion, psychology, and science are provided, since many of the terms are used in the book.

CHAPTER 1

REPUBLICAN CONFUSION IN DIFFERENTIATING FACT VERSUS FICTION

Introduction

Republicans talk about fact versus fiction. It is interesting they even discuss the two because more than 50 percent of Republicans in Congress cannot separate fact from fiction. President Donald Trump has told thousands of lies to the American people, and Republicans in his footsteps have done the same. The American people have been fed a steady diet of misinformation and conspiracy theories, and it has made them confused and fearful. Representative Devin Nunes from California released a podcast titled "Fact versus Fiction." In this chapter, we describe the difference between the two and provide a path for people to make distinctions.

Definitions in This Chapter:

> **Fact**—a thing that is known or proven to be true.
> **Nonfact**—a thing that is known or proven to be untrue.
> **Fiction**—something that is invented or untrue.

A fact is something that is known to be consistent with objective reality and that can be proven to be true with evidence (Wikipedia).

Facts versus Nonfacts

Facts come in various formats (e.g., words and definitions are linguistic facts, recipes are gastronomic facts, and drugs are pharmaceutical facts).

Fiction is the antonym for fact. However, it is more appropriate to consider the term *nonfact* for several reasons. Fiction has a special definition that does not include all of the synonyms that oppose facts. For example, true-or-false tests measure a person's understanding of fact versus fiction. But more specifically, these questions ask whether something is a fact or a nonfact. The purpose of this chart is to show the reader linguistic terms to differentiate fact versus nonfact.

Fact	Nonfact
true	false
nonfiction	fiction
truth	lie, untruth
honest	dishonest
trick	illusion
right	wrong
truth	deceit
genuine	fake
logic	illogical
sincerity	hoax
reality	fantasy, delusion
real	imagined
truth	perjury
honest	fraud
truth	scam
goodness	con
goodness	slander

goodness	bribe
good	evil
fair	cheat
order	chaos
knowledge	belief

Facts can be documented in the following ways:

- observation
- identification
- documentation
- analysis
- investigation
- experimentation (types)
- statistical methods
- verification

Observation

According to the *Oxford English Dictionary*, the definition of *observation* is the action or process of closely observing or monitoring something or someone. Our own observations are dependent on our senses. We use our eyes in most observations, but certainly smell, taste, and hearing—as well as the sensory portion of your nervous system, touch—play a role in observation as well.

Vision is the most common method of observation. Seeing water bubble in a pot on a hot stove indicates the water is boiling. Vision is like a camera. The eyelid is the shutter; the pupil is the aperture; the lens is built in; the retina is the sensor; the occipital lobe of the brain is the processor; and the hippocampus is the memory card. The difference is that the human brain has a frontal lobe that can determine what is a good picture and what isn't. Can vision be fooled and not factual? It can. It is possible to observe something that is a nonfact.

Take, for example, illusions. An illusion, as the *Oxford English Dictionary* explains, is "1. An instance of a wrong or misinterpreted perception of a sensory experience. 2. A deceptive appearance or impression." We think of illusions as being visual. Things like art, pictures, and nature can cause illusions. So while we still observe these things visually, they can trick the brain.

Magicians make us think they pulled a rabbit out of a hat. However, observing the trick more closely provides the fact behind the illusion. Magicians are dishonest in their trade, but people enjoy being tricked and pay money for these illusions.

Art can also create illusions. One of the most well-known artists to produce an illusion was Leonardo da Vinci. When you look at his famous painting, the *Mona Lisa*, she has a subtle smile, but if you look at it with peripheral vision, the smile changes and becomes much deeper.

Photographers can use camera tricks to make two-dimensional pictures look three-dimensional. All types of photography can cause illusions.

Drawing illusions is also possible with perspective drawing. As kids, we learned how to draw a three-dimensional box by drawing a box within a box and connecting the lines. We learn how to make the three-dimensional box, and in the process, we analyze how it is drawn.

Illusions occur in nature. As an example, you may be walking on a trail in the woods and look down at a tuft of grass next to the trail and see what appears to be a rabbit. But as you approach the rabbit, it turns out to be rocks that simply looked like a rabbit. Nature has an abundance of illusions. Many creatures use camouflage for survival. You may look directly at a creature and not see it until it is frightened and moves.

Vision provides the most tricks to our brain, but smell, taste, and hearing may also instigate illusions.

Knowledge, experience, and analysis turn our illusions to facts.

These illusions can be considered fiction, untruths, or nonfacts. However, knowing an illusion exists is a fact in itself.

In the process of making observations, things must be identified. This is important for the purposes of documentation, analysis, experimentation, and verification.

Identification

Identification is defined as follows: 1. The action or process of identifying someone or something or the fact of being identified. 2. A means of proving a person's identity, especially in the form of official papers.

Identification is a large part of observation. This includes vision, smell, taste, feeling sensations, and hearing. Vision is the most important tool for identification. Everything we see is identification. Everything we see is a fact, real, or unreal (illusion).

Identification is a method of labeling things. The animal and plant kingdoms are useful examples of humans processing things into order. Humans continue to observe, identify, and label things. We label and classify anything from a new bacteria two miles deep into the earth to a new galaxy many light-years away.

Things can also be misidentified. This can be intentional or unintentional. Unintentional misidentification may occur, for example, if two microbiologists discover a new microorganism and have two different terms for it. In such cases, an agreement is usually reached through scientific reasoning.

Intentional misidentification is the result of dishonesty. Art forgery, for example, relies on misidentification. Identity theft is a real problem. When Vice President Al Gore introduced us to the internet in the 1990s, it all looked incredibly positive. However, over the past thirty years, evil has been introduced to the World Wide Web, and bad things are happening, especially with social media. It is easier than ever to steal someone's identity.

Documentation

Documentation is material that provides official information or evidence or that serves as a record, whereas a document is a piece of written, printed, or electronic matter that provides information or evidence or that serves as an official record. To document is also a verb meaning to record (something) in written, photographic, or other form.

Recording information is important to documenting facts. Practically everything we do is documented in some way. It is written, typed, or recorded some other way.

One must always be careful with legal documents. With the purchase of a house, we get hundreds of papers of small print. We often do not comb over every minute detail but trust the person representing the mortgage company. In the first decade of this century, people were signing papers with balloon mortgages intentionally written into the fine print. Everything was fine until the third year when one had to pay off the lender. This led to multiple foreclosures and damage to the housing market.

We get messages on our phones and computers regarding terms of service, updates, and so on. There is a lot of legal language in small print, which most of us do not read, yet we agree to allow the update to continue. As consumers, we trust many legal documents without reading the fine print.

Documentation is especially important in science, medicine, law enforcement, law, government, and media.

In science and research, methods and results must be recorded to determine factual results. Fraud occurs when records are falsified. Dishonesty always has a role in presenting false facts.

With documentation, there is no presumption or assumption. These arise when documentation is falsified. However, interpretation of the documented facts can lead to the assumption that the fact is most likely true. However, further proof is needed.

Documentation is extremely important in medicine as well as other professions. For example, if a patient goes to see their doctor and complains of sadness and periodic crying, the doctor documents this in the patient's chart. The doctor would assume the patient is depressed, which is highly probable. However, it is a presumption. Is the patient depressed or sad for some reason? More investigation is needed. The doctor takes a history by asking questions that address the how, where, and when the sadness occurred. Perhaps the patient's best friend died three weeks prior, there is no history of depression in the patient's family, and the patient wasn't depressed prior to the incident. The patient is examined, and no physical cause for the sadness is determined. The doctor then makes the diagnosis of adjustment disorder with depression, and the doctor helps the patient deal with the sadness through support groups, counseling, and possibly a short-term antidepressant. This documentation is then used for future reference, and should the patient require further treatment, another health care provider can use this documentation.

Documentation occurs in the present and is frequently used in the future. That is, facts that are documented today may be helpful in the future. Documents are often disputed and argued, especially by professionals. However, the more details the document contains, the less chance there is for dispute.

Analysis

Analysis is the key to observation and fact-finding. It is defined as a detailed examination of the elements or structure of something.

Most people use analysis every day, whether at home or work. For example, you're driving your car, and it suddenly sputters. You look at the gas gauge and see that you have enough gas. What could it be? You take the car to a mechanic, and the first analysis is that the problem is the spark plugs. They are replaced, and the engine no longer sputters. You and the mechanic went through an analytical process to determine the fact the spark plugs were worn out. Experience plays a role, because if this happened to you in the past, you may be able to determine the problem. Knowledge also plays a role, because if you are a mechanic or mechanically inclined, you would know to replace the spark plugs before they wear out.

Assumptions and presumptions do not have a role in the analysis of facts. For example, you awake in the morning and find the ground, driveway, and road are all wet. You assume it rained during the night. The probability is that it rained. However, you have no proof or facts that it rained. You did not see, feel, or hear the rain because you were asleep. It could have snowed or hailed during the night and melted by morning. The inquisitive will further investigate or find evidence. You may walk out in the yard and find evidence of residual snow or hail in the cold, dark areas of the yard. Factually, it snowed during the night. Since you are not sure why the ground is wet, the weatherman on the morning news can provide the reason for you. Suppose they say it rained with pockets of hail. Examination in detail will provide the facts. You cannot assume or presume anything in fact-finding.

Analysis is an important part of our lives used to determine facts and truth. The normal brain wants to know the truth and facts. A con artist will present false facts to manipulate us. A con artist may say something like "You need to buy this stock now, because the company was just issued a patent, and it will make you a lot of money." Did the company have a new patent? To find the truth and facts, one would need to conduct a patent search. The product may not be desirable in the marketplace. The company may be going into bankruptcy. The con artist preys on people who do not do their analytical homework. Lack of knowledge, experience, and failure to analyze play into a con artist's hands.

The antonym to analysis is synthesis. Synthesis can also be useful in the creation of facts. It is a different methodology. Analysis breaks down information or elements to facts and truth, whereas synthesis takes elements of information and creates the sum total of something. It takes facts and builds a truth.

The example above with the con artist selling stocks requires vigilance and knowledge. The person can take patents, plus financial company strength, and tell you that you will make money. The con is taking false elements or information and arriving (synthesis) at you making money. But this is a false synthesis. However, as we return to investigation of elements or information, facts and truth will prevail.

Investigation

Investigation is the act of investigating something or someone, formal or systematic examination or research.

Investigation is an important element to identifying facts. It is the process of collecting information. Investigation occurs in four major areas: medicine, law enforcement, science, and news/journalism. The key to investigation is knowledge.

In medicine, a doctor uses several tools to investigate and provide a diagnosis. The first step is to take a good medical history and ask what the person is feeling. A thorough examination of the patient is essential. This provides the basis for further investigation, such as laboratory tests, x-rays, radiology studies, biopsies, questionnaires, specialty consults, and procedures.

For example, if a person comes into the doctor's office gasping for air, many people's first thought will be asthma. However, once the questions are answered, things change.

"When did this begin?"

"Just now."

"Where did it start?"

"I was in an orchard photographing peach blossoms."

"What happened?"

"I felt a sting on my arm!"

The doctor knows that beekeepers often place beehives in orchards to pollinate blossoms and suspects a bee sting. The doctor's examination is positive for pulmonary issues. The patient gets an injection of Epinephrine, and the symptoms subside. The doctor prescribes the patient an EpiPen to use on any future bee stings. This is a simple example regarding the investigative processes for medicine.

Law enforcement also uses tools to investigate crimes. Videos, fingerprints, DNA testing, and witnesses are only a few. Again, knowledge and training are imperative to finding the facts.

Science has many tools used for investigation, depending on the scientific area. Agriculture, weather, chemistry, and astronomy all have their methods and tools for investigating a problem.

We hear all types of investigation in the news each day. This can be anything from reporting a crime on the local news to more detailed investigative reporting like *60 Minutes*. The intent is to present the facts to educate the public.

Can there be false investigation? Absolutely! This is probably most common in law enforcement, where the facts can be skewed, especially by witnesses, who are notoriously unreliable.

Experimentation (Types)

An experiment is a procedure designed to test a hypothesis as part of the scientific method. There are three main types of scientific experiments: experimental, quasi-experimental, and observational/nonexperimental. Experimental experiments are the most detailed, and they show cause and effect.

Experiments must have a design. We call this experimental design. It should have the following protocol or steps:

1. Make observations.
2. Formulate a hypothesis.
3. Design and conduct an experiment to test the hypothesis.
4. Evaluate the results of the experiment.
5. Accept or reject the hypothesis.
6. If necessary, make and test a new hypothesis.

This process will generate facts, not fiction. As the experiment plays out, it will be determined whether the facts it generates are expected or unexpected.

The following is from *Thought Commodification* by Anne Marie Helmenstine, PhD. Dr. Helmenstine holds a PhD in biomedical sciences and is a science writer, educator, and consultant. She has taught science courses at the high school, college, and graduate levels.

Updated September 20, 2018: https://www.thoughtco.com/what-is-an-experiment-607970.

Science is concerned with experiments and experimentation, but do you know what exactly an experiment is? Here is a look at what an experiment is … and isn't!

Types of experiments:

1. *Natural experiments:* A natural experiment is also called a quasi-experiment. A natural experiment involves making a prediction or forming a hypothesis and then gathering data by observing a system. The variables are not controlled in a natural experiment.

2. *Controlled experiments:* Laboratory experiments are controlled experiments, although you can perform a controlled experiment outside of a lab setting. In a controlled experiment, you compare an experimental group with a control group. Ideally, these two groups are identical except for one variable, the independent variable.
3. *Field experiments:* A field experiment may be either a natural experiment or a controlled experiment. It takes place in a real-world setting, rather than under lab conditions. For example, an experiment involving an animal in its natural habitat would be a field experiment.

Where experiments are mostly conducted:

- biology
- chemistry
- physics
- ecology
- geology
- astronomy
- weather
- agriculture
- medicine

Variables in an Experiment

Simply put, a variable is anything you can change or control in an experiment. Common examples of variables include temperature, duration of the experiment, composition of a material, amount of light, and so on. There are three kinds of variables in an experiment: controlled variables, independent variables, and dependent variables.

Controlled variables, sometimes called constant variables, are variables that are kept constant or unchanging. For example, if you are doing an experiment measuring the fizz released from different types of soda, you might control the size of the container so that all brands of soda are in twelve-ounce cans. If you are performing an experiment on the effect of spraying plants with different chemicals, you would try to maintain the same pressure and the same volume when spraying your plants.

The *independent variable* is the one factor that you change in an experiment. It is *one* factor because usually in an experiment, you try to change one thing at a time. This makes measurements and interpretation of the data much easier. If you are trying to determine whether heating water allows you to dissolve sugar in the water, then your independent variable is the temperature of the water. This is the variable you are purposely controlling.

For example, take three two-quart pots and add one quart of water to each pot. Heat one pot of water to 50°F, another to 100°F, and the third to 200°F. These temperatures are the independent variable. Take a half cup of sugar and add it to the first pot and with a stopwatch time how fast the sugar dissolves. You may get a reading of forty-five seconds in the first pot, twenty seconds in the second pot, and five seconds in the third pot. As noted, the independent variable is temperature, but other variables were also controlled, such as the amount of water, size of the pot, and amount of sugar.

The *dependent variable* is the variable you observe. The times at which sugar dissolves are the dependent variables, because they were dependent upon the independent variable, the temperature of the water. Similarly, you could use one pot and heat the water to 200°F and add different amounts of sugar to see how fast a half cup versus a whole cup of sugar takes to dissolve. The independent variable in this example is the amount of sugar, and the dependent variable is the time for the sugar to dissolve.

Examples of Things That Are *Not* Experiments

- making a model volcano
- making a poster

- trying something, just to see what happens (On the other hand, making observations or trying something, after making a prediction about what you expect will happen, *is* a type of experiment.)

Do all scientific studies provide accurate facts? The importance of experimentation is to find the true facts. By controlling variables, the results become accurate facts. However, because something is an experiment does not guarantee that the results are true facts. Fraud and cheating to produce desired results are not facts but rather nonfacts. Using the example above with the sugar and water experiment, the investigator could make up times to produce the results they want to convey. Fraud can also occur in science and medicine.

A prime fraudulent medical publication is the link between vaccines and autism. One of the largest and most damaging fraudulent medical claims is the link between vaccines and autism. Dr. Andrew Wakefield published a paper in in the medical journal *Lancet* describing eight children who showed signs of autism within days of being inoculated for measles, mumps, and rubella. A gastroenterologist by training, Dr. Wakefield went on in further studies to suggest that the virus from the vaccine was leading to inflammation in the child's stomach and intestines that then impeded normal brain development. He obtained blood samples from different children, failed to pass ethics review committees, and was paid by attorneys to litigate companies producing the vaccines. Meanwhile, some parents around the world—especially in the United Kingdom and the United States—keep their children from being vaccinated out of this fear of their child developing autism. In fact, autism results from a genetic mutation, not from a vaccine or inflammation of the brain. But because of this fraudulent and dangerous claim, there are measles outbreaks throughout the UK and the US as well as other countries.

It took decades to disprove Dr. Wakefield's study and publications, but many comparative studies were performed that found no link between vaccinations and autism.

The Famous Animal Transplantation Scam

Dr. William Summerlin, a dermatologist by training, was studying as an Immunology Research Fellow under the renowned immunologist Dr. Robert A. Good at Memorial Sloan-Kettering Cancer Institute in New York City.

Dr. Summerlin's research was in transplant immunology, which involved transplanting tissue between animals without rejection of the transplanted tissue.

In 1974, Dr. Summerlin claimed he had transplanted skin from black mice (high in melanocytes—cells that cause black skin) into white mice. His claim was that he placed the black skin into a special media for a period of time and then transplanted it onto the skin of white mice. As a result, the white mice grew black hair. The mice were genetically different, and normally when tissue is transplanted between two different species, the tissue is rejected by the host's immune system.

Experienced transplant immunologists questioned Dr. Summerlin's discovery, but Dr. Good was not properly informed, and the claim was published. Everyone thought this was a breakthrough in transplantation, because after transplantation, rejection occurs unless medications are used to suppress the immune system in the transplanted animal. How did it come about that there was falsification of data in the study?

The fraudulent claim was discovered when a technician wiped alcohol over the black skin and hair of the white mouse with the transplanted black skin. The alcohol removed the colored hair. Dr. Summerlin had used a black marking pen to create the area of transplanted skin.

Dr. Summerlin was investigated. He had been under a lot of pressure to publish a dramatic finding in transplant immunology. This is a common issue in academic settings where there is a lot of pressure to obtain grants and funding for research. There is a lot of pressure to publish and find a new discovery.

How can scientific fraud be prevented? Measures such as knowledge, experience, analysis, investigation, logic, and reasoning can prevent falsification of data (facts). In medicine and science, data is reviewed by experts in the area of the experiment. Usually, three experts review the manuscript before it is published. This is called peer review, and it occurs in reputable journals. Even experts can be fooled. *Lancet* is a peer-reviewed journal, but the vaccine/autism data was published in *Lancet,* which later retracted the publication.

One of the best methods to be sure of the data (facts) of any experiment is verification. Several studies were performed to prove/disprove the data that was published showing that vaccines did not cause autism. Dr. Andrew Wakefield, who fraudulently linked vaccines to autism, lost his medical license, a small price to pay considering the rise in measles and the public health crisis his false research caused.

References:

Bailey, R. A. 2008. *Design of Comparative Experiments.* Cambridge: Cambridge University Press.
Beveridge, William I. B. 1950. *The Art of Scientific Investigation.* Heinemann: Melbourne, Australia.
di Francia, G. Toraldo. 1981. *The Investigation of the Physical World.* Cambridge University Press. ISBN 0-521-29925-X.
Hinkelmann, Klaus, and Oscar Kempthorne. 2008. *Design and Analysis of Experiments, Volume I: Introduction to Experimental Design* (2nd ed.). Hoboken, NJ: Wiley.
Shadish, William R., Thomas D. Cook, and Donald T. Campbell. 2002. *Experimental and Quasi-Experimental Designs for Generalized Causal Inference.* Boston: Houghton Mifflin.

Statistical Methods

There are three important terms necessary for understanding statistics and statistical methods: sample size, independent variables, and dependent variables.

Sample size is a count of individual samples or observations in a statistical setting, such as a scientific experiment or a survey distributed to the general public. When it comes to surveys, sample size more precisely refers to the number of completed responses a survey receives.

In an experimental design, the independent variable is the variable that is manipulated by the experimenter to determine its relationship to an observed phenomenon, called the *dependent variable*. The dependent variable is also called the response variable.

Sample size (n) is extremely important to the legitimacy of any scientific study or survey. Suppose twenty people come into Baskin-Robbins for ice cream. Ten of them buy Rocky Road, and the other ten buy other flavors. A male customer comes in and asks the ice-cream attendant, "What is Baskin-Robbins's most desired flavor of ice cream by patrons?" The attendant tells him that it is Rocky Road. The attendant assumes that he is asking about his store. However, the question is general in that it asks the question regarding the favorite flavor of customers who buy ice cream at Baskin-Robbins. The sample size for that store is adequate because it is more than ten. Ten percent is the absolute number in sample size for evaluation in statistics.

If the question was "What is the favorite flavor patrons are choosing in your store today?" the answer from the attendant would be correct. But going back to the original question, "What is Baskin-Robbins's most desired flavor of ice cream by patrons?" Baskin-Robbins would need to do a survey of their 7,500 stores worldwide. The accepted sample size for this number of stores would require a survey of no less than 10 percent of their stores, or 750. The favorite might be determined to be strawberry. That is worldwide data. What about in the United States, where there are 2,500 stores? The same question could be asked, but the location must be stipulated.

One must consider independent variables. Independent variables for the Baskin-Robbins survey could include time (season) of year of the survey, the time of day, South versus North, and what day of the month it is. Baskin-Robbins has thirty-one flavors, a new flavor for each day in a month (thirty-one days). For example, strawberry may be the favorite in July, and coffee may be the favorite in January.

There are many independent variables that must be known to provide facts. In science and medicine, experimental investigation must control for independent variables in order to come to factual conclusions.

We have been describing surveys. The news is inundated with presidential polls, which are also surveys with applied statistics. We will hear a report such as "Biden is leading President Trump by 10 percent." How factual is this statistic? Again, there are many independent variables, and we do not know, as viewers, how the study was conducted. There are 350 million Americans. Did they use the minimum sample size of 10 percent and survey 350,000 Americans? Maybe they only used 3,000 Americans. Is this poll accurate or factual? No, because they did not follow the 10 percent sample size rule. Why do we accept perceived facts without full information? We base it on trust that the surveyors followed the rules of statistics, but trust can be manipulated.

Accuracy is important in statistical analysis. If you shoot target practice and you shot the center of the target, the bull's-eye, ten out of ten times, this would display excellent accuracy. Polling 350,000 Americans in ten locations and receiving the same results would indicate the polling is accurate.

Accuracy is precise, but precision is not necessarily accurate. A baseball pitcher can throw a ball in the same location just outside the strike zone three times in the same location. That is precision, not accuracy. He did not throw the ball accurately in the strike zone three times.

When comparing facts within or between surveys, one must consider the margin of error. This takes into consideration the sample size. A *margin of error* tells you how many percentage points your results will differ from the real population value. For example, a 95 percent confidence interval with a 4 percent margin of error means that your statistic will be within four percentage points of the real population value 95 percent of the time.

Margin of error is important in coming to a factual conclusion. The *margin of error* around an estimate is important because it helps you draw conclusions about the data. Small differences between two estimates may not be statistically significant if the confidence intervals of those estimates overlap.

Accuracy again enters into the outcome in margin of error. The number of acceptable errors in an experiment or survey tells the accuracy of truth. A smaller margin of error indicates accurate or trustworthy results, and a larger margin of error means the results are not as well considered.

Returning to our Baskin-Robbins example: We want to know what flavor Americans most desire. There are 2,500 stores in America. An accepted sample size of stores is 250. We want to survey 40,000 patrons. We need to choose a sample size because we do not want to survey 400,000. We pick 4,000 patrons, which is an acceptable 10 percent. Suppose 60 percent choose Rocky Road. The margin of error is the square root of the sample size sixty-three divided into the standard deviation of our population times the score of the confidence level of 95 percent to equal about 2 percent margin of error between other flavors. This shows the higher the sample size, the lower margin of error.

Let us take sample size into our elections. As an example, the popular vote is seventy million votes, and the Electoral College is 538 votes. Seventy million is a high sample number with a low bias and low margin of error, whereas the Electoral College is unrepresented, biased, and has a high margin of error, just by sample size alone. For example, the state of California is underrepresented just by population alone.

Science and medicine are similar to surveys. The absolute minimum test is ten; sample size should be larger than 10 percent; experimental design, methods of investigation, data evaluation with statistics are all important to compiling the fact(s). The reasoning for all this is to prevent precarious assumptions.

Let's say I have a drug X that I claim will correct blood pressure to 120/80 millimeters of mercury (mm Hg), which is normal. I take ten patients with high blood pressure (hypertension) who have blood pressures over 120/80 mm Hg, and all ten patients drop their blood pressure to exactly 120/80. Is drug X really working that well, or is this a fluke? We can solve this by taking one hundred patients with hypertension (say 130/85 to 220/120 mm Hg). In ninety out of one hundred, the patients responded with a blood pressure of 120/80 mm Hg, five had a blood pressure of 90/60, and five had a pressure of 140/90. We now must evaluate the independent variables. In the five with low blood pressure, did they take more drug X than prescribed or was their blood pressure borderline (i.e., 130/85) in the study? The same investigation must also be evaluated on those five patients who did not drop their pressure to 120/80. A huge independent variable would be race. African Americans have a higher prevalence of hypertension than Caucasians. All variables must be controlled. One way of controlling this variable would be to use drug X to test hypertensive African Americans versus hypertensive Caucasians.

There are many independent variables to be considered in a study—not only race but age, sex, food, salt intake, pharmacology of the drug, and on and on.

Suppose I discovered this new drug. I formed my own company to get grants and money to perform the studies above. I got patents to protect it, and I have spent $500,000 to determine all the facts concerning the drug. I would like to recover my money and help patients with hypertension, because I found drug X to be more effective than any other antihypertensive drug. I want to get the drug approved by the Food and Drug Administration (FDA). The FDA needs efficacy and safety of the drug to be proven.

The FDA will decide how to prove efficacy and safety. They provide the parameters (controlled independent variables) and experimental design. The FDA promotes double-blind studies. A double-blind study is one where a control group with hypertension does not get drug X (but instead gets a placebo, often called a sugar pill), and the hypertensive study group receives drug X. No one knows who is receiving which drug. The FDA decides the number of patients studied. They will pick several study sites. This all adds up to lots of money until drug X passes for marketing. The average cost of getting a new drug to market is $2–$4 billion.

Congress wants to know why drugs in America cost more than other counties, like Canada. Canada does not pay the billions of dollars to get the drug to patients. The FDA is powerful, and they get paid and force companies to pay this amount of money to be sure the drug is safe and effective. Then when it is approved, suppose ten people have crippling side effects. The product liability attorneys now force the company to pay out a billion dollars. Does anyone now know why new drugs are expensive in the US? The truth is that one can go through extensive testing and fact-finding, and there is still an X factor, or the unknown.

This establishes the fact that knowledge, experience, and verification processes are important in establishing accurate facts, true facts, and not made-up, untruthful, and fraudulent facts.

Verification

The process of establishing the truth, accuracy, or validity of something is called verification. Verification is the absolute truth in a fact. If something can be repeated with the same results or remarkably similar results, it is a fact. We already described accuracy; hitting the center of the target multiple times denotes accuracy. This cannot be refuted, because it is documented, verified, analyzed, interpreted, and concluded.

Verified facts must be clear and not left to semantics. I could be conversing about Delicious apples and say that I have ten red apples in a row. One can assume that I have Red Delicious apples in a row. However, I could have nine Red Delicious apples and one Macintosh apple. They are all red, which is a fact, but they are not all the same apple. Appearance and taste would verify that nine are Delicious and one is Macintosh. Talking about Delicious apples also requires designation between Red Delicious and Yellow Delicious apples, because when talking about Delicious apples, one can assume we are talking about Red Delicious apples.

Fact-finding is also time-consuming. Establishing a fact takes time, and verifying facts takes even longer. Before the advent of the internet, one would have to go to a textbook or the library to verify facts. In medicine, to research an area of interest, one had to go to a medical library and look up references in thick books called Index Medicus that comprised all research publications. Using the internet, PubMed indexed all of these publications from the National Medical Library. Research these days is less time-consuming thanks to search engines like Google and websites like Wikipedia. Nevertheless, verifying something factually takes time.

We have noted the importance of time in verifying facts. The example of vaccines versus autism is a good one. It took nearly a decade to prove that vaccines do not cause autism. We are still working on reversing the damage from the faulty information that was published. Measles could have been eradicated like polio, but measles continue to spread in 2020, all as a result of the false statement that autism is caused by the measles vaccine and parents thus refusing to vaccinate their children. This has caused some state health departments to force vaccinations.

Time is saved when two independent research groups work together on the same or similar problems and arrive at the same factual conclusion. This is commonly found with Nobel Prize winners who share a similar discovery.

Facts are also substantiated with several references. One frequently finds more than three hundred references in a medical textbook to substantiate the topic discussed.

People who accept information without verification allow misinformation to spread.

Viral Testing as It Applies to Two Viruses: Hepatitis and Coronavirus—Sensitivity and Specificity

Testing for viruses is an extension of how well verification operates in medicine and public health. We show the accuracy through verification processes using test sensitivity and specificity and the importance of the verification process to viral diseases. Utilizing viral testing is historic in public health and other aspects of medicine. We will use the test for hepatitis as an example.

Testing for a viral infection can be used diagnostically, for screening, or as response to the virus in the body to monitor treatment. A virus has an inner core of genetic material—deoxyribonucleic acid (DNA) or ribonucleic acid (RNA). This is the genetic material that allows the virus to replicate when it enters the body. The virus also has a core or shell around it that is made up of proteins and other chemicals. The capsule has receptors on the surface that the human body recognizes. The immune system is a complex system that protects the body. When the virus enters the body, the immune system responds by making antibodies, which attack the virus. However, the antibody response is a slow process, taking from a week to a month. After the antibody response, the immune system will remember the antibody, in some cases, for many years.

Testing for the virus itself in the body is the earliest method of detection. There are two methods now available to test for a virus. The most precise and accurate method is to test for the DNA and RNA of the virus. This kind of testing is polymerase chain reaction, or PCR testing. It is used to make millions of copies of a target piece of DNA or RNA. It is an indispensable tool in modern molecular biology and has transformed scientific research and diagnostic medicine. However, this method is expensive and labor-intensive.

The second method has been available for many years. This method inactivates the virus but keeps it intact. The inactive virus is then injected into rabbits or goats to create an immune response by forming antibodies. These antibodies are collected from the blood of the animal. The animal antibody is linked to an enzyme dye. The human sample with the suspected virus is added to the enzyme-linked antibody, a color is activated, and the presence of the virus is determined. A similar reverse method can be used to detect the antibody to the virus. One of the earliest seminal viral explorations in testing started with hepatitis B in the 1960s. Hepatitis B testing was unique in that it could be used diagnostically to monitor the disease and as a screening test.

In terms of diagnosing the disease, one had to recognize symptoms and signs of hepatitis.

Symptoms and signs are used by doctors to preliminarily diagnose a disease. Symptoms are something a person experiences, such as cough, fatigue, or joint pain. Signs are the findings or observations of a person, such as elevated temperature, percussing the liver for pain, urine sample with dark urine, and a dip stick of the urine.

Hepatitis signs and symptoms may include:

- abdominal pain over the liver
- dark urine
- fever
- joint pain
- loss of appetite
- nausea and vomiting
- weakness and fatigue
- yellowing of skin and the whites of the eyes (jaundice)

It should also be noted that these symptoms may be extremely mild and unassociated with hepatitis.

When a patient presents with these symptoms, a differential diagnosis is made with viral testing. There are three types of viral hepatitis: hepatitis A (infectious), hepatitis B, and hepatitis C. All three are detected either by antigens (the virus) or by the antibody to the virus. Hepatitis A is extremely rare. Hepatitis B and C have been transmitted through IV drug use, dirty needle tattoos, blood transfusions, and male-to-male sex.

Hepatitis B Testing for Diagnosis, Monitoring, and Screening

We noted earlier that all viruses contain nucleic acid, either DNA or RNA (but not both), and a protein coat, which encases the nucleic acid. Some viruses are also enclosed by an envelope of lipid (fat) and protein molecules. The encasement has a surface with receptors used to infiltrate a human cell. With the hepatitis B virus, there is a center DNA with a core, and the encasing portion has a surface. When the hepatitis B virus is tested in the blood, the test looks for hepatitis B surface antigen (the virus), also called HBsAg. The body mounts an immune response by forming several antibodies. One of the first antibodies is an antibody against the surface antigen called anti-hepatitis B surface antibody or anti-HBs antibody. This antibody kills the virus and protects the infected person from ever developing a hepatitis B recurrent infection. Another antibody that develops from the virus is an antibody against the core portion of the virus where the DNA is contained. This antibody is called anti-hepatitis B core antibody or anti-HBc antibody. Both anti-HB surface antibodies and anti-core antibodies remain in the body for life, but the core antibody is usually used to detect previous exposure and monitoring hepatitis B infection. If the immune system cannot kill the virus, hepatitis B antigen and hepatitis B core antibody tests remain positive. This means hepatitis B is present and continues to cause damage to the liver, eventually progressing to cirrhosis and liver cancer. All the tests for hepatitis B have 100 percent sensitivity and specificity.

Hepatitis B vaccinations are completed with three separate vaccinations at intervals. The vaccination produces antibodies to hepatitis B surface antigen, which is a marker of immunity. Its presence can be detected for thirty years, indicating an immune response to hepatitis B virus infection as an immune response to the vaccinations. The hepatitis B vaccine is also known as the first anticancer vaccine because it prevents hepatitis B, the leading cause of liver cancer worldwide.

Hepatitis B Screening

Nobel Prize winner Dr. Baruch Blumberg discovered hepatitis B in 1967. It was discovered that hepatitis B could be transmitted through blood transfusions. Mandatory testing of all blood donors began in 1972, which reduced the transfusion of hepatitis B from about 20 percent to 45 percent to less than 2 percent. However, recipients of blood transfusions developed a form of hepatitis even though the hepatitis B surface antigen was negative in transfused blood. This was called non-A, non-B hepatitis. It took over a decade to identify this virus as hepatitis C virus (HCV). Mandatory blood screening began in 1990. This was done by using an antibody test to detect hepatitis C. False positives were noted, and as a result, a test called Western blot was used to confirm the test as a true positive versus a false positive. A more specific test called the nucleic acid test for HCV ribonucleic acid found in the virus is now used. This is also known as PCR (polymerase chain reaction). A rapid PCR test, Nucleic Acid Amplified Test or NAAT, is used to confirm HCV, and this test can detect virus particles from ten to millions of viruses.

Hepatitis C Testing for Diagnosis, Monitoring, and Screening

Hepatitis C is transmitted in the same manner as hepatitis B: blood transfusions, IV drug use, and tattoos. It was first recognized in patients who received blood transfusions. As noted, blood donations were screened for hepatitis B, but patients were developing hepatitis unassociated with hepatitis B. This was called non-A, non-B hepatitis. In 1990, hepatitis C was discovered, and immediately the antibody to hepatitis C was mandated by the Food and Drug Administration for all blood donations screened for the hepatitis C antibody.

The interesting aspect of this virus is that it stays in the body undetected for years without symptoms, until a patient develops cirrhosis or liver cancer. Unlike hepatitis B using the surface antigen to detect the disease, hepatitis C uses the antibody test to screen for the virus. Why not use an antigen test? The antibody test has a 98 percent sensitivity and 100 percent specificity. Testing for the virus uses the nucleic acid amplification test (NAAT), which is more expensive. Finally, doctors started using the hepatitis C antibody test to diagnose hepatitis in their patients.

If the antibody is positive, the NAAT test is used to detect the virus. Using NAAT, six different variants containing different RNA sequences called genotypes have been identified. These genotypes are only useful to the physicians who treat hepatitis C.

Hepatitis C can now be cured with antiviral drugs. The first drug used to eliminate hepatitis C was interferon. Interferons are substances produced by cells in the body that help fight infections and certain cancers. Interferons do not directly kill viral or cancerous cells; they boost the immune system response and reduce viral production. Interferon alfa-2b injection was used initially to treat hepatitis C. The main problem in treatment was the extensive treatment time and side effects, such as severe fatigue, and interferon did not eliminate hepatitis C infection.

Direct-acting antivirals (DAAs) against hepatitis C were available in 2014 to treat patients with hepatitis C. These drugs prevent replication of the virus, which in turn kills hepatitis C viral infections. As mentioned, there are different genotypes of the virus, some more damaging and more difficult to eliminate, but there are several of these drugs that kill all genotypes. The most common genotype in America is type 1, and the drug Harvoni kills the virus without any significant side effects. Intense research and development went into discovering and implementing these drugs with the approval of the Food and Drug Administration.

As a result of extensive verification of testing, hepatitis B is prevented with vaccinations, and hepatitis C is being eliminated with drug therapy. With highly specific and sensitive tests, the blood supply for patients is the safest it has ever been.

When hepatitis C is detected with the hepatitis C antibody test, the NAAT test is used to confirm the diagnosis, and the same test is used to determine the genotype, which is useful for determining which antiviral drug to use. In addition, the NAAT test is used to quantitate the virus particles in the blood. Suppose a person with hepatitis C has a million virus particles before treatment. If, after treatment with a drug like Harvoni, the quantitative NAAT test found no viral particles, there is a presumed cure. If testing the patient a few months later indicates no virus particles in the blood, there is a cure of hepatitis C. Again, none of this can be completed without verification of tests and drugs used to cure hepatitis C.

COVID-19 Testing for Diagnosis, Monitoring, and Prevention

The coronavirus, COVID-19, is a 2020 pandemic that caused numerous deaths in a short period of time. Testing for the virus using PCR was paramount in preventing the disease. The PCR testing has a sensitivity and specificity of 100 percent. This test, in order to be accurate, cannot be done within three days of exposure, because it will return a false negative. A test will be positive between five to seven days after exposure. Also, at the beginning of the pandemic, many laboratories were start-up labs, which caused unreliable testing.

South Korea used one test and pushed testing to the highest level, which prevented many deaths. The US, with its poor leadership of the Trump administration, was negligent in its pursuit of testing. Despite the incompetence of the Trump administration, science and research from private companies such as Roche (testing) and Pfizer and Moderna (vaccines) moved rapidly to test for the virus and develop vaccines. President Trump attempted to get credit for the speed of vaccine development by calling it "Operation Warp Speed," but the vaccine technology has been in research and development for decades. The warp speed was a result of years of research by the National Institutes of Health, the premier medical research center in the US funded by Congress.

After the carnage COVID-19 has caused, it would seem obvious that when the vaccine was approved, everyone would rush to be vaccinated. But, in fact, that was not the case. The Freedom Riders and Libertarians believe it is their right to abandon any recommendations for vaccinations, using opposition defiance or narcissism. There is also a fear of science and a mistrust of reality. Anything associated with the government cannot be trusted. The only reasons for opposing COVID-19 vaccinations are a result of Donald J. Trump's lies. Smallpox has been eradicated by vaccinations; polio has been eradicated by vaccinations; and hepatitis B has almost been eradicated with vaccinations. The only way COVID-19 can be eradicated is through vaccinations or antiviral drugs like those used for treatment of hepatitis C.

The Gray Area of Facts: Opinion, Belief, and Quasi-Facts

People often accept opinion as fact, which is a mistake. This is especially true in law and politics. The definition of opinion delineates the two.

Opinion

Opinion: 1. A view or judgment formed about something, not necessarily based on fact or knowledge. 2. A statement of advice by an expert on a professional matter.

The two words are without facts or knowledge. I have been stressing the importance of combating nonfacts through experiments, surveys, experience, education, and knowledge.

Law is especially prone to opinion. In a court case, both sides of the argument are presented to the judge or jury, who forms an opinion that may be final. We see phrases such as "he is of the opinion" that something is true. This only provides a belief and not a fact. Or, you may hear "a difference of opinion," which means there is a basic argument about something that is not a fact.

Everyone has an opinion about something. The issue here is making a distinction between facts and opinion. I can say that thoroughbred horses are the fastest of all horses. That is not a fact but rather an opinion that I hold. To state this as a fact, one would either conduct a survey of horse lovers or determine if my opinion is factual by researching the library or internet. If I were to research on the internet, I would need to understand the relevancy of the publication. To satisfy my opinion, the publication should have references and verification of my opinion.

Belief

Beliefs can only be addressed by way of understanding knowledge (epistemology) and reality (ontology). Definitions are helpful for this understanding.

Belief. The acceptance that something exists or is true, especially without proof. Something one accepts as true or real, a firmly held opinion. A religious conviction. Trust, faith, or confidence in someone or something.

Experience. Practical contact with and observation of facts or events. The knowledge or skill acquired by a period of practical experience of something that is gained in a particular progression.

Existential. Relating to existence.

Epistemology is the study of the nature and scope of knowledge and justified belief. It analyzes the nature of knowledge and how it relates to similar notions, such as truth, belief, and justification. It also deals with the means of production of knowledge, as well as skepticism about different knowledge claims. Epistemology is the philosophical field revolving around knowledge and how to reach it.

Knowledge. 1. Facts, information, and skills acquired through experience or education; the theoretical or practical understanding of a subject. 2. Awareness or familiarity gained by experience of a fact or situation.

Ontology is the philosophical field revolving around the study of the nature of reality and the different entities and categories within reality. It looks at the very nature of things—their being, cause, or identity.

Thinking. The process of considering or reasoning about something.

Truth. That which is true or in accordance with fact or reality.

Belief Perspective

Individual belief is the acceptance that something is true or exists without proof of existence or without evidence of fact (or in the absence of fact). Faith and trust are the forerunners of beliefs.

Collective beliefs. The collective perception of fundamental truths governing behavior. The adherence to accepted and shared beliefs by members of a social system will likely persist and be difficult to change over time. Strong beliefs about determinant factors (i.e., security, survival, or honor) are likely to cause a social entity or group to accept rules and norms.

Traditionally, psychology treats belief as if it were the simplest form of mental representation and therefore one of the building blocks of conscious thought. Philosophers tend to think of belief in a more abstract form.

In reality, both are true. They both apply to the existence of mental states. Psychologists divide belief into core beliefs, which are those actively thought about. They also entertain beliefs in the form of depositional beliefs, which may be defined as someone who has not thought deeply about the issues. I would argue the core belief premise. The beliefs actually result from a child developing a belief system based on the parents' beliefs, such as religion. For example, Christians believe in Jesus, and therefore their children will believe in Jesus and associated Christian values. The same is true for other religions.

The dispositional belief is one in which the person does not think about any situation. For example, people going to work each day believe that they will not have a traffic accident. As a result, the person is forced to think about why they hold the belief.

Philosophically, beliefs along with truth, justification, and propositions have been argued. This is the foundation for epistemology.

To better understand the origin of beliefs, research indicates that beliefs occur from three areas of the brain: the prefrontal and frontal cortex, the amygdala, and the hippocampus. This makes perfect sense as that is where information and facts originate. This is also the cognitive portion of the brain. The amygdala is involved in fear and fear memories. The hippocampus is associated with declarative and episodic memory as well as recognition memory.

The left side of the brain is responsible for controlling the right side of the body. It also performs tasks that have to do with logic, such as those used in science and mathematics. On the other hand, the right hemisphere coordinates the left side of the body and performs tasks that have do with creativity and the arts. Beliefs come from more than one part of the brain. It appears to be prefrontal, right-sided brain along with the memory centers of the brain that are involved in belief.

There are two forms of belief systems: positive true beliefs and false or negative beliefs. Positive true beliefs consist of mindfulness, resilience, moral and ethical thinking, and values. Whereas negative false beliefs consist of failure in thinking, unrealistic beliefs, evil thinking, and immoral and corrupt thinking. Belief is often misrepresented in knowledge. This is further discussed in the next section.

Epistemology

Justification. The action of showing something to be right or reasonable. Good reason for something that exists or has been done.

Verification. The process of establishing the truth, accuracy, or validity of something. Validity of a proposition.

Proposition. A statement or assertion that expresses a judgment or opinion. A statement that expresses a concept that can be true or false. A formal statement of a theorem or problem, typically including the demonstration.

Epistemology is the study of knowledge. It delineates boundaries between knowledge, beliefs, and opinion. In the philosophy of epistemology, there is a delineation between truth and belief of something, and both are central to "justified belief with knowledge," which is present within justified belief.

Epistemology dates back to Plato but became more prominent in the Enlightenment in Europe with Rene Descartes (early 1600s). It has also come to light in the twentieth century.

Justified true belief is considered the definition of knowledge. The concept of justified true belief states that in order to know that a given proposition is true, one must not only believe the true proposition but must also have justification for this belief.

As an example, agent S knows that proposition P is true only if P is true, S believes that P is true, and S is justified in believing that P is true.

Epistemology philosophy uses an example of a woman crossing a bridge. The proposition is a footbridge that the woman can cross. A footbridge is safe to cross (P = proposition). The woman (S = subject) has the proactive belief that the footbridge (P = proposition) is safe to cross. The woman (S = subject) safely crosses the bridge and is justified that the (P = proposition) bridge was safe to cross. Therefore, the woman believes that crossing the bridge is safe. But what if the woman crosses the bridge and the bridge collapses? The woman lacked knowledge regarding the safety of the bridge.

What if a 285-pound man crossed the footbridge? He believed the footbridge was safe, and sure enough, he got to other side without the bridge collapsing. He then comes to the second footbridge, and there is a sign that states, "Maximum weight three hundred pounds." He sees a small-statured couple crossing the bridge; the maximum weight for both persons is 265 pounds. He believes the footbridge is safe to cross, and he crosses the footbridge without incident. He comes to the third footbridge, and this also states, "Maximum weight three hundred pounds." He crosses the bridge, and the bridge collapses. So, the question now becomes, why did the bridge collapse? Suppose we weigh the man, and he weighs 310 pounds. That could be an explanation. Further investigation indicates that the footbridge was fifteen years old and had more than one thousand people cross the bridge. Of the one thousand people, one hundred persons weighed three hundred pounds. We now have three variables, which include the weight of the man crossing the bridge, which was greater than the maximum three-hundred-pound weight for the bridge. We have the bridge maintaining foot traffic for fifteen years. And we also note that the footbridge was crossed by a maximum of three hundred pounds several times. These are considered variables. Had the sign read "Maximum three hundred pounds, bridge is fifteen years old, foot traffic heavy," would the man have crossed the bridge? Suppose the man actually weighed 285 pounds and the sign entering the bridge stated a maximum weight of three hundred pounds. Built fifteen years ago. Heavy use. The man decides that crossing the bridge is safe, and as he crosses, the bridge collapses. We now have knowledge that everything was safe; however, the bridge collapsed. This then becomes randomness, and randomness is unexplainable.

In the first bridge crossing by the man, the man justified his true belief because he got to the other side without incident. Coming to the second bridge, the man justified his true belief with knowledge, and he crossed that bridge without incident. On the third bridge, he thought he had substantial knowledge and justified his true belief, but the bridge collapsed. We will argue that epistemology is confused between belief, truth, and knowledge. In the first bridge crossing, the man only had belief. He believed; in other words, he had faith or trust that the bridge was safe. In the second bridge crossing, there was truth that the bridge was safe to cross. In the third case, hundreds of people had the knowledge that the bridge was safe and was crossed safely; however, when he crossed the bridge, it collapsed.

Consider belief. We get in our motor vehicles every day and drive to work or the store and believe that nothing will happen and everything is safe. However, based on randomness, accidents happen. When bad things happen to people, they often say it was meant to be. When they do happen, we find that our belief system fails. Human beings then turn to their faith to alleviate mental anguish and pain.

Returning to the third bridge crossing, suppose the bridge was maintained on a yearly basis. This would eliminate randomness from occurring. All across the United States today, we have bridges and tunnels that are not maintained, because the government would rather spend the money on defense than on maintaining infrastructure. Someday, the inevitable will occur randomly, but most likely, people will attempt to explain the root cause.

In the 1960s, there was an argument against justified true belief being used as knowledge. Edmund Gettier is known for his 1963 paper titled "Is Justified True Belief Knowledge?" He used an example to argue against justified true belief. In his example, he stated that two men, Smith and Jones, had ten coins in their pockets. Smith knew that Jones had the ten coins in his pocket but failed to count his own coins. They interviewed for a job and were told by the interviewer that whoever had ten coins in his pocket would get the job. Smith was certain that Jones would get the job because he knew he had ten coins in his pocket. However, Smith got the job. Smith did not understand why he got the job, because he knew he had coins in his pocket, but he did not know how many. This is a perfect example of a person failing to identify the facts and believing something else is true. This generally happens in politics and religion. People fail to get or ignore the facts and rely on their own beliefs.

In general, belief is not truth, and truth has no part in belief. Knowledge is separate from both and can only be used in terms of facts and truth.

Believing should not be confused with thinking. Thinking is a rational process in consideration of something being true or false, whereas beliefs are irrational and mythical. There is no thinking in beliefs, only acceptance of those things that are unproven.

Quasi-Facts

Quasi. Resembling or seeming but not really. "Having some, but not all of the features of" and used in the formation of compound words: *quasi*-definition; *quasi*-monopoly; *quasi*-official; *quasi*-scientific.

Fact. A thing that is known or proved to be true.

Therefore, quasi-facts are facts that are subjective or relative.

Eye color is a fact. As is a person's birth date. Someone may factually have brown eyes and have been born on July 1, 1970. A quasi-fact is age, which is always changing. It is subjective unless stated that I have been alive fifteen thousand days, four hours, and thirty-six minutes. This comes out to roughly 44⅔ years old. Age is a quasi-fact because it is relative.

Things like weather are considered quasi-facts in that the prediction is rain, but where, when, and how it rains is subjective.

It is a fact that water is H_2O. It is unchanged unless another oxygen molecule is added, which would then make it hydrogen peroxide, H_2O_2. There is nothing subjective or relative about this fact.

Other examples of quasi-facts are surveys, polls, and the census, or societal or social questionnaires, and sampling.

There is nothing bad or wrong with quasi-facts. One must simply be aware of facts that are absolute and those that are subjective.

Knowledge

Knowledge. 1. Facts, information, and skills acquired through experience or education; the theoretical or practical understanding of a subject. 2. Awareness or familiarity gained by experience of a fact or situation.

Experience. Practical contact with and observation of facts or events. The knowledge or skill acquired by a period of practical experience of something especially that is gained in a particular progression.

Aptitude. Ability to do something.

Cognition. The mental action or process of acquiring knowledge and understanding through thought, experience, and the senses.

Metacognition. Awareness and understanding of one's own thought processes.

Memory. The faculty by which the brain stores and remembers information.

Learning. The acquisition of knowledge or skills through study, experience, or being taught.

Understanding. Comprehension. The power of abstract thought; intellect.

Retention. The fact of keeping something in one's memory.

Analytical. Relating to or using analysis or logical reasoning.

Logic. Reasoning conducted or assessed according to strict principles of validity.

Reason. The power of the mind to think, understand, and form judgments logically.

Recitation. The action of repeating something aloud from memory.

Mindfulness. The quality or state of being conscious or aware of something.

In epistemological mathematics, there is knowing *that* 2 + 2 = 4, but there is also knowing *how* to add two numbers. In other words, the addition of two numbers is a concept; knowing that and knowing how is the understanding of how to add two numbers. Epistemology philosophy makes knowledge abstract and difficult.

The argument is that adding two numbers is not a concept until it is learned. Showing an infant 2 + 2 = 4 makes no sense to the child. But when mom gives the child two Hershey's Kisses and dad gives the child two Hershey's Kisses, the child can now count two Kisses and two Kisses equals four Kisses. Suppose as an adult you see: Èr + Èr = Sì. You know the concept of adding, but unless you know Chinese, you do not know how what that means.

Michael Polanyi, a Hungarian physician who also had a PhD in physical chemistry and was a chemistry professor at Oxford and the University of Manchester, was known for his contributions to the theory of knowledge (epistemology) and philosophy of science (identification of the "structure of tacit knowing"), as well as his contributions to physical science (potential adsorption theory). He was also considered a twentieth-century philosopher.

Professor Polanyi argued for the epistemological relevance of knowledge how and knowledge that; using the example of the act of balance involved in riding a bicycle, he suggests that the theoretical knowledge of the physics involved in maintaining a state of balance cannot substitute for the practical knowledge of how to ride and that it is important to understand how both are established and grounded.

The problem is that both are not intertwined and established, because of other factors involved in knowledge. For example, we will use the balance of bicycle riding. We have three young boys who want to learn to ride a bicycle. One boy is overweight, and the other two of normal weight. Each has a bicycle that fits their size. The concept of balance and riding a bike is explained to all three. Each are shown how to ride a bicycle. The overweight boy tries to ride and balance but has a lot of difficulty. After many attempts, he finally rides. The second boy attempts to ride and falls. He is afraid to try again. Training wheels are placed on the bike, and he feels secure, eventually learning to ride. The third boy gets on the bicycle and rides away without any difficulty, turning around on the bike and returning without incident. All three had the concept, and all three were taught *how to*, and only one rode his bicycle using both concept (knowing that) and knowing how. All three had the epistemological requirements for knowledge, but only one filled the criteria immediately.

It could be argued that we are basing knowledge on success. For the most part, knowledge is the infinite progression of successes. However, failures do occur with knowledge. With mindfulness, failures can be overcome with resilience. Again, infinite progression leads to further knowledge—that is, we learn from mistakes and become street-smart.

Modern philosophical/psychological epistemology considers that knowledge can be explored under four categories: factual, conceptual, procedural, and metacognitive.

The first two types, factual and conceptual, constitute knowledge of what, and the last two types, procedural and metacognitive, constitute knowledge of how to.

We argue for modern-day considerations of knowledge that subscribe to the definition of facts, information, and skills acquired through experience or education, the theoretical or practical understanding of a subject. There are many terms that fit into the description of knowledge, such as experience, observation, understanding, and retention.

Knowledge should fall into the following categories:

- genetics and aptitude
- cognition and metacognition
- experience reflected in observation, analysis, learning, understanding, and retention
- memory
- recitation or composition

This model is supported by what we know about brain function. Knowledge is involved with many parts of the brain. The prefrontal cortex sits above the eyes and nose and processes sensory information, as does the occipital lobe for vision. It also initiates the process for cognitions, which is present in the executive portion of the frontal lobe. Learning and memory are associated with the hippocampus. The left lobe of the cerebral cortex is responsible for analytic thinking and mathematics, and the right lobe for creativity. Parts of the limbic system, such as the hippocampus and amygdala, are involved in cognitive thinking, and these areas are also involved in emotions.

The limbic system is a large part of the brain, including the hypothalamus, and much of this system is involved with emotions, as well as many other functions. An example of this is a bad memory stored in the hippocampus that can be regulated by the amygdala to cause sadness.

A major issue is the contradiction between knowledge and belief. It is puzzling that emotion often outweighs knowledge and reason. There are many examples of this problem:

1. Investments in the stock market by intelligent people. The stock market operates entirely on emotion and beliefs.
2. Why do Catholic athletes give a sign of the Holy Trinity before a game when that has nothing to do with the outcome?
3. Why do evangelicals support a Republican who breaks every commandment?
4. Why do intelligent people vote for and support President Trump?
5. Why are we so emotional over HIV and coronavirus infections? Because we are concerned and feel sympathy for people.

The only explanation we can provide is that the limbic system is very ingrained with emotions and beliefs that overpower rational and analytical thinking.

Fiction

There are no facts in fiction. We become involved in fiction every day. The issue is separating fiction from facts. This is done by critical thinking, analytic thinking, and investigative thinking. This type of thinking can be arduous and time-consuming. Many people are lazy and will believe things without verifying them. With knowledge, fiction can be overcome.

Fact versus fiction has been used in politics to show that one party believes in facts while the other uses fiction. This is totally incorrect, and although we were caught up in this for the title of this chapter, fiction is a part of nonfact. Fiction is defined as generally understood as not adhering precisely to the real world, which also opens it up to various interpretations. Characters and events within a fictional work may even be set in their own context entirely separate from the known universe: an independent fictional universe.

Metafiction. Fiction in which the author self-consciously alludes to the artificiality or literariness of a work by parodying or departing from novelistic conventions (especially naturalism) and traditional narrative techniques. The act of telling a story becomes part of the story.

Historically, the oldest form of fiction is mythology, which dates back to before Christ. This will also be addressed.

In contrast to fiction is its traditional opposite, nonfiction, in which the creator assumes responsibility for presenting only the historical and factual truth.

Fiction is invented or untrue. Fiction can also be perceived as a make-believe reality. It is an inventive construct of an imaginary world.

Like truth, fiction is dependent on our senses. In order to determine fiction, we must be able to see (observe), hear, smell, and taste. Our brain then determines what is real. Fiction is usually thought of as the opposite of fact.

Fiction is a medium that relates to an imaginary world or reality. The medium refers to a novel or short story. More encompassing are plays, movies, films, comics, cartoons, audio, recordings, live theater, animation, television programs, video games, videos, and social media. The internet has had a major impact on the creation and distribution of fiction. A prime fiction example is Facebook and other social media sources.

Some fiction authors attempt to make their audience believe their work is nonfiction or otherwise blur the boundary of facts. Fiction can have themes, such as lessons learned, values, and principles. Although fiction is untrue reality, it can often send ethically and morally useful messages using imaginary characters. For example, in *Star Wars*, we see the war between good and evil; Luke Skywalker represents good, while Darth Vader is evil.

A children's fairy tale, *Pinocchio*, sends a message that if you lie, your nose will grow. If this were the case, President Trump's nose would have grown long enough to wrap around his body and squeeze him to death like a boa constrictor.

Fiction has several genres, including science fiction, which is sometimes seen as a prediction of the future. Science fiction predicts science and technologies that are not reality at present. One excellent example is Jules Verne's novel *From the Earth to the Moon*. This novel was published in 1865, but it was not until 1969 that astronaut Neil Armstrong set foot on the moon. It would not be surprising should some of the things in *Star Wars* become reality.

Realistic fiction is more concerning in that people who lack critical thinking may believe the stories they read. Realistic fiction will take a true location and event but substitute untruths in the story setting. The event(s) could feasibly happen in a real-world setting. In other words, nonrealistic fiction involves a story where an imaginary universe and alternative history appear real or true. Those persons who have a high-level belief mentality will believe the story is real or true. The challenge of differentiating fiction from nonfiction remains. The best way to do this is to verify facts. This can be done using Google, Wikipedia, Encyclopedia Britannica, PubMed, the local library, or any source where factual data and information are found. This requires work, but it is worth it.

Another means of determining fact is knowledge and analytical thinking. The author never attributed autism to vaccinations. Signs of autism can be recognized before a child is vaccinated. Signs like delayed speech, total withdrawal, and lack of response to commands can be observed. The purpose of vaccines is to turn on the immune system to provide future memory for the immune system to fight a virus. This has no bearing on the brain.

Definitions, description, and examples of fiction clearly indicate that fiction is specific to untrue literature and various media. Fiction is not the same as untruths expressed by politicians. It is not any of the other prescribers of nonfacts. It is specifically one part of nonfact.

Separation between fiction and nonfiction was traditionally more distinct. However, in the twenty-first century, it has become blurred.

Mythology

Myth. 1. A traditional story, especially one concerning the early history of a people or explaining a natural or social phenomenon and typically involving supernatural being or events. 2. A widely held but false belief or idea.

Mythology is the oldest form of fiction. It dates back to 3000 BCE. *The Epic of Gilgamesh* is one of the most well-known Mesopotamian myths and is often regarded as the oldest known piece of literature in the world. It was initially a number of individual short stories and was not combined into one cohesive epic until the eighteenth century.

Myths are stories that are not true. However, they may start out as true and change intentionally to embellish the story or may do so unintentionally over time. The initial story is fact, but as people tell and retell these stories, they may have changed some parts.

Myths are like the childhood game we played called "Whisper down the Lane." This is a game in which a message is passed on, in a whisper, by each of a number of people, so that the final version of the message is often radically changed from the original. For example, six people may be standing in a row, and the first person may say something like "A cat is in the tree" to the second person. This phrase is repeated until it gets to the last person, who is to repeat the same phrase. The last person may say something like "A bat flew into the tree." It may start out as true but ends as something else entirely.

We think of mythology in terms of Greek mythology in the form of Greek gods and Greek creatures. The Greek god Zeus represented a correlation between God and man. Zeus had powers over lightning and storms. Whenever Zeus wanted to, he could make a storm, and he made storms to show his anger.

While Greek mythology is the most famous, every country and culture has its own myths.

The main characters of myths are gods, part god, part humans (demigods), and supernatural humans. Myths were often endorsed by rulers and religions. In the seventeenth and eighteenth centuries, myths were prominently promoted by kings and religious leaders like priests.

Mythology is the central component of religion. Religion incorporates mythology and ritual. Mythology does not necessarily incorporate religion. Rituals in religion provide a complex relationship between recital and enactment of the ritual(s).

Prominence of the word *myth* originated in the Greco-Roman world. By the time of Christ, myths were considered fables, lies, fiction, or areligious stories, but to believers, myths are considered Holy Scriptures. They are narratives used to explain and justify a belief or ritual. These mythological religious stories occur in different religions and cultural belief systems. As examples, it is unjustified to believe Buddha was conceived in a dream by a white elephant. Although perhaps believable by Christians, it is logically unbelievable that Jesus was born from the Virgin Mary.

Traditional sacred stories by most religions are believed to represent profound truths. Practitioners of religious groups often believe that some or all of their traditional stories are not only sacred and true but also historically accurate and divinely revealed. These practitioners believe that calling their religious stories myths is disrespectful to their religious beliefs.

We mentioned in the section on belief that beliefs are extremely strong, especially when it comes to religious beliefs. Some religious believers (especially Christians) take offense when historical aspects of their faith are labeled myths. Most of the time, these devoted believers have difficulty distinguishing religious fables from sacred narratives, which are described by their tradition as history or revelation. Evangelical Christians have a strict, unwavering belief system that cannot make a distinction between religious fables and traditional historical writings. Myths are considered pagan.

Jesus Feeding the Multitudes

A perfect example of biblical mythology is Jesus feeding the multitudes, which is a term used to refer to two separate miracles of Jesus reported in the Gospels. The first miracle, "Feeding of the 5,000," is reported by all four Gospels (Mathew 14:13–21, Mark 6:31–44, Luke 9:12–17, and John 6:1–14). The second miracle, the "Feeding of the 4,000" with seven loaves of bread and fish, is reported by Mathew 15:32–39 and Mark 8:1–9 but not by Luke or John.

How can this be factual or true? Either the fish were whales and the bread was as large as a house or the author missed a few decimal points. These are two myths in which authors frequently exaggerate their story to prove something. We also recognize that fiction frequently provides moral and valuable messages. In analyzing the stories of feeding the multitudes, Jesus appears to have a good heart, filled with compassion.

Many believe that Jesus most likely existed, but Aristotle, Galileo, Michelangelo, and Newton definitely existed. There is scientific and historical evidence that all those mentioned with the exception of Jesus are real. All of these men have a strong connection to God, but they are not enigmatic or mythical like Jesus. It appears reasonable and logical that humans *need* myths and rituals to believe in and connect to God.

The myth of Jesus coordinates with other myths of human connection to God, such as the myths of Muhammad, Buddha, and others. This raises the question of distinguishing God's myths from humans' myths. God's myths have a superhuman connection with God, whereas humans' myths are more pagan, generally related to animals and nature.

Many Christians (especially evangelical Christians) will have strong objections to the biblical mythology connection because it challenges their belief system. They are terrified by words such as *myth*, because the word represents fantasy. This takes away from what they perceive to be the Word of God. It seems more apparent to accept the myth for its worthiness of principles than to be caught up in the literal interpretation of the Bible.

Joseph Campbell, a modern twentieth-century philosopher and mythologist, believed that people could not understand their individual lives without mythology to aid them. By recalling the significance of old myths, he encouraged awareness of them. In responding to the question "How would you define mythology?" Joseph Campbell answered: "My favorite definition of mythology: other people's religion. My favorite definition of religion: misunderstanding of mythology."

A myth did not hold religion back; that myth was an essential foundation of religion, and eliminating that myth would eliminate a piece of the human psyche.

The next mythological concept is creation mythology. A creation myth (or cosmogonic myth) is a symbolic narrative of how the world began and how people first came to inhabit it. This is a universal myth that is present in every religion, society, and culture. Though all cultures have a creation myth, the substance of the myth varies. A myth is considered a false or untrue story. But the creation of earth and humans is true. The myth is in the belief system, which is unknown. Creation myths explain in metaphorical terms our sense of purpose about who we are in the context of the world.

Conspiracy Theory

This is another form of untruth and misaligned facts. It is worth presenting, because this has become a norm for right-wing extremists and many in the Republican Party.

Conspiracy. A secret plan by a group to do something unlawful or harmful.

Conspiracy theory. The theory that an event or phenomenon occurs as a result of a conspiracy between interested parties; specifically, a belief that some covert but influential agency (typically political in motivation and oppressive in intent) is responsible for an unexplained event.

A conspiracy theory is an explanation of an event or situation that invokes a conspiracy by sinister and sometimes powerful people, often dishonest and political in motivation, when there are truthful or factual explanations. The term has a pejorative connotation, implying that the appeal to a conspiracy is based on prejudice or insufficient evidence.

Psychologically, the conspiracy theorists suffer from psychological projection and paranoia. Additionally, they gain recognition that is also present in insecure, narcissistic personalities. They are extremely harmful and hurtful to others, especially who they perceive as opponents. Their audience is complacent, trusting, and less educated and therefore believes and supports the theorist. The captive mind that feels powerless in society now possesses power.

In the United States, conspiracy theories by prominent hyper-nationalist and religious fundamentalists are prominent.

Conspiracy theorists perform on the fringe of society, and they have become more prevalent in the twenty-first century as result of media and social media. The problem is that there is a great amount of information flowing around, which becomes the subject of questionable belief. As previously discussed, the battle to fight this problem requires fact-finding/investigation, and that takes time and energy.

Michael Barkun wrote that conspiracy theorists see themselves as having privileged access to special knowledge or a special mode of thought that separates them from the masses who believe the official account (Barkun 2016, *Conspiracy Theories as Stigmatized Knowledge*).

The conspirator has a strong need for projecting their belief onto other people, which gives them a sense of power. They project a significant event with a significant cause. They will demonize their cause against the common good.

Fear is an important tool for the conspiracy theorist. It may come out in its severest form with paranoid personality disorder. There is a cognitive disconnect where the emotions of fear override reason, logic, and critical thinking.

Conspiracy theories may be emotionally satisfying by assigning blame to a group to which the theorist does not belong and so absolving the theorist of moral or political responsibility in society. We can also claim the conspiracy theorist is a creator of mythology, twisted mythology.

Conspiracies serve the needs of diverse political and social groups in the United States and elsewhere. They identify powerful elites, blame them for economic and social catastrophes, and assume that things will be better once popular action can remove them from positions of power.

Belief in conspiracy theories has no basis in evidence but is instead based on the faith of the believers. There is no analysis, factual documentation, verification, or institutional analysis.

There are many examples of conspiracy theories. They can develop between or within groups and can be found in nearly every facet of life.

Popular examples of conspiracy theories include the John F. Kennedy assassination, the moon landing, 9/11, HIV/AIDS, and the coronavirus pandemic.

David Vaughan Icke published many documents detailing his conspiracy theories, including his belief that earth would be destroyed by earthquakes and tidal waves.

Summary

The terms fact and fiction should be eliminated because only facts and nonfacts exist. This chapter should have provided a better understanding of facts.

CHAPTER 2

REPUBLICANS BEHAVE LIKE TODDLERS

Introduction

The purpose of this chapter is to recognize the difference between normal and abnormal development in two- to five-year-old children. This is helpful as we explore the development of some traits in children that lead to personality disorders and other mental health issues in adults. We shall begin with basic neurophysical development along with emotional and behavioral development. This progresses into behavioral and development disorders. This is simply observational and descriptive. There is no medical or psychological advice, which can be obtained from specialized health care providers.

Early Development

Babies express emotions by crying, smiling, and undistinguishable sounds (babbling). Their emotions are primitive because their brains are undeveloped. They spit up and throw food. Laughing and cooing indicate they are happy. They start crawling and become inquisitive of their surroundings. By the time they turn two, they generally start walking and saying a few words. There is no significant emotional activity until they approach two years old. Much of the discussion progresses from two- to five-year-olds. The proper name for a three-year-old is a toddler. At age two, there is a swift change in a child's emotions. This transition from baby emotions to the toddler emotions is fast, because the emotional part of the brain (limbic system) is developing.

Development of Two-Year-Olds

The two-year-old stage is a transition between total dependence and newfound independence. At this stage, children begin to explore their world. They do it both with and without the adults. They generally start talking. Most, but not all, toddlers can say about twenty words by eighteen months and fifty or more words by the time they turn two. By age two, they are starting to combine two words to make simple sentences, such as "Want candy" or "Come, Daddy." They begin to recognize differences in shapes and sizes. It is not until age three that they start recognizing a few colors, especially red. This is all a normal progression of brain and vision development.

The neurophysical development at age two includes walking, running, and starting to jump. Toddlers carry toys and can pull little wagons. They love to step on tiptoes and kick balls. They climb onto chairs and play with playground equipment. They start practicing proper hygiene, such as washing and drying hands and brushing their teeth with some help.

As two-year-olds progress to age three, these activities progress to easily walking up and down stairs, catching balls, hopping, running more confidently, and riding a tricycle.

It should be noted that every child is different. A child may be able to do extensive physical activity at two but not say a word, while others may say a full sentence at two but have difficulty with physical activities. You know when your child is gifted when they start playing the violin at age three.

Language and Delayed Speech

By age three, most children should know about two hundred words. At age two, they start combining two words to make simple sentences. However, they frequently leave out a verb. They say, "There Daddy" instead of "There is Daddy." A child gifted in language may say "There is Daddy."

Two-year-olds can recognize sizes, shapes, numbers, and textures, but it will take to age three or four before they can say a color or number. They can say their age and name.

What if a two-year-old only says a few words until three? This is called speech or language delay. This occurs when a two-year-old says 50 percent fewer words for their age. In other words, if they say fewer than ten words by eighteen to twenty-four months, speech is considered delayed. Boys have later language skills than girls. About 20 percent of toddlers have some delay in communication skills, dependent on the maturity of their brains.

Delayed speech can be divided into primary and secondary conditions. Some causes of primary speech delay are physical. They may be due to problems hearing caused by ear infections. In addressing hearing, there is also a condition called auditory processing disorder. Prematurity can be a reason for speech delay. Extreme environmental deprivation with minimal adult interaction will often delay speech. Delayed speech alone should not be confused with autism. A subset of late talkers may be highly intelligent. They may be focused on such things as math, memory, or music.

Secondary conditions of speech delay are usually associated with other conditions affecting the brain. Speech delay is not the single factor, but rather other behavioral and developmental symptoms are associated. This includes mental retardation, Down syndrome, autism spectrum disorders, and others.

Terrible Twos

The terrible twos is a normal developmental phase experienced by young children. This phase is characterized by tantrums, defiant behavior, and lots of frustration. The terrible twos don't necessarily occur right when a child turns two. The two-year-old alternates between reliance on adults and a newly developed feeling of independence. It is a stage that most two- to three-year-olds go through to varying degrees.

Temper Tantrums

Two-year-olds can have troublesome emotions, such as shyness, stress, strange eating habits, and temper tantrums. All of these can occur as a normal part of a child's development.

Temper tantrums are characterized by stubbornness, crying, screaming, violence, defiance, angry ranting, a resistance to attempts at pacification, and, in some cases, hitting. Temper tantrums are unpleasant and disruptive behaviors or emotional outbursts. They often occur in response to unmet needs or desires. Tantrums usually begin in children twelve to eighteen months old. They get worse between age two to three, then decrease until age four. After age four, they rarely occur. The reason they decrease by age four is a result of improved language skills and a child's ability to express their feelings.

This is the time in a child's life when they are learning independence, but at the same time, they are restrained by and dependent on adults. They are learning control, and part of their vocabulary is saying no. The more emotional and communicative skills a child has, the less intense and frequent the tantrums.

A distinction should be made between a temper tantrum and a meltdown. The main difference between the two types of outbursts is that tantrums usually have a purpose. Toddlers are looking for a certain response. Meltdowns are a reaction to something and are usually beyond a child's control. The length of the outburst is longer with a meltdown, and as a result, the child isn't likely to stop when they get what they want.

When temper tantrums are severe or persist beyond about four years of age, they may indicate a behavioral disorder.

Four- to Five-Year-Olds Are Considered Preschoolers

The neurophysiological development in a four- to five-year-old is becoming adaptive to the surrounding and environment in which they live. They are now considered preschoolers. Four-year-old children should be running, jumping, throwing a ball overhand, kicking balls with force, climbing in the playground, swinging without help, and swimming with adult help. They should be able to climb jungle gyms at the playground (but still need close supervision).

Other neurological skills include hand-eye coordination and fingering, such as with activities on a piano or iPad. They can draw simple objects and use scissors.

A huge neurophysical development is for a four-year-old to go to the bathroom unassisted. The American Association of Pediatrics reports that kids who begin potty training at eighteen months are generally not fully trained until age four, while kids who begin training at age two are generally fully trained by age three. Many kids will not master bowel movements on the toilet until well into their fourth year.

A four- or five-year-old child is also learning to focus. They should be able to stay focused on a task between four and twenty minutes, possibly more, depending on the task.

At this age, they are starting to form sentences and will start knowing the meaning of some words. They know what *stop* means and they are familiar with the concept of *time-out*.

Emotional Development in Four and Five-Year-Olds

It is important to understand normal development from the instigation of mental disease. This is true with emotional development as well as language and reading development.

At this age, children have some difficulty sharing but are starting to learn to take their turn. They are learning about performing tasks, but they may have problems focusing at times. They may be quick to anger but are starting to understanding anger and how to deal with it through words. They also want to please.

The emotions of temper tantrums in four- to five-year-olds are associated with emotional distress typically characterized by stubbornness, whimpering, crying, screaming, defiance, angry ranting, a resistance to attempts at pacification, and, in extreme cases, hitting and other physical behavior.

Temper tantrums and meltdowns will start to dissipate by this age. Meltdowns should have stopped. With independence comes defiance. Children may be absorbed in an activity, and if asked to come to lunch, they may defiantly say, "Not now." This sort of defiance also normally goes away as children become more self-confident and know that they can return to the same activity after they have done what they've been asked to do. Their independence is learning boundaries.

When tantrums occur at this age, it may be due to a child's difficulty in expressing themselves. Their language skills are not fully developed, leading to frustration. Other causes may be that they are exhausted, hungry, or scared. Severe stress, parents' divorce, the death of a parent, or other emotional upsets may also prompt tantrum-like behavior.

Temper tantrums after age five should be gone. If they do occur, they should only last a few minutes and be relatively infrequent. If they remain for more than twenty-five minutes, 90 percent of the time, parents should consider seeking treatment for an emotional disorder.

Language and Reading

A child's vocabulary significantly increases between three and six years of age. Vocabulary grows to be about seven hundred to a thousand words by the time a child is three years old. The typical four-year-old child will have a vocabulary of about 1,500–1,600 words.

Five-year-olds can start to learn more words and read simple sentences. Typically, they should have about 1,500–1,800 words they know and can speak. They can read "see puppy," "see cat," "see Dick run," and the like. Pictures along with words help them learn.

A child's speech should become clearer as they get older. Speaking should become clear by age four, with some mispronunciation in as many as half of a child's basic sounds; however, this is not a cause for concern until age five.

Sentences become progressively longer between age four and five. They may be able to say, "My mom bought me a toy."

In addition to speaking short sentences, most four-year-olds are capable of learning how to write their names, the letters of the alphabet, and some numbers. They can also learn to recognize simple words in books and remember them. They are able to memorize some of their favorite words. They understand how to read and write both uppercase and lowercase letters.

Developmental and Behavioral Disorders in Two- to Five-Year-Olds

Ontogenesis is the development of an individual's anatomic or behavioral features from the earliest stage of maturity. Abnormal development of the brain is either developmental or behavioral. Developmental disorders should be thought of in terms of dysfunction in physical and/or brain development. Behavioral problems or disorders include the way one acts or conducts oneself, especially in relation to others. A behavioral disorder is an emotional disability characterized by the inability to build or maintain satisfactory interpersonal relationships with peers and/or teachers. This can be as serious as total dysfunction or disability.

Development disorders can be physical, mental, or both, thought of as primary (genetic) or secondary/acquired (e.g., chemical or infections). Behavioral disorders can overlap with developmental disorders. The disabilities found in developmental disorders often involve learning and language. The following list includes several common developmental disorders as provided by the Centers for Disease Control and Prevention (CDC).

Developmental Disorders
Attention-Deficit/Hyperactivity Disorder
Autism Spectrum Disorder
Cerebral Palsy
Fetal Alcohol Spectrum Disorders, Acquired
Fragile X Syndrome
Down Syndrome
Hearing Loss, Infection (Acquired) versus congenital
Intellectual Disability
Lead Poisoning in Childhood, Acquired

Further details about each of these disorders can be reviewed at https://www.cdc.gov/ncbddd/developmentaldisabilities/specificconditions.html.

In psychology, five of the mental development disorders have been grouped into pervasive development disorder (PDD). This group is characterized by severe delay in the development of multiple basic functions including socialization, language (speech), and learning. The inclusive group consists of autism, Asperger's syndrome, all autism spectrum disorders not otherwise specified, childhood integrative disorder, and Rett syndrome. The problem with this categorization is that all five could be considered autism spectrum disorders.

Behavioral Disorders

Some children have extreme difficulty and challenging behaviors that are outside the normal behavioral development for their age. The most common disruptive behavior disorders include oppositional defiant disorder (ODD), conduct disorder (CD), and attention deficit hyperactivity disorder (ADHD). It should be noted that most developmental and behavioral disorders are not fully recognized until age three or later.

Some of these disorders can be temporary, and others can last into adulthood. Temporary behavior problems can be stress, anxiety, and depression. Most of the others evolve into adulthood-ADHD, autism, conduct disorder, oppositional defiant disorder, and bipolar disorder. Almost all of these disorders that progress into adulthood have a genetic component.

There are at least seven behavioral problems and disorders. These include oppositional defiant disorder (ODD), conduct disorder, attention deficit hyperactivity disorder (ADHD), autism spectrum disorder (ASD), anxiety disorder, depression, and bipolar disorder.

We will go into more detail for obstinate-oppositional defiant and conduct disorders because of the high prevalence of both in some of the members of the current Republican Party.

Oppositional Defiant Disorder

As mentioned, the temper tantrums that begin to dissipate by age four should be totally gone by age five or six. However, if this type of behavior persists along with other behaviors, it may be a sign of oppositional defiant disorder (ODD). ODD can persist into the teenage years and can be recognized by a frequent and persistent pattern of easy anger, annoyance, irritability, arguing, defiance, or vindictiveness toward adults, especially authority figures.

The exact cause of ODD is not known, but it is believed that a combination of biological, genetic, and environmental factors may contribute to the condition. Some studies suggest that defects in or injuries to certain areas of the brain can lead to serious behavioral problems in children. Such children refuse to obey rules. Many deliberately try to annoy or aggravate others. They have low self-esteem but appear to compensate through their behavior. They are quick to blame others. Around one in ten children under the age of twelve are thought to have oppositional defiant disorder (ODD), with boys outnumbering girls two to one. This behavior in late teens can lead to drug abuse, impulsive behavior, and suicide. The persistence of this behavior into adulthood is likely genetic, but it could be carried over from environmental issues.

Conduct Disorder

Normal toddlers and preschoolers learn to develop friendships and socialize. They are able to understand feelings and start recognizing right from wrong. This becomes more apparent as they grow out of the terrible twos and temper tantrums.

Children with conduct disorders (CD) start exhibiting very abnormal behavior that can be recognized between the ages of six and fifteen. CD is a behavioral disorder that causes some children to engage in antisocial behaviors. They have trouble following rules and struggle to show empathy to others. They may threaten the safety of pets, others, or themselves.

Children with conduct disorder are diagnosed in adulthood as having antisocial personality disorders. The prevalence in children is obscure, because not all children get seen by child psychologists since they are often thought of as a "bad kid." Prevalence in adults is 2 percent to 3 percent in the population, and this may be the same for children. CD is found in boys more than girls.

CD is likely a genetic disease. The prefrontal and frontal cortex is malfunctional in individuals with CD. MAO inhibitor variant genes are abnormal. These features are found in adults, so the same is probably true in children. Research studies have not been completed.

The behavior of individuals with CD is difficult to change. Frequently, the boys wind up in military schools.

Environmental factors can influence the severity of the disorder, but it is usually not the cause of the disorder, with the exception of brain damage or trauma to the brain. The environmental factors that may influence the severity of the disorder include child abuse, family violence, poverty, and parental substance abuse.

Typically, the behavior of individuals with CD includes aggression, such as starting fights. They destroy property with disregard for rules or laws. Chronic lying and dishonesty is often part of their behavior. They engage in bullying and cause harm to others. These behaviors give them substantial pleasure. This includes injury to animals/pets by pulling their tails or throwing them. In extreme cases, this can result in the killing of animals. These individuals lack remorse and do not exhibit empathy. Teenagers who have access to firearms may use them. They may force someone into sexual activity and set fires to cause property damage. Approximately 25 percent of individuals with CD eventually end up in prison.

A diagnosis should not only include a psychiatric evaluation but also genetic studies and functional brain scans to determine the function of the prefrontal and frontal cortex.

Treatment is difficult since this is a genetic disorder. Family counseling, behavior modification, and cognitive behavior therapy may help. One should not consider themselves a failure if treatment is not successful, because CD is currently difficult to treat. Teenagers should not have access to firearms.

At this juncture, the rest of the behavioral disorders will be only briefly described for completeness and to differentiate oppositional defiant disorder and conduct disorder from the other behavioral disorders.

Summary

Normal toddler and preschooler development is used to make the distinction between normal behavior and behavioral disorders. As previously indicated, most of these disorders progress into adulthood. The two disorders that arise in childhood and carry over into adulthood in some of the members of the Republican Party are oppositional defiant disorder and conduct disorder.

References for further information:

National Institute for Mental Health website
Mayo Clinic website
WebMD website
Wikipedia
Centers for Disease Control and Prevention website

CHAPTER 3

PSYCHOLOGY OF REPRESENTED PERSONALITY DISORDER ASSOCIATED WITH REPUBLICANS

Introduction

Psychological descriptions in this chapter apply only to personality disorders. There are several personality disorders, but only three will be discussed in detail: paranoia, narcissism, and antisocial personality disorders. These three personality disorders are prevalent in some members of the Republican Party.

Some sections of the three pertinent personality disorders are extrapolated from the *Diagnostic and Statistical Manual of Mental Disorders*, fifth edition, American Psychiatric Association, copyright 2013, also referred to as DSM-5. Definitions of paranoia, narcissism, and antisocial disorder all come directly from the manual. The rest are from the author.

Personality Disorders Introduction

According to DSM-5, *personality disorder* is an enduring pattern of inner experience and behavior that deviates markedly from the expectations of the individual's culture, is pervasive and inflexible, has an onset in adolescence or early adulthood, is stable over time, and leads to distress or impairment.

The following personality disorders as described in DSM-5:

- Paranoid personality disorder is a pattern of distrust and suspiciousness such that others' motives are interpreted as malevolent.
- Narcissistic personality disorder is a pattern of grandiosity, need for admiration, and lack of empathy.
- Antisocial personality disorder is a pattern of disregard for, and violation of, the rights of others.

For purposes of exact and specific diagnoses for paranoid, narcissist, and antisocial personality disorders, the following is reproduced from the *Diagnostic and Statistical Manual of Mental Disorders*, 5th edition, American Psychiatric Association, copyright 2013. The exception is sociopathy and psychopathy.

Paranoid Personality Disorder

Diagnostic Criteria

A pervasive distrust and suspiciousness of others such that their motives are interpreted as malevolent, beginning by early adulthood and present in a variety of contexts, as indicated by four (or more) of the following:

- Suspects, without sufficient basis, that others are exploiting, harming, or deceiving him or her.

- Is preoccupied with unjustified doubts about the loyalty or trustworthiness of friends or associates.
- Is reluctant to confide in others because of unwarranted fear that the information will be used maliciously against him or her.
- Reads hidden demeaning or threatening meanings into benign remarks or events.
- Persistently bears grudges (i.e., is unforgiving of insults, injuries, or slights).
- Perceives attacks on his or her character or reputation that are not apparent to others and is quick to react angrily or to counterattack.
- Has recurrent suspicions, without justification, regarding fidelity of spouse or sexual partner.
- Does not occur exclusively during the course of schizophrenia, a bipolar disorder or depressive disorder with psychotic features, or another psychotic disorder and is not attributable to the physiological effects of another medical condition.

Prevalence

An estimate for paranoid personality based on a probability subsample from Part II of the National Comorbidity Survey Replication suggests a prevalence of 2.3 percent, while the National Epidemiologic Survey on Alcohol and Related Conditions data suggest a prevalence of paranoid personality disorder of 4.4 percent.

Development and Course

Paranoid personality disorder may first be apparent in childhood and adolescence with solitariness, poor peer relationships, social anxiety, underachievement in school, hypersensitivity, peculiar thoughts and language, and idiosyncratic fantasies. These children may appear to be "odd" or "eccentric" and attract teasing. In clinical samples, this disorder appears to be more commonly diagnosed in males.

Narcissistic Personality Disorder

Diagnostic Criteria

A pervasive pattern of grandiosity (in fantasy or behavior), need for admiration, and lack of empathy, beginning by early adulthood and present in a variety of contexts, as indicated by five (or more) of the following:

- Has a grandiose sense of self-importance (e.g., exaggerates achievements and talents, expects to be recognized as superior without commensurate achievements).
- Is preoccupied with fantasies of unlimited success, power, brilliance, beauty, or ideal love.
- Believes that he or she is "special" and unique and can only be understood by, or should associate with, other special or high-status people (or institutions).
- Requires excessive admiration.
- Has a sense of entitlement (i.e., unreasonable expectations of especially favorable treatment or automatic compliance with his or her expectations).
- Is interpersonally exploitative (i.e., takes advantage of others to achieve his or her own ends).
- Lacks empathy: is unwilling to recognize or identify with the feelings and needs of others.
- Is often envious of others or believes that others are envious of him or her.
- Shows arrogant, haughty behaviors or attitudes.

Prevalence

Prevalence estimates for narcissistic personality disorder, based on DSM-IV definitions, range from 0 percent to 6.2 percent in community samples.

Development and Course

Narcissistic traits may be particularly common in adolescents and do not necessarily indicate that the individual will go on to have narcissistic personality disorder. Individuals with narcissistic personality disorder may have special difficulties adjusting to the onset of physical and occupational limitations that are inherent in the aging process.

Gender-Related Diagnostic Issues

Of those diagnosed with narcissistic personality disorder, 50 percent to 75 percent are male.

Antisocial Personality Disorder

Diagnostic Criteria

A pervasive pattern of disregard for and violation of the rights of others, occurring since age fifteen years, as indicated by three (or more) of the following:

- Failure to conform to social norms with respect to lawful behaviors, as indicated by repeatedly performing acts that are grounds for arrest.
- Deceitfulness, as indicated by repeated lying, use of aliases, or conning others for personal profit or pleasure.
- Impulsivity or failure to plan ahead.
- Irritability and aggressiveness, as indicated by repeated physical fights or assaults.
- Reckless disregard for safety of self or others.
- Consistent irresponsibility, as indicated by repeated failure to sustain consistent work behavior or honor financial obligations.
- Lack of remorse, as indicated by being indifferent to or rationalizing having hurt, mistreated, or stolen from another.

- The individual is at least age eighteen years.
- There is evidence of conduct disorder with onset before age fifteen years.
- The occurrence of antisocial behavior is not exclusively during the course of schizophrenia or bipolar disorder.

Prevalence

Twelve-month prevalence rates of antisocial personality disorder, using criteria from previous DSMs, are between 0.2 percent and 3.3 percent. The highest prevalence of antisocial personality disorder (greater than 70 percent) is among most severe samples of males with alcohol use disorder and from substance abuse clinics, prisons, or other forensic settings. Prevalence is higher in samples affected by adverse socioeconomic (i.e., poverty) or sociocultural (i.e., migration) factors.

Development and Course

Antisocial personality disorder has a chronic course but may become less evident or remit as the individual grows older, particularly by the fourth decade of life. Although this remission tends to be particularly evident with respect to engaging in criminal behavior, there is likely to be a decrease in the full spectrum of antisocial behaviors and substance use. By definition, antisocial personality cannot be diagnosed before age eighteen years.

Risk and Prognostic Factors

Genetic and physiological. Antisocial personality disorder is more common among the first-degree biological relatives of those with the disorder than in the general population. The risk to biological relatives of females with the disorder tends to be higher than the risk to biological relatives of males with the disorder. Biological relatives of individuals with this disorder are also at increased risk for somatic symptom disorder and substance use disorders. Within a family that has a member with antisocial personality disorder, males more often have antisocial personality disorder and substance use disorders, whereas females more often have somatic symptom disorder. However, in such families, there is an increase in prevalence of all of these disorders in both males and females compared with the general population. Adoption studies indicate that both genetic and environmental factors contribute to the risk of developing antisocial personality disorder. Both adopted and biological children of parents with antisocial personality disorder have an increased risk of developing antisocial personality disorder, somatic symptom disorder, and substance use disorders. Adopted-away children resemble their biological parents more than their adoptive parents, but the adoptive family environment influences the risk of developing a personality disorder and related psychopathology.

Gender-Related Diagnostic Issues

Antisocial personality disorder is much more common in males than in females. There has been some concern that antisocial personality disorder may be underdiagnosed in females, particularly because of the emphasis on aggressive items in the definition of conduct disorder.

Sociopathy versus Psychopathy (Author's Description)

As noted, DSM-5 defines antisocial personality disorder in general terms. It makes no distinction between sociopathy and psychopathy. This lack of distinction creates a problem in the understanding between the two. And, clearly, in society there are distinct differences.

The term *psychopath* was coined in 1888 by German psychiatrist J.L.A. Koch (1841–1908). In German, the word is *psychopastiche*, translated to psychopath. He described it as mental disease of the soul, originating at birth.

American psychologists started using the term *sociopathy* in the 1930s. From the late 1920s, American psychologist George E. Partridge narrowed the definition of psychopathy to antisocial personality and from 1930 suggested that a more apt name for it would be sociopathy.

The generalization of antisocial personality disorder (ASPD) creates difficulties in diagnosis, etiology, understanding, and treatment. There are a few commonalities in that these behaviors begin before age fifteen and involve no empathy.

The present DSM-5 defines antisocial personality as a person having three or more of the following traits:

1. Constantly, pathologically lies and deceives others
2. Impulsive and lacks the ability to plan ahead
3. Proclivity to fighting and aggressiveness
4. Lacks regard for the safety of others
5. Irresponsible, cannot meet financial obligations
6. Lacks empathy and feels no remorse or guilt
7. No respect for laws, frequently breaks or flouts the law

There are psychiatrists and psychologists who believe there is difference in severity between psychopaths and sociopaths. That may be true for some shared issues such as manipulation. The following chart illustrates common signs and symptoms of sociopathy and psychopathy and explains how each presents in each disorder.

Signs and Symptoms	Sociopath	Psychopath
1. Narcissism	Grandiose, self-possessed	Not prominent
2. Lies	Pathological liar	Less apparent but pathological
3. Manipulation	Mild to moderate	Severe, extensive
4. Empathy	Very little, some	None
5. Cognition	Weak conscience	No conscience

6. Criminal activity	More risk—white collar	Minimize risk—serial killers
7. Regard for laws	Erratic	Disregard
8. Behavior	Impulsive, erratic, rage-prone	Appears levelheaded
9. Emotions	Anger	Lack emotions and guilt
10. Social interaction	Like-minded person interaction	Unattached but charming
Etiology	Childhood trauma and/or genetic	Genetic

The DSM-5 lists seven traits for antisocial personality disorder (ASPD), of which three suggest or indicate the disorder. The author has listed ten basic signs and symptoms that differentiate sociopaths from psychopaths, although it is possible to have overlap.

We propose the term "sociopathoid" for a person who meets five out of the ten traits. Or only one will suffice if they committed a white-collar crime. This type of criminal act distinguishes between psychopathy and sociopathy.

Sociopathy

We shall go through each sign and symptom to understand the differences and similarities between associated personality disorders.

Narcissism: Sociopaths are narcissistic, sometimes to the extent of narcissistic personality disorders (NPD), but NPD does not have all the other signs and symptoms of sociopathy. Some of the overlapping traits are manipulation and lack of empathy. Sociopaths have grandiose ideation and think they are the only person who matters or exits. This is a trait also found in con artists.

Lies: Lying and deceit are a huge part of a sociopath's life, bordering on delusion. The lies are many and chronic. Sociopaths have difficulty discerning their own reality from normal factual reality and may lash out at those who don't agree with their reality. Deception is a part of con artistry.

Manipulation: The way in which a sociopath manipulates someone is subtle. You do not realize the manipulation unless you have facts to discern it. One form of manipulation is diversion. If an event is subject to investigation, sociopaths will divert the focus to something different. This trait can manifest in many ways. If there is a disagreement between a person(s) or event, they can manipulate it in their favor. And now we return to their narcissistic, dishonest behavior. If they have money or power, their manipulation can be used successfully to their favor, usually at the expense of others. Sociopaths and psychopaths, as well as narcissists, all use manipulation. This trait is also common for con artists, who can be considered sociopaths.

Empathy: Lack of empathy is another characteristic of sociopaths. Sociopaths and psychopaths both lack empathy. They are void of this understanding of another person's hardship. A narcissist may be totally absorbed in themselves, but should someone close to them understand grief, they could feel empathy. It is not self-promoted, but they can understand it when others help them understand. However, sociopaths and psychopaths feel nothing.

Cognition: Cognitive skills are very weak in sociopaths. They have trouble distinguishing right from wrong. They have little to no guilt.

Criminal activity: Sociopaths have no regard for laws. They take risks and make every attempt to get away with their crime. Those with money will hire attorneys after they are caught. They frequently challenge laws but don't outright break them. They commit crimes like insurance fraud and hedge fund schemes.

Statistically about 25 percent of inmates in prisons are sociopaths. There are just as many who never get caught. Still others live unethical and immoral—but not illegal—lives. Famous sociopaths such as Michael Milkin and Bernie Madoff schemed and stole millions of dollars. Sociopaths often participate in corruption and white-collar crimes.

Behavior: Sociopaths are very impulsive and many times do things without thinking through the repercussions of their actions. This behavior frequently overlaps with their criminal activity. A large part of their drive is to gain money and power. Sex is often used to overpower the other person. Sociopaths can be sexual predators.

Emotions: Sociopaths have outbursts of anger, especially when something interferes with their plans. They easily become agitated with questions about their knowledge or behavior. They often call people names during emotional outbursts. These kinds of behaviors increase a sociopath's chances of being apprehended. Opposing this behavior, they are emotionally immature and insecure. Bullying and such activity may be a compensatory mechanism. They are emotionally detached, causing poor family relationships. They are distant from their children and spouse. Sex is a game for control.

Social interaction: Sociopaths are usually friends with like-minded people. If they are committing fraud, they will interact with other people who also commit fraud.

Etiology: A sociopath's signs and symptoms originate from childhood abuse, physical and/or psychological abuse. Varying degrees of abuse may also lead to varying signs and symptoms. However, some children who have severe abuse, such as being locked in a basement for years, overcome their situation without symptoms of antisocial behavior. Based on PET brain scans on psychopaths, sociopaths may also have a disconnect between the executive prefrontal area of the brain and the emotional limbic system.

Psychopathy

The term *psychopath* is generally used in the criminal justice system as well as in fiction and has worked its way into everyday vernacular. As a result, much more is described about the traits of psychopaths than sociopaths. More research has been done on psychopaths since they frequently commit heinous crimes. Criminal psychologists have studied them more than sociopaths who are not serial killers. As a result, more is known about the brain pathology of psychopaths than sociopaths.

Narcissism: Psychopaths are perceived as normal and do not express narcissism to the degree of a sociopath.

Lies: Psychopaths do not have a proclivity to pathological lying, although they are highly deceptive and better at lies.

Manipulation: Psychopaths are highly manipulative.

Empathy: Psychopaths feel no empathy for anyone's hardships or personal losses. They feel absolutely no guilt.

Cognition: Psychopaths cannot distinguish right from wrong. There is complete dissociation from cognitive thinking. As a result, they have no guilt or remorse.

Criminal activity: Psychopaths do not significantly engage in obvious criminal activity. The risk is especially minimized. This is not to say that they are not dangerous. They are more dangerous than sociopaths, because their criminal activity is overshadowed by what appears to be normal behavior. Serial killers are generally psychopaths.

Behavior: Psychopaths exhibit fairly normal behavior. They are family persons and hold down jobs.

Emotions: Psychopaths lack emotional involvement. They totally dissociate from the pain of others. If they harm someone, they do not apologize. Their emotions are completely detached from the main event.

Social interaction: Psychopaths have difficulty forming relationships with anyone. They are shallow and withdrawn. When they form relationships, they are superficial and artificial and are usually manipulated in a way that promotes their psychopathic gains. Nevertheless, people may see them as charming, friendly, and well educated.

Etiology: Psychology researchers generally believe that psychopaths tend to be born—it is likely a genetic predisposition—while sociopaths tend to be made by their environment. (Which is not to say that psychopaths may not also suffer from some sort of childhood trauma.)

Some of the most famous psychopathic serial killers are David Berkowitz (a.k.a. the Son of Sam), Albert DeSalvo (the Boston Strangler), Ted Bundy, Jeffrey Dahmer, John Wayne Gacy, Ed Gein, Herman Webster Mudgett, and Aileen Wuornos.

Studies of the brains of psychopaths using specialized functional PET brain scans show decreased brain activity of the prefrontal orbital cortex of the brain. This is the part of the brain that controls morality (moral and ethical decision-making) and impulse control. When brain activity is lacking in this area, the brain cannot control or prevent the amygdala and violent parts of the brain from becoming overactive. This same finding may also be true to some extent in sociopaths.

There is another scientific fact that also plays a role in psychopathic behavior: genetics. There are genes in our DNA associated with violence. One of these genes is called the MAO-A (monoamine oxide-A) gene. This gene is also called the warrior gene. The MAO-A gene is responsible for producing serotonin, a chemical in the brain that has a calming effect. A variant of the MAO-A gene may reduce serotonin and cause violence. Obviously, there is much, much more to be learned regarding the behavior of psychopaths.

The most research in criminality has been conducted on psychopathy. Psychopaths are killers, as opposed to sociopaths, who generally commit nonviolent crimes. Criminal psychologists have devised checklists to diagnose psychopaths.

Criminal Psychology of Psychopaths

Criminal psychologist Dr. Hare developed the Hare Psychopathy Checklist (PCL-Revised), used to assess cases of psychopathy. Each behavior described in the following list is worth two points. Meeting all the criteria would be a score of 40. A score of 30 to 40 is considered diagnostic of a psychopath. However, it appears that this checklist is inclusive of psychopaths and sociopaths.

A score of between 30 and 40 denotes psychopathy.

1. Glib and superficial charm—smooth talker, great storyteller, insincere and shallow words.
2. Grandiose self-worth—huge egos, confident, arrogant, feelings of superiority and entitlement; huge braggers of things they have done (and not actually done).

3. Seek stimulation or prone to boredom—risk-takers, sensation seekers.
4. Pathological lying—skilled liars, unafraid of being caught; lie to manipulate.
5. Conning and manipulativeness—"callous ruthlessness"—deceive, cheat, con, and defraud others for personal gain.
6. Lack of remorse or guilt—they feel pain for themselves but not others; coldhearted with no empathy for their victims—only disdain for their victims.
7. Shallow affect—friendly and charming with no feelings for others.
8. Callousness and lack of empathy—callous, heartless, contemptuous, indifferent and tactless.
9. Parasitic lifestyle—they live off others with no sense of responsibility or accountability; will manipulate and exploit others for their own gain.
10. Poor behavioral controls—aggression, verbal abuse, outbursts of anger and temper tantrums.
11. Promiscuous sexual behavior—sex encounters are often viewed as conquests and they boast about them; attempts to coerce people into sexual relationships.
12. Early behavior problems—antisocial behavior before age thirteen—lying, stealing, cheating, vandalism, bullying, cruelty to animals or siblings.
13. Lack of realistic, long-term goals—lack real direction but talk about big plans, sometimes a drifter.
14. Impulsivity—reckless and unpredictable, cannot control impulses, cannot resist temptation; seek instant gratification.
15. Irresponsibility—repeatedly fail to honor commitments or obligations—legally, morally, and financially.
16. Failure to accept responsibility for own actions—no sense of duty or conscientiousness, deny their responsibility and even play victim.
17. Many short-term marital relationships—inability to maintain a long-term relationship.

18. Juvenile delinquency—crimes that are manipulative, aggressive, violent, or callous between the ages of ten and eighteen.
19. Revocation of condition release—probation may have been revoked due to lack of responsibility and accountability—failing to appear, etc.
20. Criminal versatility—often involved in diverse criminal activities, boasting about getting away with crimes.

According to the author's differentiation between the sociopath and psychopath, psychopaths kill people, and sociopaths do not!

See this reference for further explanation on psychopathy versus sociopathy: http://www.scholarpedia.org/article/Psychopathy#Psychopathy_vs._Sociopathy.

Borderline Personality Disorder

Manipulation is a large part of borderline personality disorders. People with borderline personality disorders use manipulation to gain nurturance, whereas those with antisocial personality disorder (ASPD) use manipulation to gain profit, power, or some other material gratification. Individuals with ASPD tend to be less emotionally unstable and more aggressive than those with borderline personality disorder, although antisocial behavior may be present in some individuals with paranoid personality disorder. Manipulation is not usually motivated by a desire for personal gain or to exploit others as in ASPD but rather is more often attributable to a desire for revenge.

Criminal behavior is not associated with borderline personality disorder. Antisocial personality disorder must be distinguished from criminal behavior undertaken for gain that is not accompanied by the personality features characteristic of this disorder. Only when antisocial personality traits are inflexible, maladaptive, persistent, and cause significant functional impairment or subjective distress do they constitute antisocial personality disorder.

Con Artistry

According to the DSM-5, narcissism and antisocial personality disorders fit the personality of con artistry.

In her book *The Confidence Game: Why We Fall for It ... Every Time*, Maria Konnikova discussed con man characteristics and personality disorder. She states that the con man is characterized by a triad: a combination of narcissism, Machiavellianism, and psychopathy.

The triad is described as follows:

1. **Machiavellian.** Uses clever but often dishonest methods that deceive people so that he/she can win power or control. They are aggressive, manipulative, exploiting, and devious in achieving personal gains.
2. **Narcissist.** These people have an exaggerated sense of self-importance. They lack empathy, are entitled, and believe others are envious. They engage in promiscuous behavior. They are unable to tolerate criticism and often become enraged when challenged. Instead they seek confirmatory admiration.
3. **Psychopath.** These people are considered to have antisocial personality disorder. The two terms are interchangeable.

Bill Eddy, LCSW, JD, a lawyer and therapist, associates con artists with narcissism and sociopathy. In the legal system, narcissists and sociopaths create significant conflict. He calls this "High Conflict Personality." This is a subtype of sociopaths that incorporate con artistry. Nevertheless, Bill Eddy does not include psychopaths in con artistry.

The author argues that there are con man traits in the psychopath but not psychopathic traits in the con man. Sociopaths and con artists cause extreme emotional and financial pain to many people, but they do not physically kill people as does the psychopath.

Con artists can best be described as narcissists and sociopaths with Machiavellian traits.

Do not play with a con artist; they know what they're doing, they believe that what they are doing is justified, and they celebrate the con. You will not win.

The con man or con artist is present in all aspects of society. A common area of interest is business. Many on Wall Street, business CEOs, and salespeople are con artists. They are attorneys and politicians. Another prevalent area of con artistry is evangelism.

Evangelism is one of the more prevalent forms of con artistry. The Bible talks about preaching the Gospel. That does not mean that persuasive communication be used to force inconsistent mythological beliefs onto others (including those not of the same belief system). Persons who are leaders of evangelism are called evangelists. They usually have a large following across all forms of media.

Evangelists gained prominence in the 1950s with Reverend Billy Graham, who would hold large meetings in tents and stadiums for all those who wanted to be "saved" by God. Sinners could be saved for a price.

As television entered nearly every household, so did the evangelists. Evangelists such as Oral Roberts played on people's fears and health conditions. He had God heal their diseases. A person in a wheelchair would walk after Oral Roberts prayed to God to heal their disease and join God. All of this came at a price. Send money; he will pray for you and your disease or fears. His TV show built an empire in Tulsa, Oklahoma, including a university. The scam is obvious. "I will pray for you, but please send me money!"

These televangelist con artists become exorbitantly wealthy as a result of money coming in. This money was tax exempt, and there was little to no supervision by the IRS or any third party.

The evangelists meet all the criteria for sociopathy. They are narcissists who believe they sit at the right hand of God. They share grandiose ideas in the name of faith in God to exploit their followers in order to make money. They are manipulative, using *faith* as the means to an end. Their empathy is fake. They have no guilt. They are dishonest and lie about their faith. Their criminal aspect to their sociopathy is that there are no laws to stop them from committing fraud. As far as their cognition is concerned, it must be weak, allowing their emotions to overrule right from wrong.

The other parameter for con artists is also met. They are Machiavellian, and they use charisma and cleverness but often dishonest methods that deceive people so they can gain power and control. They are aggressive, manipulative, exploitative, and devious.

T.D. Jakes, Franklin Graham, Joel Osteen, and Jim Bakker are some of the most notorious televangelists. One of the most egregious examples is Creflo Dollar, a televangelist and leader of the World Changers Church based in Georgia. He is a pastor / con artist who recently petitioned members of his church for donations so he could buy a $70 million private jet in order to fulfill the mission of the ministry. The thirty thousand members delivered on the principle that giving one's own money to the church will result in the subsequent flourishing of personal wealth. This is the whole mantra of religious con artists.

Summary

Antisocial personality disorder should be reevaluated regarding its generality. Sociopathy and psychopathy are distinctive in terms of criminal description. Psychopaths kill other humans, while sociopaths do not take their criminal behavior to that extent. Separation of the two began in the nineteenth and twentieth centuries for a reason, and it is reasonable to continue those descriptive separations.

Distinguishing the two is also beneficial for purposes of research and treatment. Perhaps medications could be designed to increase brain activity in the prefrontal cortex. Functional PET brain scans, as well as genetic studies, should also be used to distinguish the two.

CHAPTER 4

WHY REPUBLICANS CALL DEMOCRATS SOCIALISTS: UNDERSTANDING SOCIALISM VERSUS UTILITARIANISM

Introduction

The intent of this chapter is to provide a brief explanation of both socialism and utilitarianism and the ways in which they can be interchangeable. Both of these reflect social values; however, socialism involves political, economic, and social structuring, whereas utilitarianism is more philosophical and has moral implications. Both address social issues, values, and similar goals. There are many forms of socialism that exist not only as ideologies but practiced in many countries throughout the world. We will briefly explore several of these different varieties of socialism and present two extremes: radical/revolutionary socialism and democratic socialism.

Definitions

Socialism. A political and economic theory of social organization that advocates that the means of production, distribution, and exchange should be owned or regulated by the community as a whole.

Communism. A theory or system of social organization in which all property is owned by the community, and each person contributes and receives according to their ability and needs.

Capitalism. An economic and political system in which a country's trade and industry are controlled by private owners for profit, rather than by the state.

Utilitarianism is a moral philosophy that life can be made better by increasing the amount of good in society. We also use a new term for a philosophy that represents immoral and bad behavior in society, called nefariousism.

Socialism as defined by the *Oxford Dictionary* is somewhat different from the accepted political definition. The political definition is "a social and economic system characterized by social ownership in the form of a cooperative, or citizens and democratic control of the means of production." There are many varieties of socialism that provide the greatest good for the greatest number of people in an autocratic system.

Socialism is perceived by Republicans in the United States as bad, but as with any form of social government (i.e., capitalism and communism included), there are both good and bad parts. The question is the degree of utility versus oppression. A large part of socialism is dependent on the management of profits, monetary principles, and the economy.

Socialism arose from monarchies and individualism that failed to address the social concerns of poverty, social oppression, and gross inequality of wealth. Individualism has historically been considered liberal. This has repeated itself with the recent issues in America that the Republicans fail to address.

Communal socialism has been present from the beginning of human existence. It allowed everyone to be involved with production and consumption, and all had an equal share and chance to ensure their survival. It became more politicized in the 1800s in Europe.

As the working class became more oppressed in various European countries and in Britain, socialism arose with labor parties. This is how communism began in Russia, where socialism was used by Lenin in 1918 as the basis for communism. The Russian Social Democratic Labor Party was an illegal party formed in response to peasant poverty. It was formed to unite the various revolutionary organizations of the Russian Empire into one party in 1898. It fought against the autocracy, organized meetings and strikes, and printed illegal newspapers blaming the Tsar and his government. Many members of the party were arrested, imprisoned, or condemned to penal servitude. The party was split into two, the Bolsheviks and the Mensheviks. The Bolsheviks became the dominant party. The Bolsheviks were a radical, Far Left, and revolutionary Marxist faction founded by Vladimir Lenin and Alexander Bogdanov. This Bolshevik faction eventually became the Communist Party of the Soviet Union.

The appearance of the Communist Soviet State motivated and strengthened communist parties across the world that previously had varying levels of political and social influence. Among those that grew stronger were the communist parties of France, Spain, Italy, China, Germany, Mexico, and Brazil. In 1919, the communist party of Ukraine was formed.

Today, the existing communist states in the world are found in China, Cuba, Laos, and Vietnam. These communist states often do not claim to have achieved communism in their countries but to be building and working toward the establishment of socialism.

There are anywhere between eighty-two and 107 communist parties or groups throughout many countries in the world, depending on membership numbers. This breaks down to about eighty-five million communists in the world.

Karl Marx in *Das Kapital* and Vladimir Lenin in his essays in *Imperialism, the Highest Stance of Capitalism* were opposed to capitalism. Both were defendants of the working class. Lenin wrote that capitalism was a monopoly and created globalization. He observed that as capitalism had further developed in Europe and America, the workers remained unable to gain consciousness of their class because they were too busy working and were concerned about how to make ends meet. He therefore proposed a social revolution.

These socialist ideas from the nineteenth and twentieth centuries can be applied today. There is no question that there is a huge discrepancy between the working class and poor and the wealthy in America. The Republicans want to keep it that way because they are imperialists. But what is healthiest for the country is to strengthen the middle class and elevate the poor to make a stronger America. The Republicans view this idea as socialist. But when it is utilitarian socialism that generally works in a democracy anyway, why not join it to a capitalist system?

Radical left and Far Left socialism has historically originated from monarchies. The monarch oppresses and suppresses the working class, and the working class revolts in the form of social democratic factions. Radicalization and revolutionary forms of socialism then generate power in the form of communism.

China is another example. The communism in China originated from a revolution, a result of the oppression of the Qing Dynasty of the early 1920s. There was Japanese invasion and civil unrest until 1949. The Communist Party grew in strength, and in 1949, the Chinese Revolution occurred, eventually forming the People's Republic of China. China did not evolve from an emperor to socialism and finally to communism. The communist party in China formed directly from the oppression of a monarchy.

The United States has tried to stop radical left socialism and communism throughout the world. A lot of money and lives were spent to fight the communist party in Vietnam, which failed. There was an attempt to do the same in Nicaragua.

Lessons should be learned from the history of oppressing the working class in many countries. Republicans have been oppressing the working class in the United States, and the response has been the rise of socialist ideals. The Democrats have been champions for the poor and working class, and the Republicans call Democrats *socialists* to create fear among Americans. Americans need to be educated regarding social programs.

Socialism is not necessarily nefarious. Socialism, democracy, and capitalism can all coexist. After World War II, good socialism developed in many European counties. At the time, social democratic governments introduced social reform and monetary distribution in the form of state welfare and taxation. The social democratic parties came to fruition during the postwar period in many countries, including France, Italy, Czechoslovakia, Belgium, and Norway.

The British Labor Party gained power in 1945. It created many social programs and nationalized several public utilities, including mines, gas, coal, electricity, rail, iron, steel, and the Bank of England. British Petroleum was officially nationalized in 1951. However, employees were gradually involved in a percentage of ownership. Over time, between 1979 and 1987, British Petroleum was made public.

The Nordic socialist model, including Norway, Sweden, and Finland, also evolved after World War II. Of all the Nordic countries, Sweden is the prime example used for reform socialism. There are two social democratic parties in Sweden: the Norwegian Labor Party founded in 1887 and the Swedish Social Democratic Party founded in 1889. The majority Swedish Social Democratic Party gained power in 1936 and held the majority until 1976, as well as from 1982 to 1991 and 1994 to 2006. The minority party, the Norwegian Labor Party, held power briefly from 1976 to 1982 and 1991 to 1994.

The Nordic counties have adopted a nixed economy, which is variously defined as an economic system blending elements of a market economy with elements of a planned economy, free markets with state interventionism, or private enterprise with public enterprise. This allows enhancement of individual autonomy, ensuring the universal provision of basic human rights, and stabilizes the economy. It is distinguished from other welfare states with its emphasis on maximizing the labor force participation, promoting gender equality, and extensive benefits, such as education and health care. Although Sweden has higher taxes, there is a high level of transparency with balanced budgets, economic education, and health care. The Swedes take care of their children and senior citizens, unlike the United States.

The Far Left is associated with communism, and the Far Right with fascism (discussed in chapter 7). The Left is said to be liberal. They called themselves the New Left in Great Britain and the United States in the 1960s and 1970s. They were activists for social justice, including antiwar, gay/lesbian rights, abortion/women's rights, gender rights, racial equality, and marijuana legalization. Compare this to radical Marxist Left. It should be obvious that democratic socialism attempts to create equality in principle.

The 1968 American protest against the Vietnam War, the military, and powerful capitalist leaders created a huge social movement. The Black community organized the Poor People's Campaign concerning economic disparity in America, leading a coalition against the elite in support of the poor and the civil rights movement for the Black community. This represents democratic socialism.

Socialist International wrote *Progressive Politics for a Fairer World*. It stated: "Democratic socialism is an international movement for freedom, social justice, and solidarity. Its goal is to achieve a peaceful world where these basic values can be enhanced and where each individual can live a meaningful life with the full development of his or her personality and talents, and with the guarantee of human and civil rights in a democratic framework of society." Who wouldn't want to have these values? It is unclear why Republicans keep calling Democrats socialists when the values for citizens should be the same.

Democratic Socialism versus Social Democracy

Democratic socialism is a broad political movement that seeks to promote the ideals of socialism within the context of a democratic system. This is differentiated from social democracy. Modern social democracy emphasizes a program of gradual legislative modification of capitalism in order to make it more equitable. This is promoted in a pro-capitalist or mixed economy. Social democracy is not totally linked to the economy but rather social issues. It is a political movement that seeks to establish an economy based on economic democracy by and for the working class. Wealthy Republicans are fearful of having their money go to helping the middle and working class. They fear democratic socialism. Wealthy Republicans control the Republican Party in the United States.

Social democracy is an ideology that originated from socialism. The systems in northern and western Europe that have a mixed system of capitalism and social democracy have provided a higher standard of living and more happiness than American capitalism.

Social democracy can perform in a hybrid form. There is a peaceful, gradual reformist evolution to socialism in the social democratic form of democratic socialism that creates reform to capitalism. It would provide economic democracy in the form of an increased standard of living for the working class and poor.

Social democracy opposes the excesses of capitalism, such as inequality, poverty, and oppression of various groups, and supports a fair and just free market economy. It promotes universal rights to public services, such as education, health care, child care for working families, elder care, and farmers' rights and land protection. Social democracy is also connected with the trade union and labor movement and supports collective bargaining rights for workers.

Modern democratic socialism is a broad political movement that seeks to promote the ideals of socialism within the context of a democratic system. Democratic socialists seek a modification of capitalism in order to make it more equitable and humane. Theoretically, the end goal of social reform is pro-capitalist. The possibility of a complete socialist system in capitalism is unlikely unless capitalism becomes so disengaged from the wealthy becoming powerful and the middle class, working class, and poor being abused, so much that it inspires a revolution with socialism overtaking capitalism. It is apparent that the social democratic direction of Democrats in the United States would actually prevent socialism. But Republicans want the power and use nefarious behavior to keep it.

The major difference between social democracy and democratic socialism is the object of their politics: contemporary social democrats support social equality, social support, employment equality, and unemployment insurance as a means to a more just and humanistic capitalism. Democratic socialists seek to replace capitalism with a socialist economic system.

Liberal socialism does not seek to abolish capitalism, but instead, it supports a mixed economy that includes both public and private property in capital goods. It challenges monopolies and opposes deregulation. Liberal socialists blame capitalism for economic inequality and greed. Among the most famous philosophical promoters have been John Stuart Mill and John Dewey.

Religious Socialism

Religious socialism should not be confused with the fact that many religions meet the definition of socialism. Religious socialism is a type of socialism based on religious values. Based on this definition, several religions hold the same values and principles as socialism, including Buddhist socialism, Christian socialism, Islamic socialism, and Jewish socialism. Adopted into these religions are social and economic doctrines, including public rather than private ownership or control of property and natural resources. Typically, production is for all and shared by all in a cooperative means. It is considered communal under a specific religion.

Buddhist Socialism

The moral principles of Buddhism are nearly identical to Buddhist socialism. Both seek to diminish human suffering and equalize personal gains, while capitalism seeks personal gains as its main objective. Dharmic socialism believes that socialism is a natural state, meaning all things exist together in one system. Buddhist socialist ideology is not significantly different from Buddhism itself.

Christian Socialism

Modern Christian socialism, as explained in Wikipedia, is "a religious and political philosophy that blends Christianity and socialism, endorsing left-wing politics and socialist economics on the basis of the

Holy Bible and the teachings of Jesus of Nazareth." Many Christian socialists believe capitalism to be idolatrous and rooted in the sin of greed.

Christian socialism dates back to Jesus and the formation of the church. The early church essentially formed groups of Christians who were economically and socially dependent on one another for their existence. The Catholic Church began in the first century in the name of Jesus under the Roman Empire. It grew in power. Medieval cathedrals were the most obvious sign of the wealth of the Roman Catholic Church. The cost of these cathedrals was huge, and the money to pay for them came from the people via the payments they made to the Roman Catholic Church. This reflects socialism by way of politics, production, distribution, building, and education. The Roman Catholic Church also merged with many governments and states in Europe. Their support of the governments that went to war is heretical to the fundamental teachings of Jesus.

Another religious group that initiated Christian socialism was the Anabaptists of Switzerland of the early 1500s. The movement originated as a radical socialist religion during the Protestant Reformation. They formed independent social groups that practiced their own political, economic, and religious socialism. The Anabaptists opposed Catholicism. Their most prominent belief was that of adult baptism. Unlike Catholicism, Anabaptists do not believe in infant baptism, because they believe that only those who truly understand and accept the teachings of God can be legitimately baptized. For them, baptism required a public acknowledgment of their faith. Catholics, Lutherans, and some Baptists believe in baptism.

The Anabaptists were a radical religious faction that developed from the teachings of Ulrich Zwingli and Martin Luther. However, both Zwingli and Luther rejected the Anabaptists because they deemed them to be too radical. They rejected that their followers were baptized in rivers around Zurich, Switzerland. As a result, the Anabaptists were persecuted and fled to other countries, such as Germany.

The Anabaptists emigrated from Europe to the United States in the early 1700s, where they settled predominantly in Pennsylvania and the rural areas of New York, Virginia, and Maryland. Different religious congregations were formed that consisted of Mennonites, Quakers, Amish, Church of the Brethren, and other factions. They formed socialist communities that produced off the land, distributed among themselves, and formed their own government system. This held until television, tourism, computers, and cell phones invaded their social ways. The Amish in Lancaster County in Pennsylvania had their social communities disrupted by tourism, causing many to leave for Canada, Ohio, and other Midwest states. They have even moved as far as Belize to form their own socialist communities.

Islamic Socialism

Islamic socialism is defined as a political philosophy that incorporates Islamic principles in socialism. As a term, it was coined by various Muslim leaders to describe a more spiritual form of socialism. Muslims believe that the Quran and the teachings of Muhammad coincide with socialism. In fact, Muhammad established a welfare state in Medina. In AD 622, Muhammad led his followers to Medina to establish order among clans and in doing so established a welfare state. Medina is located in the Hejaz region of western Saudi Arabia. To this day, Islamic socialism continues throughout the Middle East, especially in terms of anti-imperialism.

Hindu Socialism

Hinduism believes in the fundamental divinity of all forms of life. It accepts diversity of the planet. It expects human beings to be mindful of the ubiquitous presence of God in its every aspect.

Hindus fail to see the unity in a society that is organized on the basis of a caste system and on social values that are centered on the concepts of karma. They are obsessed with the ideas of caste, gender, language, beliefs, occupation, and ideology. They believe whether one is born rich or poor is a result of one's prior life. On this basis, every Hindu accepts the inequalities of their social and economic system as inevitable and justified. Because inequality is ingrained in Hindu ideology, revolutions are eliminated.

Hinduism circumvents the definition of socialism by denying the existence of socialism due to the nature of individualism in religion. Hinduism is not suitable for a political ideology that strives to establish a socialist society. It is not conducive to socialism or communism, because both are contradicted by the fundamentals of karma.

Hinduism approves of free enterprise, which is harmonious with the ideology of karma. The Hindu belief system is susceptible to corrupt leaders or invasion of foreign imperialism. Hindus endure suffering because they believe they are responsible for it in the first place. As a result, socialism, communism, and capitalism could all be involved politically in India, of which Hindus make up roughly 80 percent of the population. And indeed they all have had some activity in India. The distinction should be made between Hinduism as a religion (antipolitical) and the country of India as sociopolitical people.

Socialism in India began with Gandhi. Mahatma Gandhi was the leader of India's nonviolent independence movement against British rule. Born October 2, 1869, in Porbandar, India, Gandhi studied law and organized boycotts against British institutions in peaceful forms of civil disobedience. Gandhi promoted socialism politically in line with some aspects of Hinduism. It became known as Gandhian socialism. He was assassinated on January 30, 1948, during a vigil in New Delhi when Nathuram Godse, a Hindu extremist who objected to what he perceived to be Gandhi's destruction of Hinduism and tolerance for Muslims, fatally shot him.

In the *American Journal of Economics and Sociology*, R. Koshal and M. Koshal describe Gandhian economic philosophy. From their article: "The ideology of Gandhian socialism is rooted in Gandhi's work titled Swarai and *India of My Dreams* in which, he describes Indian society, with no one rich or poor, no class conflict, where there is an equal distribution of the resources, and self-sufficient economy without any exploitation and violence. Thus, Gandhian socialism differed from Western socialism because the latter believed in material progress whereas Gandhi considered every one materially equal."

There was also a religious aspect of Gandhi's socialism. After India's independence in 1947, the Indian government under Prime Minister Jawaharlal Nehru and Indira Gandhi (later prime minister) oversaw land reform and the nationalization of major industries and the banking sector. In 1931, the Indian National Congress adopted the principles of socialism. This was also addressed in the 1955 Congress. In 1976, socialism was added to the Indian government.

Reference:

Koshal, Raijinadar, and Manulika Koshal. "Gandhian Economic Philosophy." *American Journal of Economics and Sociology* 32, no. 2 (1973): 191–209.

Jewish Socialism

Jewish socialism occurs when the Jewish Left supports liberal causes. This is mostly individualized, since there is no organized movement. However, their major historical forces appear socialist. Jews have long promoted the labor movement, housing settlements, women's rights, and antiracism. They are opposed to fascism, colonialism, and those who are anticapitalist.

Socialist Zionism, also recognized as Labor Zionism, embodies labor as its most important movement. They believe that a Jewish state can only be created through the efforts of the working class settling in the Land of Israel. This can also be accomplished through progressive socialism.

Summary of Religious Socialism

Socialism entered into early religion initially with the Catholic Church. It began in agrarian communities based on production, distribution, consumption, and a society governed by the rules of religion. For the Catholic Church, this formed into a geosocialist and political religious force. Similarly, the Anabaptists formed as an agrarian community in Europe, separate from Catholicism, with their own social communities and their own production, distribution, and consumption as well as religious governance.

Many religions have incorporated the socialist ideology.

Utilitarianism

Introduction

Utilitarianism has been described by English philosophers, starting with Jeremy Bentham in 1780. Bentham's book *An Introduction to the Principles of Morals and Legislation* was published in 1789. A follower of Bentham, John Stuart Mill, published his book *Utilitarianism* in 1963. Both adopted the principle of utility, which holds that an action is good in so far as it promotes happiness for moral agents. Hence, actions should not be considered good or bad in and of themselves but only in reference to their utility (i.e., usefulness in achieving happiness). They defined utilitarianism as a family of consequentialist ethical theories that promotes actions that maximize happiness and well-being for the majority of a population.

Classic and modern utilitarianism are discussed below.

Definitions for Utilitarianism:

Utilitarianism (author's definition). A postulate that simply proposes the greatest good for the greatest number of people.

Good. 1. To be desired or approved of. 2. Having the required qualities; of a high standard. 3. Possessing or displaying moral virtue.

Good can also be defined as being of high standard, health, strength, usefulness, as advantageous, and beneficial in effect.

Goodness. The quality of being morally good or virtuous.

Utility. The state of being useful, profitable, or beneficial. The measure that is sought to be maximized in any situation involving choice.

Utilitarianism. The doctrine that actions are right if they are useful or for the benefit of a majority. The doctrine that an action is right in so far as it promotes happiness and that the greatest happiness of the greatest number should be the guiding conduct.

Happiness. The state of being happy.

Happy. A feeling of pleasure or contentment. Carefree; excited.

Values. The principles or standards of behavior; one's judgment of what is important in life. Principles.

Ethics (or moral philosophy). Involves systematizing, defending, and recommending concepts of right and wrong behavior. Philosophers today usually divide ethical theories into three general subject areas: meta-ethics, normative ethics, and applied ethics. Someone who is honest and follows good moral standards is said to be ethical. Ethical comes from the Greek *ethos* ("moral character") and describes a person or behavior as right in the moral sense—truthful, fair, and honest.

Morality. The principles concerning the distinction between right and wrong or good and bad behavior. The extent to which an action is right or wrong. Three common frameworks are deontology, utilitarianism, and virtue ethics. The last branch is applied ethics. It addresses specific, practical issues of moral importance, such as war and capital punishment.

The difference between the two according to our understanding, ethics is a more individual assessment of values as relatively good or bad. While morality is a more intersubjective community assessment of what is good, right, or just for all. There is a difference between what I should do in an ethical dilemma and what we should do in a moral dilemma.

Similar Theoretical Philosophies

In the early 1700s, the philosopher Francis Hutcheson arrived at the proportional idea that moral action, virtue, is in proportion to the number of people to which a particular action brings happiness. Although Jeremy

Bentham originated the concept and term of utilitarianism in 1781, John Stuart Mill expanded the term and extended the philosophy in 1861.

Utilitarianism expands on human happiness. Happiness was discussed by Aristotle. This was not a totally new concept to Bentham. Nevertheless, other theories and philosophies had similar characteristics, including ethical hedonism and consequentialism.

Ethical hedonism is the belief that our fundamental moral obligation is to maximize pleasure or happiness. Ethical hedonism is most associated with the ancient Greek philosopher Epicurus (342–270 BCE), who taught that our life's goal should be to minimize pain and maximize pleasure. As a theory of value, hedonism states that all pleasure is intrinsically valuable and all pain is intrinsically invaluable. Hedonists usually define pleasure and pain broadly, such that both physical and mental phenomena are included.

Utilitarianism is a version of consequentialism, which states that the consequences of any action are the only standard of right and wrong. Unlike other forms of consequentialism, such as ethical egoism and altruism, utilitarianism considers the interests of all beings equally. Ethical egoism is the normative ethical position that moral agents ought to act in their own self-interest. It differs from psychological egoism, which claims that people can only act in their self-interest. Altruism (also called the ethic of altruism, moralistic altruism, and ethical altruism) is an ethical doctrine that holds that the moral value of an individual's actions depend solely on the impact on other individuals, regardless of the consequences on the individual itself.

Original Classic Utilitarianism

Utilitarianism was introduced by an English philosopher, Jeremy Bentham (1748–1832). He wrote an axiom that the greatest happiness for the greatest number is the measure of right and wrong. He advocated individual and economic freedom and the separation of church and state.

The eighteenth- and nineteenth-century philosophers correlated good with happiness. Plato and Aristotle addressed happiness in 300 and 400 BCE. Aristotle used the term *human flourishing,* which he described as happiness. Plato claimed that happiness can occur in moral and virtuous people. Socrates believed that the abuse of power enslaves oneself to irrational and self-centered, harmful behavior. He also saw a type of happiness stemming from social justice and in fulfilling social functions. More obvious forms of happiness, such as leisure, wealth, and pleasure, are deemed lesser, if not completely false, forms of happiness.

The philosophy of happiness is the philosophical concern with the existence, nature, and attainment of happiness. Some philosophers believe happiness can be understood as the moral goal of life or as an aspect of chance; indeed, in most European languages, the term *happiness* is synonymous with luck.

Desire and pleasure are discussed by the early philosophers of utilitarianism. Both are described significantly in hedonism, which is defined as an ethical theory that pleasure (in the sense of the satisfaction of desires) is the highest good and proper aim of human life. Another more philosophical definition is that hedonism is a school of thought that argues that seeking pleasure and avoiding suffering are the only components of well-being. Ethical hedonism is said to have been started by Aristippus of Cyrene, a student of Socrates. He held the idea that pleasure is the highest good.

A more modern-day view is to maximize pleasure and minimize pain. The argument is that pleasure and pain/suffering are usually temporary and short-lived. These feelings have no place in utilitarianism, because they are not substantially enduring.

Modern Twentieth-Century Utilitarianism

Ideal utilitarianism arose from several sources in the early 1900s. It states that the only fundamental requirement of morality is to promote a plurality of intrinsic goods for all those capable of possessing them. This moral framework flourished in the middle 1900s.

George Edward Moore, professor of philosophy at Cambridge University, wrote about moral knowledge, epistemology (discussed in chapter 2), ethics, and ideal utilitarianism. Moore, in his book *Ethics* (London: Williams and Norgate, 1912), argued that there is a range of values that might be maximized. Moore's strategy was to show that it is intuitively implausible for pleasure to be the sole measure of what is good. He wrote that such an assumption of a world in which absolutely nothing except pleasure existed—excluding knowledge, love, enjoyment of beauty, moral qualities in which each of these are intrinsically better than pure pleasure—but that the aggregate or plurality of intrinsic goods for all those capable of possessing them.

Moore believed that it was intuitively obvious that even if the amount of pleasure stayed the same, a world that contained such things as beauty and love would be a better world. He added that if a person was to take the contrary view, then "I think it is self-evident that he would be wrong."

Mid-twentieth-century utilitarianism ushered in the rules of morality. However, rule utilitarianism proposes a more central role for rules that was thought to rescue the theory from some of its more devastating criticisms, particularly problems with justice. This became known as rule utilitarianism.

Rule utilitarianism says that we can produce more beneficial results by following rules than by always performing individual actions whose results are as beneficial as possible. This suggests that we should not always perform individual actions that maximize utility. This is paradoxical to utilitarianism as defined. This would best serve a utopian society, but unfortunately, in America, the rule follows the individual, especially when the individual is wealthy. This is ironic. Laws and justice in a utilitarian society mean that a law that is good would serve the purposes for all, and everyone would be treated the same under that law. In the United States, justice is not utilitarian. A person is presumed innocent until proven guilty. Unfortunately, this is not true in many situations. If the law is good and has been obviously broken, there is no contest. However, many situations are not just. A character assassination costs a lot of money to defend. A police officer shooting a Black person in the back only leads to the officer being put on administrative leave. Wealthy people get away with breaking laws easier than poor people. This deletes the greatest good or well-being for the greatest number of people.

In the mid-1950s, another theory was termed act utilitarianism. Act utilitarianism is a utilitarian theory of ethics that states that a person's act is morally right if and only if it produces the best possible results in that specific situation. The essential difference is what determines whether or not an action is the right action. Act utilitarianism maintains that an action is right if it maximizes utility; rule utilitarianism maintains that an action is right if it conforms to a rule that maximizes utility.

Much of the late-twentieth-century utilitarianism emphasizes the individual and not the greater good. Another variant of utilitarianism is preference utilitarianism, which is the only form of utilitarianism consistent with the important philosophical principle of preference autonomy. The principle that in deciding what is good and what is bad for a given individual, the ultimate criterion can only be his own wants and one's own preferences. For example: I, as a nondiabetic, want ice cream. I go to Baskin-Robbins, where there are thirty-one varieties. I choose Rocky Road, because that gives me the most pleasure. This totally misses the theory of utilitarianism and falls more into hedonism. It excludes well-being and responsivity in terms of irrational ethics to self. A diabetic should not be at Baskin-Robbins.

Utilitarianism, Justice, Morality, and Consequences

Some philosophers argue that utilitarianism ignores justice. Act and rule utilitarianism are the only two forms of utilitarianism that address justice, and neither do so very well.

H. J. McCloskey wrote "A Note on Utilitarian Punishment" in *Mind*, 72, 1963, page 599: "Surely the utilitarian must admit that whatever the facts of the matter may be, it is logically possible that an 'unjust' system of punishment—e.g. a system involving collective punishments, retroactive laws and punishments, or punishments of parents and relations of the offender—may be more useful than a 'just' system of punishment? In other words, if you created a peaceful and happy society, utilitarianism does not accept injustices, such as murder and robbery." This suggests confusion between utopia/dystopia and utilitarianism. Utopia is when the community or society is perfect or ideal, and dystopia is when the conditions of that society are extremely bad, with great suffering, injustice, or unpleasantness. Utilitarianism does not pursue either of these extreme societies. A utilitarian would say that a just system of punishment is more useful than an unjust system. Utilitarianism is not utopian. Classical utilitarianism made maximizing social utility the basic criterion of morality. Morality is a variable in the context of utilitarianism.

It has been said that utilitarianism makes all of us members of the same moral community. However, a person with antisocial personality disorder is also a member of the same community and causes harm to a moral person in the community. This person has no claim to the moral community when it comes to defining our concept of social utility.

Morality can only be a variable that is nonindividualized in utilitarianism. Discussing individualism in utilitarianism is nonsensical. However, one could choose a moral value for utility, like respect, love, or compassion (e.g., the greatest love for the greatest number of people). We don't have to stop there; we could say the greatest compassionate love for the greatest number of people. With COVID-19, this has become obvious with doctors, nurses, and respiratory therapists doing the greatest good for the greatest number of people. Emergency medical technicians are saving lives, grocery attendants are making sure people can buy food; the list of helpers is long. One could also say President Obama's compassion was the greatest good or quality that served the greatest number of people in America.

We should also recognize the absurdity in using a generalization of morality as the only feature of utilitarianism. For example, if a moral (good) man smokes cigarettes, is that morally good for the community? He is moral, and the community is moral, but the cigarette smoke causes harm to the community.

Consequences have been discussed with classic utilitarians Bentham and Mill. Some philosophers state that it is impossible to calculate the requirements of utilitarianism because the consequences are inherently unknown. It is believed that it would be impossible to assign a precise value to an incident because it is impossible to know what will occur at any given time.

Consequences are obtuse to the functionality of utilitarianism. They are an independent variable. If a person has high blood pressure, a blood pressure medicine is administered to lower the blood pressure. The greater good is the blood pressure medication, which is designed to lower the blood pressure in which the consequence is normalizing the blood pressure. The medication (the greatest good) is designed to provide normal blood pressure to those with high pressure (the greatest number of people with high blood pressure). Will this medication absolutely lower the blood pressure of all hypertensive persons? No, some people may take two or three medications for blood pressure. So the consequence may be variable, but the outcome is the greater good.

We have discussed vaccinations (immunizations) previously. It can be said that vaccinations provide the greatest good (protection from infectious disease) for the greatest number of people in a population. Vaccinations provide an imprint in a person's immune system, so that when exposed to the infectious agent, the person does not contract the infection. With a new vaccine, can the consequences of that vaccine be predictive in preventing infections in the general population? A very good prediction can be made using scientific knowledge. Measles, mumps, and rubella (MMR) vaccinations have nearly eliminated measles, except in the cases of antivaccination proponents who falsely believe there is a link between vaccines and autism. Many diseases, including polio, hepatitis B, smallpox, and others, have nearly been eliminated as a result of vaccinations. The consequences of vaccinations are well established. From these examples, along with rigorous science and research, the same process will occur for COVID-19. Why is there no vaccine for human immunodeficiency virus (HIV)? Again, vigorous scientific research has found that the proteins on the virus are not readily recognized by the immune system. HIV can infect many cells, including the cells of the immune system before the immune system recognizes the virus. Consequently, it is difficult to develop a vaccine that the immune system would recognize when exposed to the virus. This shows that consequences in utilitarianism can be known but only through facts and scientific principles.

Religious Utilitarianism

In terms of religion, utilitarianism is a system of morality concerned with that which is the most useful and pleasurable. Utilitarian principles do not fit into religion, but some of the moral values of religion fit into utilitarianism.

The combination of utilitarianism with the belief in God has strong consequences regarding human nature. Utilitarianism is the theory that maximization of joy is good and that everyone's interests are equally important. Since God is omnipotent, God can do everything. In short, religion is not utilitarian. Religion is based on faith and beliefs, while utilitarianism is based on rationality.

Objection and Criticism of Classic and Modern Utilitarianism

While the term *utilitarianism* was first used by John Stuart Mill, there have been many varieties, including Bentham utilitarianism, Mill utilitarianism, rule utilitarianism, act utilitarianism, ethical utilitarianism, hedonist utilitarianism, preference, total, negative, and more. Understandably, some variation in the principle originated throughout time. The *Oxford Dictionary* describes utilitarianism as a doctrine: "The doctrine that actions are right if they are useful or for the benefit of a majority. Or classically: The doctrine that an action is right in so far as it promotes happiness, and that the greatest happiness of the greatest number should be the guiding conduct." Utilitarianism is not a doctrine. Nowhere is utilitarianism used in churches. Utilitarianism is a postulate.

Author's Concept and Philosophy of Utilitarianism

Utilitarianism (author's definition). A postulate that simply proposes the greatest good for the greatest number of people. Good is considered to have high standards and possess high moral values.

Utility in the word *utilitarian* means well-being or mindfulness. Most definitions include happiness as the greatest good. This is objectionable. Happiness is more of an illusion. In reality, happiness is usually short-lived, because the reality of life is not one of constant happiness. People desire happiness, which is why they have parties and fun activities, but being happy only lasts as long as the activity. Well-being is a better term, because it means feeling comfortable, healthy, or untroubled. Well-being provides utility as an undercurrent that all is generally well. Utility is the consequence of good actions for oneself or for society.

Obviously, utilitarianism is not limited to well-being but is applied to many values of morality and to different concepts. Interestingly, Karl Marx, in his *Das Kapital*, argued that well-being does not appear to recognize that people have different joys in different socioeconomic contexts. The common denominator for any form of utilitarianism is to maximize unity, which is often defined in terms of well-being or related concepts.

The action of pleasure should not be considered in utilitarianism. This view of pleasure is hedonistic, as it pursues the thought that pleasure is the highest good in life. However, utilitarianism accepts intellectual pleasure over sensual pleasure, but only sensual pleasure is hedonistic.

The proposition that utilitarianism is included in morality must be based on facts. One cannot say that nonfacts provide the greatest good for the greatest number of people. The initial proposition is like a hypothesis, and the consequences may or may not be known. Utilitarianism only has validity to facts and not nonfacts (see chapter 2).

Consider the following examples to explain a proposition used in utilitarianism. Seat belts in motor vehicles were first introduced in 1949 by the American car manufacturer Nash. Ford followed in 1955, but seat belts were optional. At the time, there was much consternation regarding the use of the seat belt, which caused Nash and Ford to make it optional. It was presumed that the seat belt would prevent deaths in accidents, which is the greatest good for the greatest number of drivers. However, all the facts (consequences) were not clear regarding this premise. Further studies in Sweden provided more data, and the Swedish car manufacturer Saab made seat belts mandatory in 1968. This confirmed the greatest good for wearing a seat belt to the greatest number of drivers to the extent that the greatest good became mandatory.

Another premise is the airbag. One could claim that the airbag is the greater good in that it saves the greatest number of lives in a head-on collision. This is a factual statement. On the other hand, one cannot say that airbags prevent injuries for the greatest number of people in accidents. This would be an untrue statement, because airbag release causes injuries, such as bruising, hematomas, fractured noses, and concussions.

In 2020, COVID-19 become a global pandemic. It immediately became apparent that wearing masks, social distancing, and frequent handwashing could reduce transmission of the virus significantly. Other countries put these measures in place, while much of the United States did not. The incompetent American leadership did not make these measures mandatory. Many Americans refused to follow these recommendations because they felt mandatory government regulations would interfere with their freedom and personal rights, even as these irresponsibly defiant people interfered with the health of others. They refused to follow the postulate of the greatest good (wearing masks, etc.) for the greatest number of people. Hence, much illness and over half a million American deaths occurred.

If we return to the example of seat belts, the opposition-defiant people got in their cars every day and were forced to wear seat belts. What about the loss of this freedom? What about those who intentionally run a red light, because the red lights violate their freedom to drive how and where they want? These people who are fixated on the childish oppositional defiant disorder are a menace to the greatest number of people. And who was leading the crowd with defiance about wearing a mask and such?

The Republican president, congressional Republicans, and Republican state leaders. These people need courses in logic, science, reason, ethics, and cognitive therapy.

Utilitarianism only postulates goodness, not badness. Problems arise when comparisons are made between good and bad in utilitarianism. Outcomes or consequences can inadvertently be good or bad, but the usual premise starts with something good.

It should be apparent that one cannot initially compare good versus bad. For example, Peter Singer, in his book *The Life You Can Save*, wrote that it is more instinctive to save a drowning child than it is to save starving children in India and Africa. He struggles with the moral justification of lacking sympathy to what takes place in distant locations. Describing this as utilitarian makes no sense, because of course one would save a drowning child—it's immediate. Dying children in Africa are not immediate for most people in America. It would be more correct to say the intuition for saving a child from drowning is greater than for saving a drowning man, woman, Black, white, brown human being or even to go so far as saving an animal such as a dog. It would also be correct to say that feeding starving children is the greater good for the greater number of children. We have had programs like the Peace Corps in America that have helped poor countries. We have had philanthropic organizations like the Bill and Melinda Gates Foundation that have eliminated malaria in Africa.

Utilitarianism operates on the premise of moral and ethical conduct. Societies choose goodness over evil. Bad conduct, such as dishonesty, corruption, and injustice, have no place in utilitarianism, because the good of the whole disapproves. This is best said in John Stuart Mill's book *Utilitarianism*. In the final chapter, Mill concludes that justice, as a classifying factor of our actions (being just or unjust), is one of the certain moral requirements, and when the requirements are all regarded collectively, they are viewed as greater according to this scale of "social utility."

Utilitarianism is a philosophical view or theory about how we should evaluate a wide range of things that involve choices people face.

Utilitarianism and Socialism

The reason utilitarianism was chosen in concert with socialism is that socialism in general attempts to provide good for the population involved. In general, socialism is a political and economic theory of social organization that advocates that the means of production, distribution, and exchange should be owned or regulated by the community as a whole. It provides the greatest social equality for the greatest number of people. In theory and as an ideology, this is all good. However, with almost everything regarding the nature of human beings, there is good and there is bad.

Bad socialism evolves from oppression. It starts with monarchies oppressing the masses. It is revolutionary without reformation. It becomes autocratic, and from that point, it is either autocratic socialism or evolves into communism. This bad form of socialism has no ideology in utilitarianism. Bad socialism only has a transference of power from a monarchy to an autocratic socialist system. The greatest good is for the autocrat, although the population may experience a better good than with a monarchy.

Republicans love to throw the term *socialist* around when talking about Democrats. They do this to insinuate that socialism is bad and that Democrats are therefore bad. Their intent is to produce fear in the American people, so they can exert control. Of course, a group of Americans play into this fear.

Democrats should educate Americans that they are not socialists but utilitarians who support a social democracy. Social democracy is a governmental system with similar values to socialism but within a capitalist framework. The ideology, named for a democracy where people have a say in government actions, supports a competitive economy that provides for minimum wage, equal pay, free bargaining, and equality for working-class people and preventing employer abuse with reasonable unions. Many other issues like racial equality, gender equality, education, health care, child care for working families, elder care, farmers' rights, national forest protection, and natural land protection are also important.

Social democracy is connected with the trade union and the labor movement and supports collective bargaining rights for workers.

Democrats have long supported these issues. Theodore Roosevelt, a Republican, was the most conservationist US president. What went wrong?

The question is, are capitalist oligarchies, racism, LGB phobia, xenophobia, propaganda, gender inequality, religious inequality, female rights, and injustice utilitarian, or are social policies such as health care, education, and global warming prevention utilitarian?

Nefariousism

Nefariousism is our theory about creating the greatest bad for the greatest number of people. This is associated with unethical and immoral human behavior. Certainly, bad things occur in nature, and that can affect human behavior, but nefariousism is about intentional immoral behavior.

Bad. Failing to conform to standards of moral virtue or acceptable conduct.

Badness. Lack of or failure to conform to moral virtues or values; wickedness, evil.

Nefariousism associates and endorses such behaviors as deceit, deception, dishonesty, false information, hatred, hypocrisy, lies, conspiracies, killing, blame, bribery, extortion, authoritarianism, cheating, crimes, corruption, oppression, fraud, racism, inequality, deregulation, slander, terrorism, treason, tyranny, and any other unethical or immoral practice or behavior. Whereas utilitarianism operates under morality, nefariousism condones immorality.

Immorality is a violation of moral laws, norms, or standards. Immorality is normally applied to people or actions, or in a broader sense, it can be applied to groups or corporate bodies and works of art. Moral law is a system of guidelines for behavior. For example, murder, theft, prostitution, and other behaviors labeled immoral are also illegal. Moral turpitude is a legal term used to describe a crime that demonstrates depravity in one's public and private life, contrary to what is accepted and customary. Moral laws encompass regulations on justice, respect, and sexual conduct. All people will be held accountable to these laws. First Corinthians 6:9–11 is about dealing with God's moral law, which says that the unrighteous should not inherit the kingdom of God.

In all religions, immorality is denounced. In fact, in Christianity, sin is a central concept to understanding immorality. Morality in Christianity is often associated with sexuality. This has been a long struggle linked to dancing, homosexuality, intoxication, and the physical act of sex.

Pornography has long been condemned by Christians. Child pornography is illegal. Another form of illegal sexual activity is prostitution.

Morality is also considered when discussing abortion and *Roe v. Wade*. Using the postulate that abortions are the greatest bad for the greatest number of women creates a larger moral dilemma. Repealing *Roe v. Wade* would cause significant health problems that would be medically unethical. Women causing their own abortions would lead to significant health issues and death. Not to mention cases of unwanted pregnancy in instances of incest or rape. Eliminating *Roe v. Wade*, which members of many religions want to do, would exemplify totalitarianism. A woman has a right to her own body, and men in government have no right to interfere. Creating a law that eliminates all abortion creates the greatest bad for the greatest number of women.

Criminal Justice and Law Enforcement Nefariousism

Punishment in the criminal justice system is largely the purview of the United States. However, there are unethical practices that occur, including failure ensuring impartiality, profiling, failure to protect citizens' rights, and abuses of power.

There is failure of law enforcement to determine a necessary amount of force to use when restraining arrested suspects and ensuring that public servants maintain a principled lifestyle outside of work. Kneeling on the necks of suspects and using choke holds is unethical. Those who engage in these behaviors cause a bad reputation for all law enforcement officers.

Capital punishment is also considered bad. Sentencing someone to death is immoral because it allows the state to choose who deserves to die. Death is too permanent a punishment, especially considering how easy it is for an innocent person to be convicted of a crime. DNA technology is constantly exonerating innocent people who have been wrongfully convicted of crimes. Although persons who commit crimes and are sentenced to prison have done harm to the greatest number of people, rehabilitation has largely been successful. This shows that the bad can become good.

Racism and Terrorism Nefariousism

Hate and prejudice provide the greatest bad for the entire population. Like a great African American leader once claimed, there are three great evils in this world among us. There can be evil of poverty, racism, and war. Many Americans want democracy as long as there is dictatorship among the African American community. He goes on to say that progress has been made with desegregation. Civil rights have been slow. In 1875, a bill was passed, but it wasn't totally established until 1964. Today, America is still struggling with racial equality. This is a place for utilitarianism to proceed.

The evil of terrorism has no place in society. It is a malignant cancer that infiltrates crowds of people and carries no moral values. Terrorists believe their values are supreme.

Government and Politics Nefariousism

America has created its own set of evil acts. The massacres of Native Americans; this was the origin of white supremacy. It has not stopped. Native Americans have been placed on unwanted land, and all the good land was taken from them by white people. They are treated like second-class citizens. How many Native Americans have farms and businesses? Have we allowed them to live the way they want to live or the way we have forced them to live? It was nice of America to give them casinos.

PSYCHOSOCIAL POLITICAL DYSFUNCTION OF THE REPUBLICAN PARTY

The internment camps for the Japanese during World War II were also very bad. However, the evil that has been occurring for the past five decades in the Republican Party and has culminated in an autocratic fascist president is the most worrisome period in the history of the United States.

When we think of nefarious leaders, we think of Hitler and Mussolini, who both created the worst evil for the greatest number of people. This kind of rule still goes on in North Korea, South America, Russia, and many other countries. President Trump and the Republicans have paved the way for this kind of nefariousism in the United States.

Religious Nefariousism

Religion by its own definition functions on morality. But that is not to say that nefariousism does not exist in religion. This can be heretical. Take a wealthy businessman who attends church every Sunday and contributes money to the church but underpays and mistreats his employees. Or the developer who builds houses without observing codes and pays off the inspector, and his houses have water leaks and other problems, but he sits in church every Sunday and donates money. Then there is the charismatic evangelist who has hundreds of thousands of followers and begs for money during every service from poor, working-class people so he can have a lavish lifestyle. There are the Catholic priests who molest altar boys. This is badness that harms the greatest number of people.

Obviously, many examples can be explored in Nefariousism. Nefariousism representing immorality, but can it be reversed? It is more difficult than becoming bad from good. Greed and ignorance cause people to transition from good to bad. Socrates stated, "There is only one good, knowledge, and one evil, ignorance."

There is no organized study of immorality, but Nefariousism could be used. We have shown different forms, but Aristotle had his own opinion. He distinguishes between two types of immorality: wickedness and weakness. Weakness could be equated with ignorance.

Republicans and Far Right Nefariousism

The title of this chapter can be summarized in this section. Nefariousism expresses hate, radicalism, corruption, dishonesty, blame, ignorance, immorality, name-calling, and more badness.

Name-calling is especially ugly, as is hatred. Hatred is expressed toward Democrats by over half of the Republicans in Congress. They call Democrats evil, socialist, and the radical Antifa. Ignorance and lies are rampant. The Republicans blamed the terrible attempted coup of January 6, 2021, on Antifa, when the mob was clearly composed of Far Right Trump supporters.

President Trump and his Republican followers in Congress have called Antifa a Far Left radical group. Anytime there is violence, the Republicans call it Antifa, such as the looting during Black Lives Matter protests and the attempted coup at the US Capitol on January 6, 2021. This is ignorance and another big Republican lie. Some Democrats have countered that Antifa is an idea, which is not totally correct either. Antifa, by definition, stands for antifascism or against fascism. It is not a radical group, and it is not organized. There may be those who are more vocal (i.e., activists), but it is not an idea, because there are people who are actively opposed to everything fascists represent.

Antifa began with the Anti-Racist Action group organized in the late 1980s to oppose white supremacists of the 1970s. Antifa as an identity was used until 2007. The mission has been to counter the Far Right, especially the white supremacists and neo-Nazis. This has been done by identifying individuals and calling for them to be fired from their jobs or attending rallies to bring public attention to their cause.

Generally, members of Antifa are opposed to those people or groups who support fascism, nationalism, Far Right ideologies, white supremacy, authoritarianism, racism, homophobia, and xenophobia. Overall, they are nonviolent, but when Antifa activists confront white supremacists, violence can occur. This occurred at the white supremacy rally in Charlottesville, Virginia, in 2017 and in Portland, Oregon, in August 2020. Very few Antifas are activists, and those who are should know one cannot fight hate with hate. It is difficult to accept the evil of ignorance, but the only deterrent is education, policy reform, and patience.

With the exception of extreme hatred against white supremacists and fascism, how can any American not oppose fascism? Republican Senators Ted Cruz and Bill Cassidy introduced a resolution in 2019 calling for Antifa to be labeled a domestic terror organization. President Trump voiced his support on Twitter. By definition, this indicates that all three support fascism.

The FBI and Department of Homeland Security have the Far Right at the top of the list of domestic terrorist groups. The January 6, 2021, attempted coup by Far Right extremists justifies this. Antifa is not included, because they don't bear arms or bombs.

The opposition has called them Marxists, communists, anarchists, and anticapitalists, but these are not the operations of Antifa. There is no comparison, but Antifa is not responsible for the violence at the nation's capital.

The Republicans fear Antifa as a real threat to democracy, but those who represent the Far Right are the real threat. It is estimated that there are only two hundred small Antifa groups in the United States. The real Far Left radical groups are Black Guerrilla (Marxist), Black Liberation Army (socialist), Black Panther Party (Leninism), Black Revolutionary Assault Team, John Brown Anti-Klan Committee (radical left), Seattle Weather Collective (communist), White Panther Party (socialist), and United Freedom Front (Marxist). If the Republicans want to talk about the radical left, why don't they call out these groups? The reason is that Donald Trump and his Far Right supporters were confronted by Antifa activists who wanted Americans to witness the type of supporters in his orbit. Using the term *Antifa* then spreads to Far Right and conservative Republican congresspeople.

Summary

Nefariousism could become the study of immorality. The only other comparative study is metaethics and a few of its variations. Metaethics is the attempt to understand the metaphysical, epistemological, semantic, and psychological presuppositions and commitments of moral thought, talk, and practice.

1. Moral nihilism, also known as ethical nihilism, is the metaethical view that nothing has intrinsic moral value. For example, a moral nihilist would say that killing someone, for whatever reason, is intrinsically neither morally right nor morally wrong.
2. Emotivism, in metaethics (see ethics), is the view that moral judgments do not function as statements of fact but rather as expressions of the speaker's or writer's feelings.
3. Metaethical relativism holds that moral judgments are not true or false in any absolute sense but are only relative to particular standpoints. This idea is essential to just about any version of moral relativism. Some metaethical relativists focus more on the justification of moral judgments rather than on their truth.

Of the three subtypes, moral nihilism could be addressed with nefariousism; however, moral nihilism provides more of an explanation than the fact that immorality exists.

Nefariousism is a philosophical and ethical study. It could be studied scientifically. We know from functional magnetic resonance imaging studies that psychopaths who are evil have dysfunctional prefrontal and frontal cortexes of the brain. More studies of the brain could perhaps help us to understand evil in humans.

Liberal Political Terms That Republicans Often Confuse with Socialism

Liberal. Liberalism in the United States is a broad political philosophy centered on what many see as the unalienable rights of the individual. The fundamental liberal ideals of freedom of speech, freedom of the press, freedom of religion for all belief systems, the separation of church and state, the right to due process, and equality under the law are widely accepted as a common foundation across the spectrum of liberal thought.

Modern liberalism in the United States includes issues such as same-sex marriage, reproductive and other women's rights, voting rights for all adult citizens, civil rights, environmental justice, and government protection of freedom from want. National social services, such as equal education opportunities, access to health care, and transportation infrastructure, are intended to promote the general welfare of all citizens as established by the Constitution. Some American liberals, who call themselves classical liberals, fiscal conservatives, or libertarians, support fundamental liberal ideals but diverge from modern liberal thought, holding that economic freedom is more important than equality and that providing for the general welfare exceeds the legitimate role of government.

Since the 1930s, the term *liberalism* (without a qualifier) usually refers in the United States to modern liberalism, a political philosophy exemplified by Franklin D. Roosevelt's New Deal and later Lyndon B. Johnson's Great Society. It is a form of social liberalism, whose accomplishments include the Works Progress Administration and the Social Security Act in 1935, the Civil Rights Act of 1964, and the Voting Rights Act of 1965.

Moderate liberal. Moderate Democrats are a moderate ideological faction within the Democratic Party of the United States. As "The Third Way" faction of the party, they support both social liberalism and economic liberalism. New Democrats dominated the party from the late 1980s through the mid-2010s. They are represented by organizations such as the New Democrat and the New Democrat Coalition.

According to recent polls, moderates are commonly identified as the second largest group, closely trailing conservatives, constituting between 36 percent and 39 percent of the population. Moderates are commonly defined through limiting the extent to which they adopt liberal or conservative ideas.

Conservative liberal. Conservative liberalism is a variant of liberalism, combining liberal values and policies with conservative stances, or simply representing the right wing of the liberal movement. It is a more positive and less radical variant of classical liberalism.

Left wing. Left-wing politics support social equality and egalitarianism, often in opposition to social hierarchy. It typically involves a concern for those in society whom its adherents perceive as disadvantaged relative to others, as well as a belief that there are unjustified inequalities that need to be reduced or abolished.

Far Left. Far Left politics are political views located further on the left of the left-right spectrum than the standard political left. The term has been used to describe ideologies such as communism, anarchism, anarcho-communism, left-communism, anarcho-syndicalism, Marxism-Leninism, Trotskyism, and Maoism.

CHAPTER 5

UNDERSTANDING CROWD AND HERD PSYCHOLOGY

Introduction

Crowd psychology is initially described using examples of historical presentation of various theories that have evolved over time. Herd psychology is often used synonymously with crowd psychology, but the term *herd psychology* similarly associates animal behavior with herd psychology. The term *herd immunity* further confuses the issue. We will address all of these terms. Nefarious crowd behavior, such as conspiracy theories and propaganda, are also addressed, all in the context of the behavior of the current Republican Party.

Definitions

Crowd. An audience. A group of people who are linked by a common interest or activity. Or a large number of people gathered together in an unorganized or unruly way.

Mob. A large crowd of people, especially one that is disorderly and intent on causing trouble or violence. A mafia or other criminal organization.

Group. 1. A number of people who work together or share common beliefs. 2. A number of people or things that are located, gathered, or classed together.

Crowd psychology is also called mob psychology, a term coined by Gustave Le Bon. Another term used is *herd psychology*, leadership in animal and bird behavior, including humans. Crowd psychology became a social evolutionary theory in the late 1800s and early 1900s as a result of changes in technology, social laws, and perceived natural biology. It started in Europe as a result of growing cities, photography, the advent of the light bulb and electric lighting, telephones, movies, and various activities that brought people together.

Crowd psychology can be divided into types of crowds, crowd behavior (theories), and leadership of crowds (herd psychology).

Types of Crowds

Twentieth-century scholars Momboisse and Berlonghi focused on differentiating between four different types of crowds. They called the four types casual, conventional, expressive, and aggressive. Berlonghi classified crowds as spectator, demonstrator, or escaping, to correlate to the purpose for gathering. Crowds can be active, such as a mob engaged in riots, or passive, such as audiences at a concert or movie.

Aggressive crowds or mobs are often violent and outwardly focused, as was the case with the Los Angeles riots of 1992. Escapist crowds are characterized by a large number of panicked people trying to get out of a dangerous situation, such as the sinking of the *Titanic*. Acquisitive mobs occur when large numbers of people are fighting for limited resources. An expressive crowd is any large group of people gathering for an active purpose, including peaceful civil rights protests, rock concerts, political rallies, and religious revivals.

Early Theorists of Crowd Psychology

One of the earliest founders of crowd psychology was Gustave Le Bon. He described how a person becomes incorporated into the crowd as opposed to the different types of crowds. Le Bon held that crowds existed in three stages: submergence, contagion, and suggestion.

Submergence: In this initial phase, the individuals in the crowd lose their sense of individual self and personal respect and responsibility. The incorporation into the crowd allows the person to lose their identity in anonymity.

Contagion: This refers to the propensity for individuals in a crowd to follow the predominant ideas and emotions of the crowd. Since they lose their anonymity, they lose any ability to engage in critical thinking and submit to the ideology of the crowd. This submissiveness then becomes submerged into the crowd.

Suggestion: This is the period in which the ideas and emotions of the crowd are primarily drawn from a shared human unconscious. This behavior originates from a primordial shared unconscious that is uncivilized in nature.

These three stages are limited by the cognition and morality of the least capable members. This is where the angst arises. Considering the issues regarding facts, nonfacts, antisocial behavior, and evil political practices, this presents more than a theoretical problem.

Le Bon concentrated on the negative aspects of crowds. The crowd types were excluded in his belief system. He believed that crowds could be a powerful force only for destruction.

It must be clear that Le Bon was not totally distinguishing between a crowd attending a symphony orchestra or a riot, although he was more concerned with negative issues. However, what he provided was an explanation for how an individual becomes incorporated into the crowd. Obviously, the emotion of a crowd attending a performance of a symphony orchestra versus those marching for civil rights is very different, but the incorporation into the crowd is largely the same for Le Bon. Nevertheless, his theory is the only one that discusses emotion.

Contagion Theory

Le Bon's theory is known as the contagion theory. According to Le Bon, crowds exert a hypnotic influence over their members. Shielded by their anonymity, large numbers of people abandon personal responsibility and surrender to the contagious emotions of the crowd. A crowd thus assumes a life of its own, stirring up emotions and driving people toward irrational, even violent action.

Le Bon's theory is one of the first and is still respected today by systematic sociological studies. Furthermore, although collective behavior may involve strong emotions, such feelings are not necessarily irrational. Turner and Killian argue convincingly that the "contagion" never actually occurs, and participants in collective behavior do not lose their ability to think rationally.

Sigmund Freud also considered crowd psychology. He provided a more comprehensive psychopathologic explanation for crowd behavior. He stated that becoming a member of a crowd serves to unlock the unconscious mind. As a result, the superego (the conscious moral center) is displaced by the crowd, which is replaced by a charismatic crowd leader. Individual emotional consciousness becomes incorporated into the crowd for each individual in the crowd. The emotions are simple, unidirectional, primitive, and diffuse among the crowd.

Leaders are often cognizant of the psychology of the masses and use this to their benefit. If the masses already believe in a proposition, the leader cements their beliefs. For example, if the crowd believes that African Americans are inferior, the leader doesn't need to work to subconsciously fortify this belief. Leaders, presidents, and dictators such as Mao Zedong and Joseph Stalin have used mass psychology.

Mid- to Late-Twentieth-Century Theories

Deindividuation Theory

The term *deindividuation* was coined by the American social psychologist Leon Festinger in the 1950s. Deindividuation is a concept in social psychology that is generally thought of as the loss of self-awareness in groups. Deindividuation theory argues that in typical crowd situations, factors such as anonymity, group unity, and loss of personal control or restraint (e.g., questioning, shame, self-evaluating behavior) increases a person's sensitivity to their surroundings and diminishes rational thinking and forethought. In crowd situations, people are distanced from their personal identities, and their concern for social evaluation is reduced.

Recent theories of deindividuation evaluate individual attention. It theorizes that an individual is unable, due to the situation, to have strong awareness of their self as an object of attention. Without individual attention, the person loses normal social interaction.

The three factors in deindividuation—anonymity, lack of social constraints, and sensory overload—are problematic. Anonymity is present in almost all crowd psychology theories. Lack of social constraints depends on the environment of the crowd. In unruly crowds and mobs, there are no social or moral constraints, but in a large educational meeting, they exist. Sensory overload occurs in any crowd, which frequently leads to heightened emotions.

The normal or abnormal expectations of one's surroundings play a role in the person's deindividuation behavior. The aggression at a militia meeting is far different from engineers or doctors at a large conference learning the latest technology. This is aggression versus learning. However, deindividualism arose out of fascism.

Individuation causes a person to focus, concentrate, create, and make decisions. A painter focuses on the painting. A rock climber focuses on his route up the rock face and the next move. All of these mental processes are lost with deindividuation. It further seems apparent that deindividuation does not require a physical crowd. Social media incorporates the individual into the distant crowd.

Convergence Theory

Convergence theory is a theory that explores the concept that as nations become highly industrialized, they will develop similar cultural traits. Convergence theory became popular in the 1960s when it was formulated by the University of California, Berkeley, professor of economics Clark Kerr.

Convergence theory states that crowd behavior is not a product of the crowd, but rather the crowd is a product of the coming together of like-minded individuals. Convergence theory holds that crowds form from people of similar dispositions, whose actions are then reinforced and intensified by the crowd.

The problem with the convergent theory is that not all crowds are convergent. A large group of psychiatrists convening to discuss social norms have rational beliefs and values so that the outcome of the meeting is a reasonable learning experience. The boundaries of the crowd are well defined. The issue of boundary is important. The Black Lives Matter marches were overall peaceful, but the boundary of the group was not contained, so violence, looting, and destruction occurred.

It should be noted that convergent theory and contagion are at odds with each other regarding crowd behavior. Whereas the contagion theory states that crowds cause people to act in a certain way, convergence theory says the opposite. People who want to act in a certain way intentionally come together to form crowds.

Emergent Norm Theory

Originally proposed in their 1957 book *Collective Behavior*, Ralph H. Turner and Lewis M. Killian claim that emergent norm theory has grown out of two main traditions: the Le Bonian tradition of thinking of crowds as normless entities and the collective action as irrational behavior. This led Turner and Killian to think about how norms are instituted in crowds or how norms emerge within a crowd.

Emergent norm theory hypothesizes that nontraditional behavior (such as that associated with collective action) develops in crowds as a result of the emergence of new behavioral norms in response to a precipitating crisis. The norms that develop within crowds are not strict rules for behavior. It insinuates that at the onset of the crowd, there is no unity. As time passes, and the crowd is in the process of forming, leaders or distinctive personalities create or instigate actions, and the rest of the crowd falls into the norm.

As a crowd forms, it adds legitimacy to their cause. Since humans are creatures of conformity and easily and heavily influenced by the opinions of others, the norm of the crowd is formed. This also adds to the universal phenomenon of persuasion of the idea that if everyone in the crowd is in agreement, then it cannot be wrong.

Social Identity Theory

Henri Tajfel in 1979 proposed that the groups (e.g., social class, family, football team, etc.) that people belong to are an important source of pride and self-esteem. Groups give us a sense of social identity, a sense of belonging to the social world.

Social identity theory states that a person's sense of who they are is based on their group membership(s). This is known as in-group (us) and out-group (them). The central hypothesis of social identity theory is that group members of an in-group will seek to find negative aspects of an out-group, thus enhancing their self-image. The groups have various moral and behavioral values and norms, and the individual's actions depend on which group membership (or nonmembership) is most personally salient at the time of action. If the values of the group change, the self can either follow or leave.

It becomes apparent that social identity in groups is dependent on such issues as values, morality, and other parameters. Frequently, a crowd is composed of multiple groups. The crowd in Black Lives Matter can consist of Blacks, whites, Christians, Muslims, and so on. However, the common denominator is social justice for African Americans.

This social identity crowd theory proposes that the group membership is made more salient by confrontation with other groups, which is a relatively common occurrence for crowds. A concern with this theory is that while it explains how crowds reflect social ideas and prevailing attitudes, it does not explain the mechanisms by which crowds enact to drive social change.

Contagion Theories; Behavior / Social Contagion

Contagion Theory of Disease

Contagion is a very old term that refers to infectious agents (such as viruses and certain bacteria) that spread from human to human or from animal to animal. Examples include bacteria such as Haemophilus influenza, Neisseria meningitidis, viral influenza, and so on. This led to the belief that rational ideas or irrational behavior could be transmitted among a crowd, particularly a large crowd.

Galen (AD 129–c. 199) first wrote that seeds of disease could be transmitted between humans. He observed that some people contracted a disease with fever, while others did not. This was expanded by a sixteenth-century Italian physician, Dr. Fracastoro, who wrote his famous book, *De contagione et contagiosis morbis et eorum curatione, libri III*, in 1546. He proposed that seeds (e.g., infectious agents) of disease could spread directly, indirectly, or from a distance. There was much discussion throughout the Middle Ages refuting contagion, and in fact those arguing against the theory were also correct. The bubonic plague (Black Death) disproved the contagion theory. It was also called the Black Plague because it caused large black boils on the skin from the bacterium Yersinia pestis. The Black Plague killed more than twenty-five million people in Europe in the mid-1300s. The term *plague* is only used for infections caused by the Yersinia pestis bacteria. Humans usually get the plague after being bitten by a rodent flea that is carrying the plague bacterium or by handling an animal infected with plague. This proved that those who argued against the contagion theory of disease were also correct, and their argument became known as vector transmission.

Vector-borne disease results from an infection transmitted to humans and other animals by blood-feeding anthropoids, such as mosquitoes, ticks, and fleas. Examples of vector-borne diseases include the bubonic plague, malaria, West Nile virus, and Lyme disease.

Vector transmission could also be considered a vector behavioral theory. The vector is the person who exchanges behavior from one crowd to another. We see this in President Trump's rallies. He usually asks questions of the crowd. For example, at a rally in Michigan, he may say, "Isn't Hillary a criminal?" And the crowd responds, "Lock her up!" Then he has a rally in South Carolina and asks the same question, and the crowd responds, "Lock her up!" He acts as the vector and transmits the same behavior from one group to another. This also proves that the identity of the crowd is important, because he would not get the same response from a group of scientists.

Galen described contagion nearly two thousand years ago, and today many people believe the coronavirus, COVID-19, is a hoax. They refute the three contagion transmissions of the virus: directly, indirectly, and airborne. Instead, they accept the social contagion theory. The COVID-19 pandemic is the perfect example of utilitarian contagion and nefarious contagion.

The utilitarian behavior of infectious disease experts like Dr. Fauci tell us to wear masks, maintain social distance, wash our hands, and stay away from large gatherings. The contagion is that people who understand facts and rational thinking follow the expert's lead. Doing these few recommendations prevents contagious spread. All of the health care and essential workers provide the greatest good for the greatest number of people.

The COVID-19 pandemic also combines nefarious contagion with nonfactual beliefs that the virus is only a flu virus. There has been so much disinformation generated by President Trump and his Republican followers, such as the claim that there is no need for masks and that large gatherings are fine because the infection is only mild. They spread the incorrect assumption that herd immunity is the cure for the viral infection, which is nonfactual. This disinformation was repeated many, many times until people didn't know who to believe. There were those who proposed that the N1H1 (swine flu) infected millions of people. However, N1H1 killed twelve thousand people, and COVID-19 has killed more than three million people worldwide. Many argued that wearing a mask was interfering with their freedom. Many of these people died. This nonfactual belief that is dangerous and kills people is precisely the reason regulations are created. It is the Tea Party and Freedom Party groups who follow the nonfactual information that cause regulation, and then they want to tear down regulations in a fight against the bogeyman of "big government."

The supernatural theory of disease is the belief that God is angry at people and causes disease. This serves as ancient mythology. However, it persists to this day. A woman was asked on *60 Minutes* what she thought about President Trump's handling of the COVID-19 pandemic. In defense of President Trump, she said the president had nothing to do with the virus: "It is God's will!"

Sociological Contagion Theory

As noted earlier, Gustave Le Bon arrived at the contagion theory. He believed that normal individual behavior will turn irrational or violent according to the nature of the crowd. He found that the individual loses all anonymity in the crowd and will therefore engage in the same level of behavior as the crowd.

Several social psychologists have expanded the theory. Contagion theory is a theory of collective behavior that explains that the crowd can cause a hypnotic impact on individuals.

Behavior or Social Contagion Theory

Le Bon's contagion theory of crowd behavior has been labeled behavior contagion or social contagion. It is the behavior of an individual to copy a certain behavior of another person or group of individuals either directly within the group or indirectly by exposure through social media. In the behavior contagion theory, several matrices of behavior have been introduced beyond that which Le Bon envisioned.

Two American social psychologists in the twentieth century, Robert E. Park and Herbert Blumer, expanded Gustave Le Bon's contagion theory. Park suggested that people in a crowd interact when they are responding to stress. As a result, an individual's thoughts and actions are finally affected by the members of the group, and the individuals will tend to reflect the behavior collectively. In addition, the group can become influenced by an individual, especially one with leadership qualities or by a person in the group with authority. The leader and the group position can be varied according to the situation.

Herbert Blumer states that symbolic interactionism rests on three premises: that human beings act toward things on the basis of the meanings things have for them; that the meaning of such things derives from the social interaction one has with one's fellows; and that these meanings are handled in, and modified through, an extreme collective effort. He concluded his findings with the possibility of emergence of a new social institution or a social change as the result of this extreme collective effort.

Both of these social psychologists introduced social contagion of a crowd along with the psyche of individuals in the crowd. Both also introduced the term *collective* for the crowd. Herd psychology originated from the contagion theories. Another term frequently used that originated from Park and Blumer is collective crowd behavior (which will be discussed under herd psychology).

Behavioral contagion now addresses various factors and situations where this behavior occurs. Social psychologists have divided behavior contagion into simple and complex behavior. A simple contagion is a person in the audience of a symphony orchestra who stands and claps, and the rest of the audience does the same. Complex contagion is encouragement from multiple sources, such as occurs in a riot. Complex contagion could also be the audience at a symphony who are emotionally sensitive to the performance such that the entire audience stands, claps, and cheers at the same time.

Modern social psychologists have also listed factors involved in contagion behavior. Some of the factors are density of the crowd, dominant leadership, degree of restraint, weak versus strong ties between individuals, social media influence, and competition. There are several factors one can arrive at as to why the behavior is contagious in a group or crowd.

Finally, the crowd psychology theories all share a basic idea of how individuals can act briefly unreasonable or inconsistent within a group and reassume their own individual identity when they are not in the group or crowd.

Mass Delusional Crowd Theory (by the author)

Delusions are idiosyncratic beliefs or an impression maintained despite being contradicted by reality or rational argument, typically as a symptom of a mental disorder.

If one were to include this with herd behavior, it would be equivalent to a stampede of cattle on the range and a caribou herd watching wolves devour a mother's calf. But mass delusional crowds are unlike herds. They follow a lie or are totally in denial/ambivalent to the truth. This is a human phenomenon and has no comparison to animals other than fear. The emotion of fear does play into the delusion, and in order to infiltrate the crowd, the entire crowd must have the same or similar fears. The lie(s) fuel the fears, which then leads to a fight-or-flight response.

The question is why do rational people become delusional? It is either a strong emotional or belief response. Still, nonfactual information initiates the delusion, and the tool to create the crowd is the internet and social media.

We have at least two previous theories involved in this theory: the convergence and contagion theories. With the mass delusional theory, we start with a delusion or lie. Convergence theory states that people who want to act in a certain way come together to form crowds. In convergence, people with similar delusions find other like-minded persons with whom they can identify with the same underlying emotions and beliefs. Included in this theory is cowardice. A person lacks the courage to act alone with his/her belief or lie. The crowd can provide courage and strengthen the belief/lie. The crowd then provides a critical mass of like-minded people.

Le Bon's contagion theory states that crowds exert a hypnotic influence over their members. Shielded by their anonymity, large numbers of people abandon personal responsibility and surrender to the contagious emotions of the crowd. The crowd develops a life of its own and builds on irrational and even violent behavior. Le Bon also associates his theory with mob activity.

During the Trump administration, we saw firsthand mass delusions, both violent and ambivalent. It all starts with lies and cowardice. With ambivalence, COVID-19 was called a "Big Lie" by President Trump, which caused people to ignore the science, killing hundreds of thousands of Americans. The *big lie* of telling his followers he won the 2020 election led to violence at the US Capitol on January 6, 2021, by his Far Right supporters. Unfortunately, many other Republicans in Congress adhere to the mass delusion theory.

Autocratic Leader Theory and Monetary Theory (by author)

Much of crowd theory addresses the behavior of the crowd. Different crowds have different identities, which we discussed. What can instigate crowd behavior? Autocratic leaders are usually associated with extreme political systems, such as communism, socialism, monarchies, and fascism. Two crowds occur with this form of leadership: support crowds and opposition crowds. The autocratic leader creates an aggressive or coercive, fearful, or intimidating persona to initiate total dominance over the crowd to maintain support. The predominant emotion of the crowd is fear. The supporters follow the autocrat to avoid the cost of punishment and torture. When in power for a period of time, coercive behavior is most effective in children rather than adults.

In time, autocratic leadership behavior also leads to opposition with a more benevolent leader opposing the autocrat. This causes oppositional crowd behavior such as riots and marches that can lead to violence against the crowd, including death or imprisonment. An example is Putin's Russia.

Monetary crowd theory is one in which financiers, agencies, and so forth provide money to a crowd to induce a given behavior. This type of theory can be seen in politics. Lobbyists, wealthy persons, and companies pay politicians to behave a certain way. It is possible that persons in the capital coup could have been paid to cause violence, sedition, and insurrection.

Animal Herd Psychosocial Behavior

Animal Group Behavior

There are many groups of animals in the wild as well as those that are domesticated. We have herds of buffalo, zebras, and wildebeests as well as cows, steer cattle, goats, and sheep. There are packs of wolves, coyotes, and wild dogs. There are flocks of birds or geese. Lions live in a pride. Quails form coveys.

All of these animals have some things in common as well as many differences. They stay together for protection and to protect their young. They move around or migrate for food. Wildebeests and zebras migrate long distances. Migration also happens in search of a comfortable climate, such as with Canada geese and many other birds. Animals will bed down together at night to keep warm and protect one another.

Animals experience many emotions. Fear is a frequent emotion. An attack by a predator leads to fear in the whole group. The leader(s) of the group will fight to protect all members. However, the weakest in the group may be singled out and attacked. In this situation, the leader and group may give in to the loss, but they do experience it. Steers and wild horses may fear lightning and thunder, causing a stampede.

Animals can show happiness, such as when a dog wags its tail. When injured, they cry or whine. There are loneliness and mating calls in animals such as moose and elk. A cow with full udders will moo in pain.

Animal Leadership

But how does the leader come into power in an animal group? Wild animals will follow a leader they trust to keep them safe, a leader who acts in the best interest of the group. There are similarities in animal and human leadership, especially when it comes to hierarchy. Each animal group has its own method of communicating leadership. Animals often choose their leader according to age, sex, or experience. For example, in a lion pride, the male leader that is strong, brave, and protective is chosen as leader. This establishes loyalty within the group. With humans, 70 percent of leaders of corporations are alpha males. But matriarchs (older, experienced females) also lead groups of elephants and other animals. This form of leadership represents dominance and subordination, alliance formation and decision-making. This is all part of the formation of hierarchy.

The purpose of social hierarchies is to organize social groups in order to allocate limited resources, such as mates and food, facilitate social learning, and maximize individual motivation. Hierarchies are common with humans and animals.

Male leaders are prominent in the animal kingdom. Lions, but also most mammals, including Rhesus monkeys, chimpanzees, baboons, wolves, and bison, are led by alpha males. However, there are two matriarch-led groups that oppose the hierarchy system: honeybees and African elephants. Both deserve mentioning, because with humans, women are finally becoming leaders in a historically male-dominant world.

The largest, oldest, wisest, experienced female in the elephant herd serves as the leader of the herd. The matriarch plays a critical role in the life of the other female elephants. She influences elephant behavior and decisions. She protects the herd from danger and teaches them how to care for their offspring. Where do the males fit into this female-dominant herd? After adolescence, males are on their own. Nevertheless, the males can be part of the herd for up to fifteen to twenty years. After they become adults, they join together, also with leadership from the dominant male. Their purpose as adults is mating and breeding. This presents another dynamic in that when their testosterone levels become exceedingly high, they become aggressive and fight over females. We sometimes see this behavior in human males as well.

The other matriarch-led group in the animal kingdom are honeybees. Their group system is somewhat socialist. The queen bee is the largest, strongest, and most intelligent of the bees. Male drones are used for mating. There are worker bees and home (comb) bees. The worker bees find tree and flower blossoms from which to collect the nectar and bring it back to the home bees to process into honey. All of the worker bees and home bees are female. This is a form of a democratic socialist society, because all the bees work together in the production of honey, and they all benefit. They also make collective decisions.

Growing up on a fruit farm, my father was a beekeeper. I was intrigued by the behavior and intelligence of honeybees. Watching the bees at work and seeing how one bee would come back to the same blossom indicated intelligence. Researchers have learned that bees are extremely complex and intelligent. It has been determined that when bees emerge from their hives in the spring, they find too many bees in the same hive.

Honeybee colonies grow too large for their current hives, so the group splits in two. The mother queen and half of the worker bees leave the hive to seek a new location, while the daughter queen and the remaining workers remain in place. The queen bee takes her group to a new temporary location. She sends out hundreds of scout bees who fan out and search for a new hive location. Researchers have found that scout bees intelligently and collectively report the quality of each scout's location. After they complete their scouting, they return to the temporary hive and communicate their findings. They communicate their findings to the supervisor bees by dancing, which may go on for hours or days before they reach a consensus. Researchers have not yet discovered how they come to a common agreement about where to finalize their comb. This decision-making by the bees appears to be a friendly, competitive democracy.

Some of the greatest women leaders in human history have similar inspiring qualities. They include:

Queen Hatshepsut (1503–1482 BC), one of the most successful pharaohs in Egypt.

Cleopatra (69–30 BC), one of several female Egyptian leaders.

Empress Theodora (500–548), the empress of the Byzantine Empire.

Queen Elizabeth I (1533–1603), the last monarch of the Tudor dynasty.

Catherine the Great (1729–1796), empress of Russia.

Queen Liliuokalani (1838–1917), the last monarch of the Kingdom of Hawaii.

Golda Meir (1898–1978), former minister of labor and foreign minister of Israel.

Indira Gandhi (1917–1984), prime minister of India for three consecutive terms from 1966 to 1977.

Margaret Thatcher (1925–2013), prime minister of the United Kingdom from 1979 to 1990.

Angela Merkel (1954–present), chancellor of Germany who became the first woman German chancellor in 2005.

In the United States, we have yet to elect a woman president. During the twenty-first century, women have become governors and congresspeople, which is a start. Vice President Kamala Harris is an important first step.

The last means by which leaders come to power is through inheritance. John Stuart Mill wrote that leadership is inherited rather than gained. Examples of this occurrence in animals happen with spotted hyenas. In humans, this occurs in monarchies. This phenomenon has also been found in indigenous tribes. The Nootka tribes of western Washington State and British Columbia, Canada, lead by inheritance. However, human royalty has more in common with spotted hyenas, in terms of leadership, than they do with most other mammals.

Herd (Mentality, Behavior, and Immunity)

Let's define a herd, because the word is abused and misused. The *Oxford Definition* of a herd is a large group of animals, especially the hoofed mammals that live together or are together as livestock. Also, it can be described as a large group.

The herd has separated from all of the other animal groups, because humans have coined the term for human psychology, human investing, and medical immunology purposes. A herd is a bunch of animals—or people who act like a bunch of animals. It's also a verb—when people herd animals, they try to keep them moving in the same direction. A herd usually refers to a group of animals with hooves, like cows or sheep (meat-eating animals like wolves cruise around in packs).

One of the first psychiatrists to introduce the description of herd behavior was Sigmund Freud. Herd mentality and behavior are used interchangeably, but some like to make a distinction. Herd behavior is the behavior of individuals in a group acting collectively without centralized direction. Herd mentality is the inclination for individuals within a group to follow along with what the group thinks or does. It is also known as mob behavior and group/crowd contagion. Herd psychology studies why and how herd behavior occurs in humans, such as how humans lose free will and why a group follows a leader. This is synonymous with crowd psychology. Also, when discussing herd psychology, another interchangeable term is contagion and the contagion theory, as well as collective crowd behavior.

A purist argues that if animal herds and human herds are interchangeable, the same behaviors in animals can be projected onto humans. Some behaviors are similar: we herd in housing for protection and comfort. When a caribou mother watches her newborn being killed by a pack of wolves, the herd comes together to mourn. We do the same. Male and female animals chose a mate in the herd, as do humans. Animals are migratory; some human groups do the same, such as groups in Mongolia. Many indigenous natives migrate due to weather or food. Another behavior that occurs in the herd is fear. Lightning and thunder can cause a herd to stampede. With humans, this is called mob behavior. Mob behavior occurs out of fear, rage, anger, oppression, and injustice. On Black Friday, a crowd camps out to obtain the best deals. When the door opens at the store, the group mobs the store out of fear that they will miss out on the best deal. Mob behavior can be considered in both crowd and herd behavior. Herd behavior in humans is equated to the stampede, people running together and tripping over one another, and if exits are restrictive, the herd cannot escape.

The terms herd mentality and behavior insinuate that the individuals in the group act together. This ignores the fact that herds operate with leaders. When cows are called in from the pasture to be milked, there is always one cow that leads the herd. Nevertheless, the whole concept of herds and herding in animals, fish, birds, insects, and humans is a primitive pattern of behavior.

Collective Crowd Behavior

The twenty-first century all-inclusive term for herd mentality or behavior, social contagion, and behavior contagion is *collective crowd behavior*. The idea of collective behavior originated with Robert Park in 1904 and was expanded on by Gustave Le Bon's contagion theory.

Collective behavior involves social processes and events that do not reflect conventional or social structure, such as laws, conventions, or institutions, but rather emerge with spontaneity. This includes human social herd behavior, animal social groups/herds, and flocks of birds. This behavior occurs in rallies, riots, mob violence (extreme anger), or an impromptu jazz musical group in a park or mall. The term has also been used for animal migration.

Turner and Killian's approach is that social forces are not really forces. Instead, "The actor is active: He creates an interpretation of the acts of others, and acts on the basis of this interpretation."

Herd behavior encompasses the contagion theory, a theory of collective behavior that explains that the crowd can cause a hypnotic impact on individuals, thus incorporating the individuals into the crowd. This whole process is more descriptively called *collective crowd behavior* by social psychologists.

Research on collective behavior is limited. Early research began with animal experiments conducted by social psychologists and biologists. John Krause and his group at the University of Leeds in England initiated animal studies that they then carried over into human experiments.

Collective crowd behavior involves consensus decisions. Consensus decision-making is when members of a group make a decision between two or more problems or actions that are considered mutually exclusive in terms of reaching a consensus. This consensus decision is more beneficial as a group than as an individual. However, the decisions are usually made by one or a few leaders providing direction with group consensus. Leadership may either be designated or emerge spontaneously as individuals possess qualities or experience in certain situations that make them ideal leaders or because they have a personality type that is more inclined to lead.

In conflict decision-making, people in larger groups have more problems making a decision about which group to follow. In small groups, the decisions are easier to make, and most will follow the majority.

Dyer et al. also studied a leader who was in the center of the group and one at the periphery of the group (mixed leaders). When both went in a specific direction, the group quickly followed. They demonstrated that the leader on the periphery is likely to be more mobile and unconstrained and can move freely around the outside of the group, quickly finding and aligning with the target, while the other leader in the center position, although initially more constrained and surrounded by people, may be able to influence more uninformed individuals through his/her movements toward the target.

The same analogy can be used for Republicans in the Trump administration. Senate Majority Leader Mitch McConnell was on the periphery, moving about with his Republican senators in a behavioral pattern that followed Trump's lies and harmful behavior. This conspiratorial behavior then trickled down to the senators and from there to the rest of the external Republicans. Meanwhile, Trump was in the center and moved the base in the direction Trump and McConnell want to take the Republican Party and its members—in this case, to autocratic nationalism, or fascism.

Findings in animal and insect behavior support the same findings in humans. I found the honeybee model to represent social democracy, but it can also represent the Trump/McConnell behavior. Beckman et al. found evidence that informed scout bees guide largely uninformed swarms to a new nest site by flying through the swarm indicating the direction of travel.

A study on consensus decision-making in human crowds was conducted at the University of Leeds, UK. Large groups of people were placed in a large hall. A few individuals were provided instructions for walking in a certain direction. The group walked randomly in somewhat close contact but could not communicate between individuals, nor with those few given instructions. The results of the study showed that in all cases, the "informed individuals" were followed by others in the crowd, forming a self-organizing, snakelike structure. They studied different ratios of participants to informed individuals and found as the participant group got larger, it required less informed individuals to lead. In the study of two hundred participants, it was found that less than 5 percent of the informed individuals could lead the crowd. The fact that none of the individuals in the crowd could talk or gesture reinforces the contagion theory. Obviously, those in the know led those who were not. And although the crowd didn't pick the leader, they followed the person who appeared to know what was going on.

Several studies show that people appear to be subconsciously swayed by the opinions of others. This is where contagion plays into these findings. The work by Krause and Dyer at the University of Leeds has also been simulated and reproduced by groups using the computer.

Since the 1970s, psychological and economic research has identified herd behavior in humans and has explained it by the phenomenon of large numbers of people acting in the same way at the same time.

Herd Behavior in Finance

In economics and finance, rational herding occurs when market participants react to information about the behavior of other market agents or participants rather than the behavior of the market and the fundamental transactions.

This phenomenon is evident in the stock market. The stock market operates on emotions, such as impulse and fear. When a few investors move up or down, many follow, as evidenced by the Dow. If Apple announces they are introducing a new iPhone, Apple stocks go up, but if Apple cannot produce enough iPhones, this negative news causes investors to sell Apple stock. Graphs and forecasts are used in stock investing, but there is no way to predict emotions and beliefs, even though there have been attempts to research this in psychology. Periods of frenzied buying produce greed, and periods of crash produce fear. Individual investors join the crowd in a rush to get in or out of the market, hence herd investing.

Many terms and descriptions have been used that can cause confusion regarding crowd psychology. It seems reasonable to categorize crowd behavior, herd behavior, contagion, collective behavior, and consensus decision-making in animals/humans as synonymous with minor differences in observations and definitions.

Herd Immunity

We have discussed herd behavior and mentality and have also studied herd psychology. This is not to be confused with herd immunity, which we will discuss below.

Definitions and Introduction

Herd immunity is defined as resistance to the spread of an infectious disease within a population that is based on preexisting immunity of a high proportion of individuals as a result of previous infection or vaccination. Herd immunity can be natural or induced. In a natural sense, we usually think in terms of a group or population of animals becoming infected with a virus or bacteria, and the majority of the population develops immunity that prevents future infections from the same organism. An example in the human population is children in daycare are vaccinated against measles and eventually develop group immunity.

Imitation herd immunity happens with the use of vaccinations. The term *herd immunity* is mostly used by health care providers to describe immunity resulting from vaccinations. They also use the term to describe the level of vaccination needed to achieve herd immunity, which varies by the type of infectious disease. Generally, this ranges from 80 to 95 percent. A better term is *population immunity*, and it should be discussed in terms of natural and induced population immunity.

To simplify the immunity event, let us consider this example: An animal or human in nature is exposed to a virus and becomes infected with symptoms, and in the process, the body's immune system fights the virus. It is a complicated system for survival that prevents death the majority of the time. As the immune system fights and eliminates the virus, it produces a memory system in terms of antibodies to prevent future virus infection. Vaccinations circumvent the process of getting sick by injecting a noninfectious portion of the virus into the person (by way of vaccination) that creates a memory of the virus in the form of antibodies that will kill the virus in any subsequent exposure.

President Donald J. Trump proposed herd immunity as the means to an end of transmission of COVID-19 in the United States. President Trump eliminated the coronavirus task force led by Dr. Anthony Fauci. Trump defended this thinking and named former Stanford Neuroradiology Chief Dr. Atlas as the head of the White House Coronavirus Task Force.

Dr. Fauci was appointed director of the National Institute of Allergy and Infectious Diseases in 1984. He oversees an extensive portfolio of basic and applied research to prevent, diagnose, and treat infectious diseases. He became the premier expert in human immunodeficiency virus (HIV) causing acquired immunodeficiency syndrome (AIDS). He has advised US presidents for years about infectious diseases, such as H1N1, Ebola, and now COVID-19 or coronavirus. However, Republicans did not want to believe his expertise and predictions about the coronavirus. Instead, they wanted to push the herd immunity theory. In fact, when Dr. Fauci appeared before Congress, Rand Paul, also a physician, stated that the reason New York had a decline in coronavirus infections was due to herd immunity. Dr. Fauci quickly explained why that statement was untrue.

President Donald Trump then confused the term *herd immunity* when he claimed during a televised town hall that "herd mentality" could make the coronavirus "disappear" with or without a vaccine. The herd mentality was convincing America that herd immunity would protect them from the infection. We now understand herd mentality and behavior. So what is herd immunity?

Medical Specifics of Herd Immunity

Herd immunity describes the point at which a population is sufficiently immune to a disease to prevent its circulation. The term was first described in 1923 by researchers in England at the University of Manchester.

Herd immunity applies more to vaccinations than to members of the population becoming infected and therefore immune to future infections. Widespread vaccination is the most reliable way to achieve herd immunity. In terms of vaccinations, the question becomes how many people in a population (the herd) require vaccinations to eliminate the infectious disease? This sounds simple but is rather complex. It has taken decades to develop vaccines for many infectious diseases, and one for HIV, first discovered in 1983, has still not been developed.

Herd immunity achieved through vaccinations can be empirically calculated. Senator Rand Paul stated that New York was no longer having COVID-19 infections because of herd immunity. But only about 5 percent of the population were infected by the virus, and in order to have complete population immunity, at least 66 percent of New Yorkers would require infections, which was not the case.

The method of transmission and virulence of the virus must be evaluated and calculated using population studies. This can be calculated using the number of people in the population who become infected from a single person. Additionally, the number of cases caused by an individual as an outbreak progresses and conditions change over time in response to the outbreak can be calculated.

The Centers for Disease Control and Prevention estimates that with COVID-19, one individual can infect three others; however, the real number is probably higher in crowds where people may be closer together. Additionally, if one person infects three others, and they each infect three people, then the number of infections soon multiplies from three to nine to twenty-seven, and on and on.

Concerning COVID-19, testing for the virus (antigen) has been very chaotic due to a lack of leadership. Testing for immunity (antibodies) has also not been very uniform. For example, if a person is exposed to hepatitis B, the virus test (antigen) is positive. One then tests for immunity (antibody) weeks later, and if the antibody test is positive, the person is immune. The antibody can be tested over time to see how long one maintains their immunity. It took years to create a vaccine for hepatitis B, and although technology has improved the vaccine for COVID-19, it takes more than months to develop. Even so, the speed with which a COVID-19 vaccine was developed was remarkable, and all built on decades of previous research and science.

Vaccinations are a perfect example of herd immunity. Measles is a highly contagious virus, meaning that one child infected with measles can easily infect fifteen others. To prevent transmission, fourteen of the fifteen or 93 percent would require vaccinations. With measles, essentially all toddlers are vaccinated, which creates a robust herd immunity. However, those mothers who prevent their toddler from being vaccinated have caused localized outbreaks.

We have seen public health successes with the vaccinations against smallpox and polio. This was due to massive, sustained vaccine programs with simple, highly effective vaccines resulting in lifelong immunity.

Natural herd immunity, the kind that involves active infections rather than vaccinations, can be studied in animals. Should the entire herd acquire a disease or infection, the herd will either survive or die. One animal can be infected and spread the infection, or the entire herd can be infected at the same time. An example of a viral infection in animals is hoof-and-mouth disease (HMD). It should be noted that, with the exception of underdeveloped countries, cattle are vaccinated for hoof-and-mouth disease, and it has been near totally eliminated.

FMD virus (FMDV) is a positive, single-strand RNA virus (similar to coronaviruses) and a member of the virus family Picornaviridae. It is a highly transmissible disease of both wildlife and hoofed animals. Sheep and goats can get the disease spread to them by one animal or the entire herd at almost the same time, since it can be transmitted through air. This does not cause death immediately in the animal, but it causes significant morbidity (e.g., severe weight loss and lack of milk production). Studies show that some animals develop immunity, but only 30 percent to 40 percent. Presumably, this is due to the timing of the antibody testing after the infection or the response of the immune system. Obviously, natural immunity from a pathogen is far more difficult to study and can lead to disinformation.

The herd immunity Republicans promoted with COVID-19 is the natural herd immunity proposition. This may only occur with nonvirulent pathogens/viruses that do not cause death and provide lifelong immunity. However, lifelong immunity is only theoretical. COVID-19 is extremely virulent and causes large numbers of deaths, which would not provide natural selection herd immunity. It has been calculated that at least 66 percent of the population would need to be infected for natural herd immunity to occur. This would also cause deaths in the millions. Promotion of natural herd immunity for COVID-19 is medical malpractice by the Republican Party. It is apparent in the legal world that this would be considered negligence and the basis for a class action lawsuit by families of those who died as a result of this misinformation spread by the Republican Party.

Vaccines are relatively safe and have only minor side effects that mostly consist of pain, mild redness, and mild swelling at the injection site. The immune system responds to the vaccine by causing fatigue, low-grade fever, and chills. It also may cause muscle and joint aches. It rarely causes a temporary headache. Tylenol and ibuprofen can treat these symptoms.

The COVID-19 vaccine has been shown to be extremely safe with a reaction rate of 0.004 percent or one out of four million vaccinations. The reactions have been similar to allergic reactions and have been treated with Benadryl or epinephrine. However, many people do not want to be vaccinated because they fear the speed at which the vaccine was made. The fear was warranted when the Trump administration called the production of the vaccine Operation Warp Speed. People believe the vaccine was created in eight months, whereas in reality, it started development during the Obama administration after the H1N1 outbreak and the Ebola virus scare. President Trump wanted to take all the credit.

The truth is that the messenger RNA (mRNA) technology for creating vaccines and immunotherapy was first published from an animal study in 1990. Thirty years of research have gone into producing mRNA vaccines. Ebola started a new program at the National Institutes of Health in Bethesda, Maryland, which is one of the largest medical research centers in America. Research centers in the United Kingdom and in Germany have also been working on this technology. The use of mRNA to produce vaccines is a fast and efficient method of vaccine production, and over the past decade, more focus has been placed on good manufacturing practices (GMP) for large-scale production. Pfizer has been producing vaccines since the early 1900s, so gearing up for the production of the COVID-19 vaccine was not difficult, especially when production facilities have $2 billion from Pfizer to use.

Operation Warp Speed should never have been used as a political strong-arm technique. After the autism/vaccination debacle, people are fearful of vaccinations, and when informed that the COVID-19 vaccine was developed so quickly, people are fearful and refuse vaccinations, thereby throwing the possibility of herd immunity in doubt. However, it is also the responsibility of the media, especially the news, to educate the public with the facts and truth. Understanding that mRNA technology has been around for thirty years should remove that fear and reassure the public about the efficacy and safety of the vaccine.

Human Crowd Psychosocial Behavior

Several theories of human crowd behavior have been presented. There has also been a discussion of animal groups and herd behavior to illustrate how human and animal behavior is more similar than dissimilar.

Adding to the understanding of collective (contagion) behavior theories, there are at least two additional theories: diffusion theory and mimetic theory. Although they may be contagious in nature, these theories only apply to humans, not animals.

Diffusion Theory

Diffusion of innovation theory is one of the older sociological theories. It was developed in 1962 by E.M. Rogers. It explains how an idea communicated over time gains momentum and diffuses (or spreads) through a specific population or social system. Some of the specific elements include innovation (ideas or knowledge), communication process(es), and channels of communication, all of which can be adopted by individuals in a social system over the passage of time. Although it dates back to the 1960s, this theory has become useful today with the prevalence of social media and other forms of media. Facebook is a good example of this theory in practice. It started as an idea that turned into a computer process for students and professionals at universities to communicate. The students spread the means of social communication to mainstream society and eventually across borders.

Mimetic Theory

The word *mimetic* comes from the word *meme*, which is a neologism coined by Richard Dawkins in *The Selfish Gene* (1976) and defined as an element of a culture or system of behavior passed from one individual to another by imitation or other nongenetic means. This theory is becoming more prominent as a result of social media. The theory advances the idea that units of cultural information (memes) survive through replication and transfer from one person to another via behaviors. In other words, a single bit of information is replicated very rapidly in social media and other media. The term *going viral* fits the mimetic theory. One can readily appreciate the contagious nature of this theory.

Both theories can be combined in the phenomenon of Pizzagate. Pizzagate began during the 2016 presidential election and involved Hillary Clinton, the Democratic candidate for president. Her campaign manager's emails were hacked by WikiLeaks and supposedly contained coded messages about human trafficking and a child sex ring at the Comet Ping Pong pizza parlor in Washington, DC. WikiLeaks published this theory, and journalists of the alternative right-wing conservative group quickly spread the conspiracy theory and called for the prosecution of Hillary Clinton. This information was spread rapidly (diffusion of information) throughout social media, cable news, newspapers, and the like. This insidious, baseless spread of a nonfactual conspiracy theory spread like a virus (memetic) and initiated a higher level of conspiracy theories from Michael G. Flynn (Michael Flynn's son) to form Pedogate. It further spread to YouTube, Instagram, and TikTok and went global. These false theories became the predecessor to QAnon.

QAnon began in October 2017 when an anonymous user put a series of posts on the message board 4chan. The user signed off as "Q" and claimed to have a level of US security approval known as "Q clearance." The theories then became known as QAnon. The messages from this user were written in a cryptic language that promoted bizarre disinformation and conspiracy theories against Democrats, journalists, and movie stars. They support President Trump's lies and conspiracy theories as well as other Republicans who support the president. The memetic theory provides an explanation for this group. The amount of traffic to mainstream social networking sites like Facebook, Twitter, Reddit, and YouTube has exploded since 2017, and indications are the numbers have gone up further during the coronavirus pandemic. This QAnon group is very dangerous, but the Republicans support this craziness, because they oppose Democrats and anything factual.

Finally, mass media can greatly influence people's opinions and amplify social contagion by reporting both factual *and* nonfactual misinformation. The last decade has propagated a significant amount of disinformation.

Important Factors in Crowd Psychology

Important factors are involved in crowds and crowd behavior, namely identity, purpose/mission, anonymity, emotion, commonality, preservation, and beliefs/trust/opinions. The identity and purpose of the group or crowd is most important in terms of behavior. The identity of crowd types has been something psychologists and sociologists have attempted to categorize.

Raymond Momboisse developed a system of four types: casual, conventional, expressive, and aggressive. The casual crowd is one that comes together without very much interaction. An example is shopping. A casual crowd forms in a store as everyone is there for the same purpose, but there is little interaction between members of the crowd. The conventional crowd is one where everyone comes together for a scheduled event, such as church or a concert. The expressive crowd is one that comes together to express emotions, such as weddings or funerals. The aggressive crowd is where they come together with a specific goal of action, such as protests or riots.

Categorizing a crowd is not an exact science, and crowds should only be characterized by their immediate identity. The identity of the crowd is observable, descriptive, and verifiable. We can categorize a football game as a sports crowd, but there is a significant difference between the crowds gathered to watch the Pittsburgh Steelers, Seattle Seahawks, or Las Vegas Raiders.

Momboisse's Four Crowd Types

Identity expresses the factual characteristics of the crowd. A crowd can be identified beyond Momboisse's four types. Crowd identity encompasses purpose, emotion, and collective beliefs. The type of crowd dictates the collective emotions. The purpose is also dictated by whatever individual beliefs come into play.

The purpose of the crowd is also factually categorized. What is the crowd's mission? This is a valid question even if the crowd isn't cognizant of their mission. The mission of a civil rights march is to make a statement about racial equality, which is their mission to social justice. The mission for a symphony orchestra is to provide symphonies to the crowd. In return, the attendees pay their respects to the orchestra. The purpose also promotes the crowd. The purpose dictates the beliefs, emotions, and, in turn, the behavior of the crowd, along with their identity.

The psychological theories of crowds include anonymity. Anonymity allows for the loss of the individual and their personality, because the individual becomes a part of the crowd. Individual thinking and appearance are lost. Anonymity is self-evident. The only individual who is apart from the crowd is the leader, a person who does something extraordinary, or when one person other than the leader contributes something to the crowd. The crowd listens to or follows the leader. An extraordinary individual in a crowd is a person who takes off all of his/her clothes and streaks through the crowd. The person loses all anonymity. An educator leading a crowd of students may ask for questions, and the person either asking or answering a question loses anonymity.

Emotions are self-evident in crowds. They can vary from rage, hate, and anger to love, joy, celebration, excitement, or anything in between. Emotions change within a crowd, such as in sports when a team makes a play, everyone yells with joy, and when the official makes a wrong call, they all boo.

There is commonality in most crowds as people sharing the same emotions, experiences, or beliefs. Identity and purpose lead to a commonality of the crowd.

Preservation of the group or crowd is important, especially where there is membership, followers, and an exchange of money. Each political party will do anything to preserve their identity, members, and followers. The National Rifle Association wants to preserve their membership, because there are financial and lobbying agendas. Businesses want to preserve their customers for financial security.

Transactional beliefs/trust/opinions occur in nonfactual crowds, such as people buying products at a store. This deserves mention, because none of the psychology theories address these types of groups.

Strong transactional beliefs are present particularly in religious gatherings, political crowds, conspiracy theory crowds, and propaganda crowds. The two detailed here are conspiracy theories and propaganda.

Conspiracy Theories

Definition of conspiracy theory: a belief that some covert but influential organization is responsible for an unexplained event.[1]

---

[1] *Oxford Dictionary.*

Conspiracy theories occur when there is an event that is vague, suspicious, and unproven (nonfactual). They are usually associated with politics, government, religion, and environment or related in some form with the universe at large, such as unidentified flying objects. The key word is *unproven*, because when an event is proven or factual, the conspiracy theory loses all energy.

Empirical Analytical Concepts of Conspiracy Theories

There has been much discussion and research concerning the concepts and principles involved with conspiracy theories in a group or crowd. There is very little discussion about the instigator of the conspiracy theory. There are the initiator(s) and the receivers (group, crowd, masses). What is the psychological makeup of those persons who start a conspiracy? The initiator is usually one or, at most, three people who start the conspiracy. They are leaders or authoritarian figures or have some resemblance of the two. It is apparent that the psychological profile of this person meets the qualifications for a personality disorder. Narcissistic, paranoid, antisocial/sociopaths have the prerequisites for originating conspiracy beliefs. Obvious features are dishonesty, self-absorption, fear, mistrust, unempathetic, and illusory thinking.

The individuals in the conspiracy theory crowd appear obsessive-compulsive, because they accept the conspiracy, obsess about those specific beliefs, and try to indoctrinate others. Research is needed to bear this out.

For individuals in the conspiracy crowd, it becomes apparent that the fundamental cerebral components of conspiracy beliefs are lack of knowledge on the subject(s) considered, lack of critical thinking, lack of analytical thinking, irrational thinking, hypersensitive belief system, and possibly illusory thinking.

Lack of knowledge allows conspiracy theories to permeate throughout society. Knowledge is knowing facts, and facts are powerful. President Trump and his followers fit this profile of conspiracy theorists.

I had a person tell me that the coronavirus and H1N1 had the same number of deaths. This falsehood was promoted on conservative media to support President Trump's theory that COVID-19 was no different from the flu. Worldwide, the number of deaths from H1N1 were estimated by the Centers for Disease Control at between 150,000 and 500,000, but in the US, there were only 12,000 deaths related to H1N1. COVID-19 has caused over half a million deaths in the US. There are also conspiracy theories about the coronavirus arising in China. The H1N1 began in the US, but we don't hear any conspiracy theories concerning the origin of H1N1. Knowledge with facts is powerful and prevents conspiracy theories.

Individuals who are part of a conspiracy theory group lack epistemic security (chapter 1), which is conducive to conspiracy beliefs. An insecure individual without a strong sense of self validates conspiracy theories if they feel comfort and support from the group.

Those who lack knowledge of the conspiracy theory are prone to accept the beliefs about it. With limited knowledge, there is a loss of control. Conspiracy beliefs provide an alternative control of the situation. This is exemplified by the security of others agreeing and supporting the belief (contagion behavior).

The lack of knowledge frequently leads to blame. People who have a predisposition to blame have become included in conspiracy theory crowds (including many Republicans in Congress, such Marjorie Taylor Greene, Mark Meadows, Matt Gaetz, etc.). Therefore, lack of knowledge (ignorance) is not the only factor, but other individual prerequisites for conspiracy beliefs include insecurity, fear, and loss of control. The fear of losing control is a big factor in the Republican Party. One way to gain control is the nefarious belief in conspiracy theories. In addition, the conspiracy crowd gains epistemic autonomy as more people join the crowd. The goal of the Republican Party is to keep control of its members and propagate more ignorance.

For those individuals confronted with conspiracy theories, it is impossible to have knowledge about every subject in the world. In the past, facts could be found at libraries, and now with the internet, facts from reliable sources are easily available and accessible. The problem with those persons who become involved with conspiracy theories is what we call *lazy brains*. People are too lazy to find the facts and the truth, and as a result, they believe everything they hear. It takes time, but if one is willing to invest the time to verify what they hear, one no longer falls into the trap of misinformation.

Lack of critical thinking arises from the impaired function of the frontal and prefrontal cortexes of the brain. This area of the brain is responsible for our thinking, emotional responses, and behavior.

Lack of analytical thinking has been thought to give rise to conspiracy beliefs. However, there is a spectrum we call *conspiracy perception reception spectrum*. This process uses analytical thinking to decipher the conspiracy beliefs. For example, the belief that Democrats eat their young would be rejected by rational, analytical-thinking people. However, the belief that the CIA killed President John F. Kennedy may cause one to consider it as a possibility. Conspiracy beliefs operate on a high level of emotion that distracts from analytical thinking. These emotions arise from the lower portion of the brain, called the limbic system, which is a group of interconnected structures located deep within the brain.

Irrational thinking also occurs when one takes part in conspiracy theories. This takes on another priority in the brain where the amygdala disables the frontal lobes and activates the fight-or-flight response. Without the frontal lobes, one cannot think clearly, make rational decisions, or control responses.

A hypersensitive belief system may be central to conspiracy thinking, because it involves beliefs. The frontal cortex of the brain has a major role in a person's beliefs. However, the subcortical information is also processed by the prefrontal cortex. The amygdala (also involved with emotions) and the hippocampus (memory portion) are involved in the process of thinking and thus help in the execution of beliefs. This memory area is going to remember all the repetitive beliefs over time from childhood to adulthood. Religion and political indoctrination and other beliefs arise from the hippocampus. Much of these beliefs are learned and remembered.

It would seem that all of these areas of the brain become hypersensitive to conspiracy beliefs. Perhaps excess dopamine plays a role. Present and future research should explore this possibility.

Preconceived beliefs can overpower rational thinking. For example, a belief that pedophiles exist in the Democratic Party can lead to the belief that Hillary Clinton is running a pedophile operation out of a pizza parlor.

Preconceived beliefs are frequently primed. A study by social psychologists at the University of Colorado divided students into two groups. One group was assigned to write an essay about a fictional student, Tyron Walker (Tyron being a name associated with a Black person), and the other group had to write an essay about a student named Brad Walker (Brad was chosen as a white person's name). Typically, the group that wrote about Brad Walker wrote about a white student, and the group writing about Tyron Walker wrote about a Black student. After completing their essays, both groups were provided with a conspiracy theory about President Obama that originated from other students: "The Anti-Christ will be a man in his forties, he will be of Muslim descent, people will flock to him and he will promise false hope and world peace, he will not have any male descendants to pass on his name, he will be an unknown man that rises to power. ... Obama ... only has daughters for children, he is a man in his forties that comes from Muslim descent, he was an unknown man who has risen to power, and he promises world peace."

The group who wrote about Tyron Walker believed this anti-Christ theory to be true, whereas the group writing about Brad Walker rejected the theory. This mental process in the brain is also important in identifying prejudice. Within-group prejudice fuels conspiracy theories.

Illusory thinking may also play a role in the perception of conspiracy theories. This also involves the prefrontal cortex located next to the visual pathway. Visual illusions may be involved with the perception of conspiracy theories. Pareidolia is when the brain perceives significant patterns or recognizable images or deciphers what they perceive to be patterns in randomness, especially in faces or accidental arrangements of shapes. For example, one may see a cloud in the sky that looks like the head of a rabbit or, walking along a path, a stone that looks like the face of a rabbit in a bush.

Understanding the location in the brain responsible for beliefs should help understand those who believe conspiracy theories. There is little research available, but 2020 being the year of conspiracy theories may prompt more research.

Research Principles of Conspiracy Theories

In "Conspiracy Theory Principles" in the *European Journal of Social Psychology*, Jan-Willem van Prooijen and Karen M. Douglas described psychological principles of conspiracy theories.

1. Conspiracy Beliefs Are Consequential: Conspiracy theories have consequences for society; these consequences are largely negative. The greatest negative consequence is the health of society. A prime example is in 2020 with the coronavirus, COVID-19. When there were only a few cases in the United States, President Trump claimed the virus would go away in a matter of weeks. This didn't happen—as medical experts warned it wouldn't—but the president repeatedly told Americans not to worry. Then he and the Republicans created a herd immunity theory that all people needed to do was to become infected, become immune, and the virus would go away. Again, this was nonfactual. The president told Americans that hydroxychloroquine (an antimalarial drug) would kill the virus. People took this drug and a few died from the side effects. Again, this was nonfactual nonsense. The conspiracy theories regarding COVID-19 piled up until over half a million Americans had died from the virus.

   Conspiracy theories can lead to numerous other consequences including negative effects on mental health and financial institutions like the stock market, as well as politics, prejudice, discrimination, and the rise of underground hate groups like neo-Nazis who kill innocent people.

Conspiracy beliefs are universal: conspiracy theories are found in all races, genders, ethnic groups, and in all countries, although America is sadly the leader in conspiracy theories. Just look at some of our congresspeople compared to other countries. The fact that these theories exist for all humans indicates they are a function of the human brain's psychological perspective of the environment. We argue that it is not adaptive but behavioral. And the behavior is universal in humans, not animals. The fact that it is behavioral explains the differences between individuals and groups to promote conspiracy theories.

Conspiracy beliefs are emotional: conspiracy theories generate a wide range of emotions including anger, hostility, hatred, anxiety, argument, mental anguish, and more. They create skepticism about those who differentiate factual from nonfactual information.

The emotions that can precipitate conspiracy theories can be societal crises, such as the assassination of a president (as with John F. Kennedy), mass shootings, terrorism, etc. Fear, anxiety, and the feeling of losing control are the emotions that generate conspiracy theories.

Conspiracy beliefs are social: crowd psychology is an important part of conspiracy beliefs. Conspiracy theories are not initiated between two individuals but rather between an individual or a few individuals and a group or between groups. It evolves from hostility and fear of the motives of the other group. The nonfactual belief becomes a domino effect within the group. The belief can avalanche and spread like a malignancy to become a larger group. Obviously, there are different identities between groups, each having opposing strong beliefs and one feeling threatened by the other. And the conspiracy theory group perceives the other group as being more powerful or more factual. The conspiracy theory becomes more powerful for the conspiracy-promoting group. Since Republicans already function on beliefs and emotion, plus childish behavior, conspiracy theories against Democrats who function on facts abound. Also, with a leader that promotes conspiracy theories, there is a contagious effect throughout the Republican party.

Supplemental Analysis

Conspiracy theories have existed from ancient times to the present. The prevalence of these theories is unchanged. However, the prevalence of awareness has increased with the increase in media. Television and social media have grown considerably over the past decade. It started when Donald J. Trump claimed that President Barack Obama was not born in the United States, thus making him an illegitimate president. From there, conspiracy theories increased as Donald Trump was elected to the White House. As conspiracy theories increased in traditional media, they grew exponentially in social media.

In the past, the prevalence of conspiracy theories between Democrats and Republicans were the same. There is no available data to prove the prevalence today is different, but observations obviously show a higher prevalence of conspiracy theories among Republicans, while Democrats depend on facts and science. The COVID-19 pandemic alone has generated numerous conspiracy theories from Republicans.

Since Richard M. Nixon's presidency, the Republicans have veered away from facts, knowledge, intellect, and academic freedom. President Nixon was paranoid about academic excellence and freedom, especially those people from Ivy League schools. The Republicans have a fear of facts, intellect, and academia. As president-elect Biden was announcing his cabinet, Marco Rubio tweeted that Joe Biden's "Ivy League" cabinet would be "polite & orderly caretakers of America's decline." This tweet is ripe for conspiracy theories that these Ivy Leaguers are going to destroy democracy. Meanwhile, President Trump and the Tea Party not only attempted to do that themselves, but they were also responsible for the half a million–plus American deaths due to COVID-19 as a result of

their willful ignorance of science. The Tea Party caucus has been trying to destroy what they perceive as *big government* and the *deep state* since their inception. However, COVID-19 has shown we need a strong, reasonable, reliable federal government.

This indicates a growing partisan divide in trust of scientific expertise over the past few decades that has, hopefully, reached its peak. In a Pew poll, https://www.pewresearch.org/science/2020/05/21/trust-in-medical-scientists-has-grown-in-u-s-but-mainly-among-democrats/, conducted in early 2020, 31 percent of Republicans expressed "a great deal of confidence" in medical scientists to act in the public interest, roughly the same level as in January 2019. Among Democrats, 53 percent expressed such confidence, up from 37 percent in January 2019 (Pew poll: *Trust in Medical Scientists Has Grown in U.S., but Mainly Among Democrats*).

Illusory Truth Effect

The bridge between conspiracy theories and propaganda is the illusory truth effect. This effect occurs when repeating a statement increases the belief that it's true even when the statement is actually false. Familiarity of the statement, whether true or false, along with repetition causes this effect on the brain. If the source of the statement or information is a leader or person of importance, one believes what is said if it's repeated. Some knowledge on the subject in which the statement is made along with ambiguity enhances the belief that the statement is true. Sensationalism in print may also serve to create the illusory truth effect. Bold or italicized print causes our brains to think in terms of truth. *The National Enquirer* uses these techniques to fortify truth from fiction. And as these sensationalist headlines are seen every time one visits the checkout counter at the grocery store, it is gradually perceived as true.

The illusory truth effect is not new, but it has been defined through experimentation. Advertising repetitively in newspaper, then radio, TV, and now the internet / social media has used this technique to sell us something, whether it be an item or idea. However, an overload of repetitive statements can also lead to a disregard for the statement. Most of us watch the stupid auto insurance ads on TV and never buy the insurance, for example.

Political ads use illusory truth, which is found to be highly effective. Used by every politician, this type of truth creates numerous false accusations. This is where illusory truth effect becomes dangerous, especially in autocratic government parties. Nazi Joseph Goebbels told repetitive lies to the German people in support of Hitler's psychopathic ideas. This has also become a tactic of President Trump, to repeat lie after lie, until his supporters believe the same falsehood. In support, Fox News reiterates these lies, and those people who watch and believe Fox News believe President Trump. One primes the other.

Repetitive indoctrination or repetitively teaching unsubstantiated beliefs to a person or group is a technique used by nefarious leaders and certain religions. A study showed that some participants exposed to false news stories will go on to have false memories. The conclusion was that repetitive false claims increase believability and may also result in errors. We have seen this with COVID-19 and many other errors by the Republicans. This causes people to lose trust in the real truth.

Propaganda

Propaganda is a form of communication intended to sway a group or crowd of people by presenting only one side of the argument. The Oxford definition is "Information, especially biased or misleading nature used to promote a point of view or political cause." As with other forms of psychological behaviors, propaganda dates back to ancient times.

As noted in the definition, propaganda is often associated with verbal or written material prepared for crowds/masses by governments, but activist groups, companies, religious organizations, the media, and individuals can also produce propaganda. With propaganda, there is persuasion, manipulation, and indoctrination.

Returning to crowd psychology and the illusory truth effect, the fact that the crowd has familiarity, biased opinions, and identified beliefs in the subject allows the propagandist(s) easy access to manipulation. The Republican love for big business and bias against small business, prejudice against Blacks, Browns, Muslims, and so forth and love for supreme whites and the religious right makes President Trump's job of manipulation and propaganda easy.

Symbolism is very effective for promoting propaganda. The Nazi sign of Germany's 1920 swastika was long used as a symbol of well-being in ancient societies, and Hitler appropriated it for nationalist propaganda. This symbol has also been promoted by white supremacy throughout the world. Many countries have banned the swastika, except the United States. How ironic that we helped allies defeat Hitler, yet we allow the symbol in America.

Red caps with "Make America Great Again" have also promoted Trump's propaganda that he is "the chosen one" to make America great, like America hasn't been great for over two centuries. Hitler's "well-being symbol" and "Make America Great Again" (MAGA) have similarities. Also, what is meant by *great*? There are arguments to be made that America is great *because* of immigrants and progressivism, not in spite of these things. Others will argue that American isn't, nor was it ever, great, and so we cannot return to a time that never existed. *Great* is such a loaded term that everyone defines for themselves. But in the case of MAGA, it's pretty clearly code for *white*. This symbolism is contagious among masses who follow the leader promoting propaganda.

The idiocy, untruth, delusion, and insanity/madness of the Republican Party is nothing new. In 1841, Charles MacKay wrote a book, *Extraordinary Popular Delusions and the Madness of Crowds*. When will this madness stop in the Republican Party?

Application of Crowd Psychology to the Republican Party

There is no one crowd theory for Republicans. Several theories apply. Convergent theory applies to Republican constants who have formulated their own beliefs and policies. Their behavior chooses a leader with the same beliefs. When congresspeople are elected, they become part of the government crowd. The leader of the Senate decides the policies, which spread like an infection throughout the Republican Congress. This is an example of the contagion theory that is common throughout many of the Republican crowds. Granted, this happens with both Republicans and Democrats, but the difference is thinking and behavior. Nefariousism is on the side of the Republicans, and utilitarianism is on the side of the Democrats. The Republicans describe themselves as the moral majority, but that is not reflected in their behavior. Instead, the opposing behavior is prominent: dishonesty, misinformation, corruption, obstructionism, hatred, violence, and conspiracy theories are not compatible with morality.

The other three crowd theories that represent Republicans are mass delusional theory, autocratic leader theory, and monetary theory.

The mass delusional theory is when idiosyncratic, unproven beliefs are incorporated in a mass of people. We have seen this starting at the top with President Trump and contagiously spreading throughout the Republican Congress and administration. The nonsensical lies spread like COVID-19. Delusional natural herd immunity and hydroxychloroquine are examples. In this situation, the spread exceeded Congress and moved to all Republican constants. The delusional conspiracy theories spread throughout Republicans nationwide.

The autocratic leader theory applies to President Trump and Mitch McConnell. From President Trump, the nefarious behavior is contagiously spread to his base through media and rallies. Former Senate Majority Leader Mitch McConnell then spread disinformation to his congresspeople. All of the people in the crowds incorporated the beliefs into their thinking and behavior. This is a simple, obvious theory that also fits to the contagion theory.

The monetary crowd theory is one where behavior of a crowd is influenced by providing money to a few members of the crowd, if not all of them. This has been blatant with Republicans in Congress. A perfect example is the National Rifle Association (NRA) paying off Republicans in Congress to prevent gun restriction laws from being passed. In addition, money was passed from Russian oligarchs through the NRA to Republican congressmen. After all the school massacres, the Republicans as a group/crowd chose money and greed over values and principles. These are obvious bribes, but since congresspeople have the power to sidestep the laws, the US Department of Justice does nothing. Any American citizen would go to prison for such corruption. Again, the Republicans represent themselves as the moral majority party, a lie sold to the American people.

The mimetic crowd theory also plays a part in the delusional neonationalist conservative Republican Party. The latest delusional lies consist of conspiracy theories spread exponentially through social media, Fox News, and far-right news outlets. Mimetics are rapid, reproductive layers of information and, in this crowd, misinformation.

The sum totality of Republican behavior in Congress and in the party consists of multiple theories. It would not be surprising if more theories are evident.

References:

Adorno, T. W. 1951. "Freudian Theory and the Pattern of Fascist Propaganda." In volume III of *Psychoanalysis and the Social Sciences*, edited by Géza Roheim. New York: International Universities Press.

Alvarez-Galvez, J. 2016. "Network Models of Minority Opinion Spreading: Using Agent-Based Modeling to Study Possible Scenarios of Social Contagion." *Social Science Computer Review* 34, no. 5: 567–581.

Beckman, M., R. L. Fathke, and T. D. Seeley. 2006. "How Does an Informed Minority of Scouts Guide a Honeybee Swarm as It Flies to Its New Home? *Animal Behavior* 71: 161–171. doi:10.1016/j.anbehav.2005.04.009 [Google Scholar].

Berlonghi, Alexander E. 1995. "Understanding and Planning for Different Spectator Crowds." *Safety Science* 18, no. 4 (February 1995): 239–247.

Blumer, Herbert. *Symbolic Interactionism: Perspective and Method.* Berkeley: University of California Press. 1969

C Couzin, I., Krause, J., Franks, N. et al. Effective leadership and decision-making in animal groups on the move. *Nature* **433,** 513–516 (2005). https://doi.org/10.1038/nature03236

Dawkins, Richard. *The Selfish Gene.* New York: Oxford University Press. 1989

Dyer, John R G et al. "Leadership, consensus decision making and collective behaviour in humans." *Philosophical transactions of the Royal Society of London. Series B, Biological sciences* vol. 364,1518 (2009): 781-9. doi:10.1098/rstb.2008.0233

John R.G. Dyer, Christos C. Ioannou, Lesley J. Morrell, Darren P. Croft, Iain D. Couzin, Dean A. Waters, Jens Krause, Consensus decision making in human crowds, Animal Behaviour, February,2008.

Dyer, J. R. G., A. Johansson, D. Helbing, I. D. Couzin, and J. Krause. 2009. "Leadership, Consensus Decision Making and Collective Behaviour in Humans." *Philosophical Transactions of the Royal Society B: Biological Sciences 364: 781-789.12 December 2009.* **https://doi.org/10.1098/rstb.2008.0233**

Freud, Sigmund. *Massenpsychologie und Ich-Analyse* (1921; English translation *Group Psychology and the Analysis of the Ego,* 1922). New York: Liveright. 1959

Henthorn, C., M. Motyl, and K. Genrow. "Is Barack Obama the Anti-Christ? Racial Priming, Extreme Criticisms of Barack Obama, and Attitudes Toward the 2008 US Presidential Candidates." *Journal of Experimental Social Psychology* 46(5): 863–866. 2010.

Kerr, Clark. *The Future of Industrial Societies. Convergence or Continuing Diversity?* Cambridge: Harvard University Press. 1983.

Krause, Jens, and John Dyer. 2008. "Sheep in Human Clothing: Scientists Reveal Our Flock Mentality." University of Leeds Press Office. February 14, 2008.

Le Bon, Gustave. *Psychology of Crowds.* 1895 [Improved edition www.sparklingbooks.com.]

Le Bon, Gustave. 1895. "The Crowd: A Study of the Popular Mind." Retrieved 15 November 2005.

MacKay, Charles. *Extraordinary Popular Delusions and the Madness of Crowds.* 1841.

Manstead, ASK, and Miles Hewstone. *Blackwell Encyclopedia of Social Psychology.* Oxford, UK: Blackwell. 1996

Marsden, Paul. 1998. "Memetics and Social Contagion: Two Sides of the Same Coin?" *Journal of Memetics* 2, no. 2: 80. 1998

Momboisse, Raymond. 1967. *Riots, Revolts and Insurrections.* Springfield, IL: Charles Thomas. OCLC 512791.

Park, Robert. 1904. *The Crowd* 1904; and *The Crowd and the Public: Masse und Publikum and Other Essays*.1904. Also: Park, Robert E., and Ernest W. Burgess. 1921. *Introduction to the Science of Sociology.* Chicago: University of Chicago Press.

Parker, R., M.J. Hugon, F. W. Porter, and D. Weissman. 2018. "mRNA vaccines for Infectious Diseases." *Nature Reviews Drug Discovery* 17, 261–279.

Perry, W. 2000. "Diffusion Theories," in *Encyclopedia of Sociology*, second ed., ed. Edgar F. Borgatta. New York: Macmillan Reference USA. 1:678–679.

Polage, Danielle. 2012. "Making up History: False Memories of Fake News Stories." *Europe's Journal of Psychology* 8 (2): 245–250.

Reicher, Stephen. 2000. Alan E. Kazdin (ed.). *Encyclopedia of Psychology.* Washington, D.C.: American Psychological Association. 2000

Rogers, Everett M. *Diffusion of Innovation.* New York: Free Press. 1962

Taifel, H. 1979. "Individuals and Groups in Social Psychology." *British Journal of Social and Clinical Psychology.* Wiley Online Library 1979.

Trotter, Wilfred. *Instincts of the Herd in Peace and War.* Guttenberg.org. At: 1916 https://www.gutenberg.org/files/53453/53453-h/53453-h.htm

Turner, Ralph H., and Lewis M. Killian. 1987. *Collective Behavior.* Englewood Cliffs, NJ: Prentice-Hall.1987.

van Prooiien, J. W., and K. M. Douglas. 2018. "Belief in Conspiracy Theories: Basic Principles of an Emerging Research Domain." *European Journal of Social Psychology.* 48(7): 897–908. 12 December 2018.

Wu, S., and Q. Sun. "Computer Simulation of Leadership, Consensus Decision Making and Collective Behaviour in Humans." PLOS. 2014. https://doi.org/10.1371/journal.pone.0080680

Emergent Norm Theory

A major criticism of this theory is that the formation and following of new norms indicates a level of self-awareness that is often missing in the individuals in crowds (as evidenced by the study of deindividuation).

Another criticism is that the idea of emergent norms fails to take into account the presence of existing sociocultural norms. Additionally, the theory fails to explain why certain suggestions or individuals rise to normative status while others do not.

Trump Contagion

There are several components of the contagion behaviors with President Trump and his followers (crowd). Like in the animal kingdom, dominance instigates behavior of the followers or the crowd. The alpha male syndrome is effective for crowd behavior.

Dominant behavior with coercion, fear, or intimidation causes people to follow dominant leaders to avoid punishment. However, such behavior is more influential among children rather than adults. Trump and the Republicans instill this fear against the Democrats when they instill fear about socialism into their supporters.

The old saying "which came first, the chicken or the egg" can be applied to Trump and his followers. Did the crowd choose Trump, or did Trump choose the crowd? It appears that the crowd chose Trump as president. The crowd was present (although factions that were more or less underground, including white supremacists) and apparent Republican conservatives and right-wing conservatives were instrumental in getting Trump elected.

Yet Trump's authoritarian behavior was obvious from the TV show *The Apprentice* on which he starred for years. He loved firing people who he thought did not meet his expectations or who did not prove themselves loyal to him.

Loyalty Issue

Prestigious behavior is contagion with Trump, because his crowd understands the intentions behind Trump's actions. Trump's followers see him as a businessman (even though he has failed financially several times). The business prestige contagion behavior is real to his followers, because he appears successful with his Trump Towers, Trump real estate, and golf courses and is a supposed billionaire. His followers see this prestige as something to follow and aspire to.

CHAPTER 6

FASCISM AND THE REPUBLICAN PARTY

Introduction

The past four years have led commentators and politicians to say that we are in an era that is endangering the fragility of democracy. But what does this mean? No one has defined this danger. This has been a long journey down a very dangerous path the Republicans have been traveling over the past five decades. That danger is described here.

Definitions

Fascism: 1. An authoritarian and nationalistic right-wing system of government and social organization. 2. (In general use) extreme authoritarian, oppressive, or intolerant views or practices.

Authoritarianism: The enforcement or advocacy of strict obedience to authority at the expense of personal freedom.

Nationalism: Identification with one's own nation and support for its interests, especially to the exclusion or detriment of the interests of other nations.

Right-wing: The conservative or reactionary section of a political party or system. "A candidate from the right wing of the party."

Descriptions

Fascism is a form of radical authoritarian ultranationalism, characterized by dictatorial power, forcible suppression of opposition, and strong regimentation of society and of the economy. It came to prominence in late nineteenth- and early-twentieth-century Europe. It grew in strength in Italy under Benito Mussolini and spread to Germany under Adolf Hitler after World War I. It is on the far right of the spectrum with a distain for anything liberal or progressive. It is on the opposing side of socialism and communism.

Most scholars focus on its social conservatism and its authoritarian means of opposing egalitarianism. Galitarianism is the doctrine that all people are equal and have equal rights, beliefs that are totally overruled by fascism. The more a person identifies himself or herself as equal among all people, the greater the likelihood that they are on the liberal ideological spectrum. The more a person considers inequality to be desirable, the further to the right he or she will be. Therefore, fascism is opposed to democracy, left-wing socialism, and communism.

Fascist ideology is racist at two extremes: fascists feel superior to other people, and they have hatred for certain other people (i.e., Blacks, Asians, Muslims, Jews, and so forth).

Fascists support violence (mob mentality), totalitarianism, radicalism, dishonesty, expansionism, psychopathic leadership, antiabortion, anti–birth control, and immigration. They support family values, which they narrowly describe as woman staying home to take care of children.

Propaganda is a tool used to suppress those with liberal ideas. There is a lot of symbolism used in propaganda. The Italian fascists used a symbol from the Roman word *fasci*, which means metal rods wrapped with metal rods. This symbolizes strength and unity.

History [1, 2]: Presented as Summary

Fascism is believed by historians to have originated in the nineteenth century. This was called the era of fin de siècle. Fin de siècle is a French phrase meaning "end of century" and is applied specifically as a historical term to the end of the nineteenth century and even more specifically to the decade of the 1890s. Historians have identified this era in history as one of the earliest examples of fascism. This was a time when people revolted against materialism, rationalism, positivity, and democracy. This period also supported emotionalism, irrationalism, and subjectivism. It rejected the rationalistic individualism of liberal society. At this early stage of fascism, violence played an important role in its formation. There is no wonder that the French social psychologist Gustave Le Bon originated the contagion theory of crowd psychology, because there were violent fascist crowds.

Early Italian Fascism

Fascism gained little strength in France, but it gained more leverage in Italy in the early 1900s. The Italian Nationalist Association (ANI) claimed that Italy's poor economy was caused by its political class, liberalism, and democracy. The ANI held ties and influence among conservatives, Catholics, and the business community.

At the beginning of World War I in August 1914, many Italians were opposed to involvement in World War I, especially the Italian Socialist Party. Benito Mussolini was prominent in the Italian Socialist Party, which promoted war against Germany. He was forced out of the party, and since fascism was becoming prominent in Italy, he moved in that direction. Mussolini founded and led the Fasci d'Azione Revoluzionaria in 1914 to promote Italian intervention in the war as a revolutionary nationalist action to liberate Italian-claimed lands from Austria-Hungary.

Ironically, the fascist group in Italy was opposed to democracy and capitalism, yet during World War I, the Allied forces, including Britain and the United States, helped the Italians gain back land the Germans had invaded during a war with Italy.

World War I

Nationalism was a huge component of World War I, as well as militarism, alliances, and imperialism. The immediate cause of World War I that made these four items come together was the assassination of Archduke Franz Ferdinand of Austria-Hungary by nationalists who wanted to end the empire. When Russia began to mobilize due to its alliance with Serbia, Germany declared war on Russia. World War I began on July 28, 1914, and lasted until November 11, 1918.

The countries in the conflict were Germany, Austria-Hungary, Bulgaria, and the Ottoman Empire (the Central powers), which fought against Great Britain, France, Russia, Italy, Romania, Japan, and the United States (the Allied powers). Thanks to new military technologies and the horrors of trench warfare, World War I saw unprecedented levels of carnage and destruction. Civilians were involved in the war, fighting and supporting the troops with food and clothing. It was a war of civilians and combatants together in the fight. By the time the war was over and the Allied powers claimed victory, more than nineteen million people, soldiers and civilians, were dead.

World War I has been referred to as "the first modern war." Many of the technologies now associated with military conflict, including machine guns, tanks, aerial combat, U-boats (undersea boats, i.e., submarines), and radio communications, were introduced on a massive scale during World War I. This led to a whole new thought process for fascism.

The technology of World War I reinforced the power of fascism. After the war, revolutionary changes in the nature of war, society, the state, and technology, along with no distinction between civilians and combatants, were observed. Fascists saw a means to an end to preserve nationalism and conservatism and to rise up against liberalism, democracy, socialism, and capitalism.

Progression of Fascism in Italy

After the war, fascism gained strength in Italy with the publication of the 1919 Fascist Manifesto. It gained more support in 1920 with a charter, which advocated national corporations align production with political views. Nevertheless, workers were not happy, causing a strike. Mussolini came to their defense to save Italy.

In the 1920s, the Italian Fascist Party ushered in support for the Roman Catholic Church, promoted family values, and placed women in the home and not the workplace. It made abortions and birth control a crime. Linking itself to right-wing politics, fascism gained more support. Despite these values, fascists supported violence and the paramilitary. It proceeded to infiltrate northern Italy. The fascists began to take over government buildings, public transportation, post offices, and so forth. They took over Rome, and Mussolini became prime minister. After becoming prime minister, he formed a coalition and gradually created a palace for the fascist party in the Italian Parliament. Fascism was overtaking all of Italy.

Voter intimidation created fascist dominance in parliament. Mussolini was in total control as a dictator, second only to the Italian king, Umberto II. The fascists agreed to a pluralistic government initially, but that didn't last long. The fascists murdered the deputy of the Socialist Party, which gave Mussolini more power.

The Catholic Church and Mussolini were initially aligned, especially with a treaty that returned land from the government to the church. However, as the Catholic Church gained more power as a result of the treaty, Mussolini felt threatened and denounced the church.

The Italian fascists were racist, believing in their superiority over Africans. They took aggressive political, economic, and military action in northern Africa, especially Libya.

Fascist movements grew in strength elsewhere in Europe, including in Hungary and Romania. The Great Depression of the 1930s caused a surge in nationalist fascism in many countries in Europe. There were also governments that borrowed elements from fascism during the Great Depression, including those of Greece, Lithuania, Poland, and Yugoslavia.

Mussolini's answer to the Great Depression was for his totalitarian fascist government to take over failing banks, industry, agriculture, and every aspect of Italian production.

Post–World War I Nationalist Fascist Germany

Germany became a republic in 1919. After losing World War I, Kaiser Wilhelm II abdicated. This democratic state was known as the Weimar Republic, which served as Germany's government from 1919 to 1933, the period after World War I until the rise of Nazi Germany. It was named after the town of Weimar, where Germany's new government was formed by a national assembly. This democratic government was faced with an economic crisis after the war.

After World War I in Germany, the Worker's Party of 1919 was formed. This party became known as the National Socialist German Workers' Party, also commonly known as the Nazi Party, in 1920. Adolf Hitler joined the party early. The party was against Marxism. A highly nationalistic group, it was also opposed to the democratic postwar government of the Weimar Republic.

Adolf Hitler rose to prominence in the early years of the party. Being one of its best speakers, he was made leader after he threatened to leave the party. The Nazi Party gained progressive power with the help of Hitler's speeches, promotion of violence (especially against liberals and Marxists), political acumen, deception, and authoritative nationalism.

Hitler promoted violence in all of his speeches. As a result, the Nazi Party created two protectors. The SS (Schutzstaffel, or Protection Squads) was originally established as Adolf Hitler's personal bodyguard unit. It would later become both the elite guard of the Nazi Reich and Hitler's executives prepared to carry out all security-related duties, without regard for legal restraint. The second group was established as a paramilitary organization that promoted violence. Intimidation played a key role in Hitler's rise to power. The second was referred to as SA, abbreviation of Sturmabteilung (German for "Assault Division"), by the name Storm Troopers. Because of Hitler's violent behavior and several of his own imprisonments, these groups were established for hypervigilance or paranoia.

The headquarters for the Nazi Party were in Munich. The liberal socialist government was also located in Munich. Hitler wanted to overturn the Munich government and take over. In 1923, Hitler and Nazi SA lead a coup d'état (called the Beer Hall Putsch) in Munich. Munich was liberal, which Hitler adamantly opposed. He had been condoning violence, and he led two thousand SA Nazis against the Munich police. The police won, and Hitler was sentenced to serve five years in prison, during which he wrote *Mein Kampf* (*My Struggle*), a book about his political views. In December 1924, having served only nine months in prison, Hitler was released. He decided to gain power through legal means, such as voting, instead of violence.

Nevertheless, violence remained a major force of the Nazi Party, with the SA opposing both the Communist and Socialist parties. In 1930, the Nazi Party became the second-largest party in Germany.

From 1931 to 1933, the Nazis combined terror tactics with conventional campaigning. The violence was mostly directed toward the communists. Anti-Semitism was also on the rise. Hitler campaigned across the nation by air, while SA troops paraded in the streets, beat up opponents, and broke up their meetings. Hitler's speeches in the form of rallies were held all over Germany.

The key reason many supported Hitler and the Nazi regime was Hitler himself. Aided greatly by the propaganda genius of Joseph Goebbels, who presented Hitler to the people, Hitler was able to present a nonpolitical, elite, superior German image.

Hitler was named chancellor in January 1933 and seized power. The Nazi SS and SA held parades and celebrations. Nationalism was strong in Germany, but they might never have imagined Hitler would become a dictator like Mussolini in Italy.

The passing of the Enabling Act in 1933 gave Hitler the freedom to act without parliamentary consent and even without constitutional limitations. After the death of the president of Germany, Hitler was in a position to pronounce himself president and chancellor—that is, dictator.

Hitler had excellent organizational skills, which the party needed to dominate Germany's political system. In addition, the Weimar Republic was growing weak. The Enabling Act of 1933 made Adolf Hitler chancellor.

Factors that played into the Nazi strength were the loss of World War I and the economic disaster after the war. Germans were defeated and struggling, which gave Hitler a platform to make "Germany Strong Again."

In summary, Germany contributed to the rise of the National Socialist German Workers' Party, which resulted in the demise of the Weimar Republic and the establishment of the fascist regime, Nazi Germany, under the leadership of Adolf Hitler. With the rise of Hitler and the Nazis in 1933, liberal democracy was dissolved in Germany, and the Nazis mobilized the country for war, with expansionist territorial aims against several countries. In the 1930s, the Nazis implemented racial laws that deliberately discriminated against, disenfranchised, and persecuted Jews and other racial and minority groups.

From 1935 to 1939, Germany and Italy escalated their demands for territorial claims and greater influence in world affairs. This led to World War II, which lasted from September 1, 1939, to September 2, 1945. It took the loss of this war for Italy and Germany to eliminate fascist states.

After World War II, democracy grew in Italy and Germany. Italy has been a democratic republic since June 2, 1946, when the monarchy was abolished by popular referendum. The constitution was promulgated on January 1, 1948.

Germany is a democratic, federal parliamentary republic, where federal legislative power is vested in the Bundestag (the parliament of Germany) and the Bundesrat (the representative body of the Länder, Germany's regional states).

Crowd Psychology of Fascism

Charismatic leadership is a characteristic of presidents in the United States. Most leaders exhibit this behavior to a degree. However, when this tendency is radicalized, the leader becomes autocratic. Narcissists and sociopaths use this behavior for power. This radical charismatic trait has been evident in Donald J. Trump for years. It was evident on his reality show when he used his power to claim, "You're fired!" over and over again. This carried over to his presidency. This same behavior was also evident in Mussolini and Hitler.

Radical charismatic behavior exudes power, which a crowd wants to follow. The crowd becomes hypnotized by the repeated propaganda from the leader. The crowd becomes so engulfed in the leader and the policies they become contagious (i.e., contagion theory). Whatever the agenda, the crowd supports. Any divergence from the leader's agenda leads to mob behavior and often violence.

Deindividuation is generally thought of as the loss of self-awareness in groups. This social theory is highly prevalent in fascism. The individuals in the crowd are completely oblivious to the evil that takes place in fascism. The fact that Mussolini poisoned Africans and Hitler killed millions of Jews, and their followers blindly went along with these things, is an example of deindividuation.

American fascism also provides an illusory identity. American fascism helps create the illusions that the real fascists, who have arrived, will be easily identifiable. That is truly an illusion, because Republicans have failed to recognize that fascism is alive and well within their own ranks.

Fascism plays into the mass delusional theory. At the core of fascism are dishonesty, fear, cowardice, and violence. The lies in Donald Trump's presidency have numbered in the thousands, but his last big lie was to tell Americans that he won the 2020 election. The other big lie was ignoring COVID-19, which lays the blame for hundreds of thousands of deaths at his feet. He has lived in a world of delusions and projected these delusions onto more than seventy million Americans who voted for him in 2020. More than 50 percent of Republicans approved of his policies, lies, and behavior. He followed Hitler's lead and almost destroyed democracy. His followers are delusional. While he secluded himself in the White House, he instigated division and violence. You didn't see Hitler carrying any bombs or keys to the gas chambers, just as you didn't see Trump himself storming the Capitol, yet both are at fault, and both are cowards.

Fascism in the Republican Party

The preceding definitions, descriptions, and history of fascism provide background material that helps to understand fascism in context so that we can responsibly ask the question, Is fascism present in America?

The behavior of the Republican Party is what we would call "incipient fascist movements." They don't wear brown suits with swastikas on their sleeves and lapels, and there is no organized fascist Republican caucus. But what we do see are subtle characteristics of fascism. These features of fascism have gradually progressed to the present. It took Donald J. Trump to openly express all the features of fascism.

Fascism also became popular in the United States in the 1930s due to the depression. People in bankruptcy, including farmers, small businesses, and young people without jobs, were hypnotized by the agenda and policies of fascism. The despair caused susceptibility to promises of a demagogue. The incipient fascism of Republicans has reached an era of deceit, leading some Americans to blind obedience.

Incipient Fascism in the Republican Party

There are factions of fascism in the United States, but there is no fascist party like that which existed in the twentieth century in Italy. In fact, there has not been a fascist party that rose to power with a dictatorship. There have been factions and a spectrum of fascist policies in several countries in the past and only a few countries today. Nevertheless, the Republican Party has been introducing several criteria associated with fascism.

Autocratic governing is part of the definition of fascism. This has been an enabling symptom of the Republican Party for the past five decades. It began in the era of President Nixon but has been slowly progressing through the rise in power of Mitch McConnell and finally President Trump. Hundreds of bills were presented to Senate Majority Leader McConnell, and he refused to hold hearings on them.

One of the key factors in their quest toward fascism was the Tea Party that sought to eliminate government and regulations, thus allowing for centralized government, a feature of fascism.

Radicalization is another strong component of fascism. We have seen a progression of radicalism in the Republican Party, especially with Donald J. Trump in office. Using fear as a mechanism for radical dialogue on

Fox News and Right-Wing media outlets has become extreme. Calling Democrats radical socialists, antidemocratic, who eat their young and form sex rings scares people, and when it is repeated ad nauseum, people start believing these lies. Calling Democrats radical is an oxymoronic statement. Republicans endorse severe emotional problems, one of which is fear. They psychologically project their fear onto Democrats. Dishonesty, conspiracy theories, and nonfactual disinformation are all used by extreme radicals. History reports this behavior with Mussolini and Hitler. Is the Republicans' behavior any different from these fascist leaders?

Nationalism has become prominent with Republicans over the past two decades. The religious right has become increasingly prominent in the Republican Party. This Far Right group is highly nationalistic, to an extent that goes far beyond patriotism. They radically promote their exceptionally conservative beliefs in the Republican Party. The white supremacists are right-wing nationalists. This group was underground until President Trump endorsed their behavior. But there is another group of white supremacists who are not as radicalized as the Proud Boys and the Ku Klux Klan. These are white people who fear losing their identity as immigration into the United States persists. These are the silent white supremacists who support President Trump.

The fascism in the party goes against the principles of a democracy (i.e., equality, racial justice, respect for laws, etc.). They view the party and nation's wealth and success as being far more important than the citizens of the country. As a result, fascists believe that rights and wealth should be reserved for only a select portion of a country's citizens. Fascists often use forcible suppression of opposition and regimentation of society and the economy.

Fascism deplores free speech in the media and attempts to suppress it and replace it with their own propaganda. President Trump has verbally attempted to suppress media that he referred to as "fake news." Another symptom of authoritarianism is suppression of truth and formation of media that promotes propaganda, such as Fox News.

Fascism supports violence that has become prominent with white supremacists. We have seen this in Charlottesville, Virginia; Ohio; Gilroy,

California; El Paso, Texas; and Pittsburgh. Republicans, aside from a select few like Mitt Romney, did not openly denounce this behavior.

Racism is another component of fascism. It was obvious during the Obama presidency, when again Mitch McConnell prevented President Obama's agendas. President Trump has repeatedly oppressed African Americans. We have Rupert Murdoch, Rush Limbaugh, Glenn Beck, and other right-wing media outlet—white people pushing a white supremacy agenda.

Voter suppression was a technique used by Mussolini to gain power. Republicans have done this for decades. Illegal methods to prevent minorities from voting have been used in many southern states for years.

Trump's Four Years of Fascism as President

The myth of Donald Trump is that he was not a politician, and Americans were looking for someone who was not a politician. His myth as a successful businessman was something many Americans were eager to follow. He was also a mythological figure with his reality show *The Apprentice* that exuded lies, but he was a familiar figure because of it. He never really represented the Republicans, because when he ran for president, he made fun of and used derogatory innuendo toward his running mates. The Republican Party adopted him, because the caucus in the Republican Party who were incipient fascists saw their chance for power. Trump was one man who cut across the many sources of anger and discontent in America. Like Hitler, Trump was initially not seen as a power-hungry racist but as someone putting America first "to make it great again." He was praised by Republican congressmen for his hateful propaganda against the Democrats, who Republicans see as left-wing socialists.

As Trump began his presidential run, he made many hateful statements about his opponents. There were those who found him funny and unique and liked his style. There were also honest, intelligent, and moral persons who suggested he was taking us into a realm of deep moral degeneration. This charismatic, magnetic leader when he became president was about to take America into the abyss of fascism. It started with racism, misogyny, and using strategic lies against his opponents to create hatred and rage in 40 percent of the Republican constituent base. In some situations, this rage produced violence, a feature of fascism and a very effective method for creating fear, especially fear of his opponents and those Republicans outside his base. In 1930s Germany during Hitler's rise to power, many well-meaning people did not choose to perceive that a new technique of conscious cynical amorality was at work. The same is true for the rise of Trump.

Trump used chaos either strategically or seemingly randomly to create fury for everyone. The chaos, repetitive lies, and fear have caused a lot of confusion for Americans. The misinformation from right-wing media and Fox News also creates confusion, and all of these outlets support President Trump.

The repeated lies in the form of propaganda are an obvious tool by President Trump to keep the behavioral engines of his Republican base constantly loyal. The propaganda rallies in just about every one of the American states created an ongoing contagion and deindividuation behavior. Propaganda was a strong feature of Hitler's fascism. Propaganda encouraged Hitler's base and provided cover for his regime's most brutal and evil aggressions. However, Hitler rose unchallenged and left carnage and chaos in his wake.

Autocratic power became the obsessive norm for President Trump. He dismembered every agency in the government as a reflection of his own power. Those agency heads who were not loyal were replaced by his most incompetent loyalists. Hitler had the same loyalty practice; the difference between the two leaders was that Hitler placed highly competent evil people in positions to support him. His love affair with dictators took on another new dimension against democracy.

Nationalism was also obvious in his leadership. Pulling out of NATO and the World Health Organization are two examples. Supporting white supremacists and the far religious right became an obvious obsession. This was also expressed by Trump's ignoring our allies, pulling out of the Iran agreement, NATO, and WHO. His support for white nationalists and hatred for immigrants is also behavior consistent with nationalism.

In 1923, Hitler and Nazi SA lead a coup d'état in Munich, and the Nazis took over the local government. On January 6, 2021, President Trump and his Nationalist Supremacists attempted a coup d'état on the Capitol of the United States. It was a sad, sad time in American history. The Republicans with all their anger and rage against the Democrats should be ashamed. And Senate Majority Leader Mitch McConnell should be held accountable.

The two main supporters of Donald Trump's presidency are Senators Ted Cruz and Josh Hawley. Both support a Trump fascist regime. These two senators are dangerous and show sociopathic behavior. They are two intelligent people with excellent educations, but their intelligence is overshadowed by an extreme devotion to a dangerous belief system. This combination can be associated with nefariousism as exemplified by their extreme support of President Trump in the Senate.

There are genuine questions about whether these two senators represent their constituents or themselves. In this scenario, they can do and say whatever they want, and the contagion theory takes effect. They can say they represent their constituents like Hitler lied about representing Germans. America is in big trouble if their constituents represent them. This would mean that everyone thinks like they think. This would represent the convergent theory, but in this scenario, I would hope all of their constituents do not think like they do.

After the attempted coup at the US Capitol, both Senators Cruz and Hawley supported Trump and his conspiracy theory about the "rigged election." These two men specifically and other Trump supporters in the Republican Party generally should be held accountable. These two senators who are supposedly experts on the US Constitution are by definition traitors to the Republican Party and have committed treason against the United States government.

As pointed out many times, sociopathy is prominent in the Republican Party, most assuredly in the Senate. Senators Cruz and Hawley have blood on their hands and failed to acknowledge it after the coup. That is clearly sociopathic behavior, if not psychopathy. To be a supporter of a psychopath in the White House makes one a sociopath.

Countries with Fascism in the Twenty-First Century

Today, very few political parties describe themselves as fascists. Instead, this term is usually used as an epithet by concerned citizens. This trend stems from the fact that there have been several fascist movements throughout history. Whether government systems recognize the traces of fascism in their ideologies or not does not take away from the reality that many systems of government still incorporate fascist ideas into their modern-day strategies.

Even democratic nations have traces of fascist movements within their histories. These nations have had fascist sympathizers, parties, and support groups with some significant influence in their respective countries. These nations include:

- Austria
- Poland
- Turkey (Implemented by Atatürk, the founding ideology of the Republic of Turkey, features nationalism as one of its six fundamental pillars. Fascism is gaining strength in Turkey.)
- Belgium
- Canada
- Ireland
- Lebanon
- Mexico
- The Netherlands
- Sweden
- The United Kingdom
- The United States

Fascism existed in many countries throughout the twentieth century around the world, including:

- Australia: 1931–early 1940s
- Austria: 1933–1945
- Belgium: 1932–1938
- Canada: 1930s–1940

- Chile: 1932–1938
- China: 1932–1941 and 1938–1945
- Croatia: 1941–1945
- Finland: 1929–1944
- France: 1940–1944
- Greece: 1936–1941
- Hungary 1932–1945
- Ireland: 1932–1933
- Italy: 1922–1943
- Lebanon: 1936–present
- Mexico: 1930–1942
- The Netherlands: 1923–1945
- Norway: 1943–1945
- Portugal: 1932–1934
- Poland: 1930s–present; evolving fascism
- Romania: 1940–1944
- Slovakia: 1939–1944
- Spain: 1936–1975
- South Africa: 1930s–1980s
- Sweden: 1926–1929
- United Kingdom: 1932–1940
- Yugoslavia: 1935–1939
- United States: 1933–1940

The fact that there was fascism in the United States might come as a shock to some. In the late 1930s, pro-German organizations showed support for fascism, and one group, the Silver Legion of America, ran candidates for president on a third-party ticket. After Nazi Germany declared war on the United States in 1941, the group was outlawed.

The peak of fascism around the world took place after World War I, with Italy introducing fascism to the world. The economy after World War I in Europe was devastated. Nationalism appeared to be a savior for many European countries. The fact that it extended to countries like Canada and the United States is dramatic, because these countries worked to defeat fascism in Europe.

The fuel on the fire of fascism was the Great Depression that took place from August 1929 to March 1933. All the counties listed above became prominent after the Great Depression. Scholars reporting on the cause of the Great Depression list failure of the American stock market, bank failure, and monetary contraction, the gold standard, and decreased international lending and tariffs. But all of these reasons were a result of the economic devastation from World War I and the cost of technology.

Methods to Prevent or Defeat Fascism

A method that has been used to denounce fascism was to rely on the capitalist courts and legislatures to stand up to the fascists. However, the tactic of the Republicans has been to place conservative judges in the courts and to have the attorney general and Justice Department follow fascist principles. The problem with the US legislature is that symptoms of fascism exist in the Republican Party within the legislature.

Another method used in Europe to fight right-wing fascists was to have the left, liberal media fight the right. That only made matters worse. In the US, the First Amendment prevents such actions.

Socialist and Marxist rhetoric has also been used to stop fascism but has largely failed.

Preventing and denying permits to the right wing and neo-Nazis to have rallies was attempted in 1960 when the mayor of New York denied the American Nazi Party, led by George Lincoln Rockwell, a permit to hold a rally. This attempt also failed.

One of the best and most successful methods of counteracting fascism is education. All secondary education should have mandatory courses in political science and US government that educates on the two extremes and provides centralist policies.

Organizations like the Lincoln Project could provide educational ads on Fox News and conservative news outlets for people to see the truth.

Right-wing news outlets have a responsibility to tell the truth and prevent the spread of propaganda. They are in the business of being greedy, spreading lies, and acting irresponsibility. They don't care if people are harmed over their lies and actions; it is self-serving greed.

For example, National Public Radio on January 15, 2021, interviewed Amy Lynn Peikoff, the conservative who is an American writer, blogger, and professor of philosophy and law. Peikoff is the chief policy officer of the social media platform Parler. Parler was removed from Amazon and others because of its association with radicalism, conspiracy theorists, and dishonesty, which led to the violent fascist mob at the US Capitol on January 6, 2021. Of course, Peikoff defended Parler as a First Amendment right and claimed that lies were okay, with the exception of radical lies. She argued that lies do not incite violence. While it is true that emotions incite violence, lies and propaganda incite the emotion that creates violence within a crowd. Parler supports lies and radicalism. With her education and background, Amy Peikoff should know better, but when big conservative money is behind Parler, one is forced to defend it. She stated that they have artificial intelligence to weed out radicalism. Perhaps their artificial should become more ethical, humanlike intelligence. But Parler is not the only irresponsible social media outlet. Facebook, Twitter, Instagram, and others have been totally irresponsible. To these companies, it is about how many billions of dollars they make. If they cannot morally and ethically censor the nefarious activity on their platforms, they should be regulated. This is not about the First Amendment but doing that which is right. Newspapers, television, and movies are censored.

Fascists and conspiracy theorists who promote or cause harm to citizens should be held accountable. However, the US democracy operates by the rule of law, except the laws are awkward. A president of the United States can commit crimes, pardon himself, and get away with murder. A police officer can shoot an innocent Black man and gets administrative leave. Wake up, lawmakers!

We must make an all-out effort to teach truth and facts. That could be another course in our educational system. The distinction between fact and nonfacts must be learned, as outlined in chapter 1.

Lies, dishonesty, disinformation, and nonfacts along with conspiracy theories can erase morality from the citizenry; this is not the same as the morality Christians and Catholics teach (often political) but rather universal principles like truthfulness, respect, empathy, and humility. This requires educators, religious leaders, ethicists, sociologists, lawmakers, and families to come together with a mission to stop this nonsense. We have had a war against drugs. Why not a war against lies and conspiracy theories?

Summary

America is a democracy, but like any other government in trying times, it can be fragile. This has been shown as both fascism and communism can infiltrate democracy. Parallel facts on fascism were presented to create awareness, not opinion.

In our democracy, even in a culture where misinformation has become omnipresent, where an angry base, supported by disparate, substantial interests, feels empowered by the relentless lying of a charismatic leader, the center still holds. The center has been strengthened by the voting of the American people in 2020 and January 2021.

Hopefully, the norm of the past four years will only last as long as the COVID-19 pandemic. Americans need to be vaccinated with a moral, utilitarian reality in search of truth, science, education, stable government, and progress. The future is progress in the twenty-first century, not regressive behavior.

References:

Blamires, Cyprian. 2006. *World Fascism: A Historical Encyclopedia, Volume 1.* Santa Barbara, California: ABC-CLIO, Inc.
Mussolini, Benito. 2006. *My Autobiography: With "The Political and Social Doctrine of Fascism."* New York: Dover Publications.
Sternhell, Zeev. 1998. "Crisis of Fin-de-siècle Thought" in Griffin, Roger, ed., *International Fascism: Theories, Causes and the New Consensus.* London and New York: Hodder Education Publishers.

Conservative Political Definitions

Much of the time, there is confusion as to what it means when a person states that he or she is a conservative or any other defining classification of conservatism. We list those here for education purposes and for convenience.

Conservative: Conservatism is a political and social philosophy promoting traditional social institutions in the context of culture and civilization. The central tenets of conservatism include tradition, organic society, hierarchy, authority, and property rights.

American conservatives believe in limiting government in size and scope and in a balance between national government and states' rights. Social conservatives oppose abortion and same-sex marriage, while privileging traditional marriage and supporting Christian prayer in public schools. Conservatism in the US is characterized by respect for American traditions, Republicanism, support for Judeo-Christian values, moral universalism, pro-business and antilabor union, antisocialism and communism, and defense of America.

Moderate conservative: Modern moderates have been known as "business conservatives," and congressional moderates are members of Main Street Republicans or the Tuesday Group. Moderates tend be conservative to moderate on fiscal issues and moderate to liberal on social issues. They sometimes share the economic views of conservative Republicans (e.g., balanced budgets, lower taxes, free trade, deregulation, and welfare reform).

Moderate Republicans differ in that some are for affirmative action, same-sex marriages, gay adoption, legal access to—and even funding for—abortion, gun control laws, more environmental regulation legislation and anti–climate change measures, fewer restrictions on legal immigration and a path to citizenship for illegal immigrants, and embryonic stem cell research.

Liberal conservative: Liberal conservatism is a political ideology combining conservative policies with liberal stances, especially on economic, social, and ethical issues, or a brand of political conservatism strongly influenced by liberalism.

Liberal conservatism incorporates the classical liberal view of minimal government intervention in the economy, according to which individuals should be free to participate in the market and generate wealth without government interference. However, liberal conservatism also holds that individuals cannot be thoroughly depended on to act responsibly in other spheres of life, therefore liberal conservatives believe that a strong state is necessary to ensure law and order, and social institutions are needed to nurture a sense of duty and responsibility to the nation. They also support civil liberty, along with some social conservative positions.

Right wing: Right-wing politics holds that certain social orders (i.e., liberal, conservative) and hierarchies (i.e., social stratifications) are inevitable, natural, normal, or desirable, typically supporting this position on the basis of natural law, economics, or tradition. Hierarchy and inequality may be viewed as natural results of traditional social differences or the competition in market economies. The term *right wing* can generally refer to the conservative or reactionary section of a political party or system.

According to *The Concise Oxford Dictionary of Politics*, in liberal democracies, the political right opposes socialism and social democracy. Right-wing parties include conservatives, Christian democrats, classical liberals, nationalists; and on the Far Right, racists and fascists.

Social stratification is a kind of social differentiation whereby members of society are grouped into socioeconomic strata based upon their occupation and income, wealth and social status, or derived power (social and political).

Far Right: Far Right politics are politics further on the right of the left-right spectrum than the standard political right, particularly in terms of extreme nationalism, nativist ideologies, and authoritarian tendencies, all sustained by an organicist vision of the world.

Generally, the left wing is characterized by an emphasis on ideas such as liberty, equality, fraternity, rights, and progress.

★ ★ ★

CHAPTER 7

PSYCHOSOCIAL ANALYSIS OF THE REPUBLICAN PARTY

Introduction

It should be noted that any name associated with a psychological description is not a diagnosis. In order to arrive at a diagnosis, a medical history and physical would need to be completed. Psychological testing and evaluations by a neuropsychiatrist and/or psychiatrist would need to be completed. Tests such as PET brain scans and genetic testing would also be useful. Associations are based on public behavior in print or media to include Fox News, NBC, CBS, ABC, NPR, PBS, the *New York Times*, *Washington Post*, published books, internet, CNN, MSNBC, or C-SPAN.

The psychological disorders described include paranoia, opposition-defiant disorder, sociopathy, psychopathy, and narcissism.

The objective is to guide us through some of the historical behaviors of Republicans, starting from the inception of the party to the present. It should be obvious how the party vacillated at times between a progressive and conservative party.

History of the Republican Party

The Republican Party came into power in 1854 when they opposed the Kansas–Nebraska Act, which would allow slavery in Kansas and Nebraska. By 1860, Republicans had taken over Congress and nominated Abraham Lincoln for president, hence the name "The Party of Lincoln." The party was against slavery and promoted human rights. Its presence was mostly in the North rather than the southern states.

It did not take long for different religions to pick sides. Presbyterians, Methodists, German Baptists, and Quakers became aligned with the Republicans, and Catholics, Episcopalians, and German Lutherans aligned themselves with the Democrats. The Republican Party supported Prohibition.

The first forty years of the Republican Party was progressive, with President Lincoln not only freeing slaves but starting the first park in 1864, Yosemite Park, which then became the third national park in 1890. The transcontinental railroad was built under his presidency. This was the initiation of socialization in America. President Lincoln represented intelligence, morality, and empathy and had a wonderful ability to articulate the truth.

The early constituents consisted of farmers, businessmen, bankers, professionals, northern evangelical Protestants, and factory workers. It promoted free labor, freedom, and free land for farmers (mostly in the West). Ironically, only white people were offered free land.

The Republicans supported business, tariffs, and banks. They supported building railroads. They wanted to destroy the Confederacy, which at the time supported Democrats in power. At the time, all of the southern governors were Democrats who supported segregation. When Attorney General Robert Kennedy and President John Kennedy proposed desegregation, the southern Democrats were fighting for segregation. As a result, this allowed the Republicans to gain power in the South. It took more than one hundred years for the South to become dominantly Republican. Heretically, the party that opposed slavery later became the party of eventual segregation of jobs, education, and social economics.

The Republican Party dominated Congress from the time of President Lincoln until 1912. President Theodore Roosevelt (1901–1909) became too progressive, and their dominance ended in 1912. The ideology of the Republican Party shifted to the right, leaving the liberal left to become the conservative right. Conservative Republicans became more vocal after Franklin D. Roosevelt took office in 1933. President Roosevelt introduced the New Deal, which was considered socialist by Republicans, because it initiated the Social Security Act. This established a permanent system of universal retirement for American citizens (Social Security). It established unemployment insurance and welfare benefits for the handicapped and needy children in families without a father present. This faced a great deal of opposition from the Republican conservatives who viewed the New Deal as socialist.

Isolationism also became a factor of the Republican Party. This began during World War II. Republican isolationists did not want to help Britain and did not want to get involved with the war. Isolationism carried over to the Reagan administration when President Reagan developed a relationship with Russian leader Mikhail Gorbachev; after the Berlin Wall came down, Republican fears subsided.

After the Civil Rights Act of 1964 and the Voting Rights Act of 1965, the Republican Party became the party of white Americans. Even though there were Democratic governors, such as George Wallace, who was a segregationist, Republicans gradually gained power. Southern Democrats wanted to preserve states' rights and the racist southern lifestyle. When the Democratic Party supported civil rights, the South moved to the Republican Party. In addition, as the Democratic Party became identified with a pro-choice position and with nontraditional societal values, social conservatives joined the Republican Party in increasing numbers.

The last progressive and socialistic president was Dwight D. Eisenhower, a general from World War II who was an internationalist. He was a supporter of NATO. He kept the programs instituted in the New Deal. He also built super interstate highways across the country (a socialist program). His attempt to move the GOP from conservatism to a more moderate party failed. One of the problems in retrospect was choosing Richard M. Nixon as his vice president. Eisenhower was not a highly involved leader in the politics of the Republican Party and left these details to Nixon, who learned to manipulate the president and the party.

Conservatism again rose with Republican Arizona Senator Barry Goldwater's conservative view. He ran against Lyndon B. Johnson for the presidency in 1964. Although he had voted in favor of the Civil Rights Act of 1957 (there were four Civil Rights Acts: 1957, 1960, 1964, and 1968) and the Twenty-Fourth Amendment to the US Constitution, he opposed the Civil Rights Act of 1964, believing it to be an overreach by the federal government. His views consisted of strongly opposing the New Deal and the United Nations, but he rejected isolationism and containment, calling for an aggressive anticommunist foreign policy.

Lyndon B. Johnson was president from November 22, 1963, to January 20, 1969. President Johnson started the Great Society while in office. This included the main goals of ending poverty, reducing crime, abolishing inequality, and improving the environment. He always had a War on Poverty because of the poverty in which he'd lived in west Texas as a child. After taking office, he passed more than two hundred bills. He obtained passage of a major tax cut, the Clean Air Act, and the Civil Rights Act of 1964. After the 1964 election, Johnson passed even more sweeping reforms, including the Older Americans Act and the Elementary and Secondary Education Act (ESEA) of 1965, both of which remain government programs. The Social Security amendments of 1965 created two government-run health care programs, Medicare and Medicaid. President Johnson's Great Society remains the largest social reform plan in modern history. As a result of the Great Society, poverty was significantly reduced in the United States. The lives of many underprivileged Americans improved.

The Republicans saw this as socialism and for forty years have attempted to eliminate these programs. They have nothing with which to replace Medicare and Medicaid. They claim to believe in a free market solution, but this has not been the case in the past. The New Deal and the Great Society were staunchly opposed by Republicans. When Reagan and Trump say, "Make America Great Again," they are referring to the Grand Old Party. However, historians have a different opinion. More than 130 professors of history were asked to rank the ten best presidents since 1900. Franklin D. Roosevelt, Theodore Roosevelt, and Lyndon B. Johnson were the top three.

In 1949, China became communist. Vietnam was trying to gain independence from the French. There were factions fighting for independence, which led to the Geneva Treaty. Peace was discussed at Geneva in 1954, and the Treaty of Geneva agreed that the French would leave Vietnam and the country would be split along the Seventeenth Parallel until elections could be held. This opened the door for North Vietnam to become communist with Ho Chi Minh, while South Vietnam was on its own.

There was significant concern by the United States concerning communism infiltrating Southeast Asia, specifically South Vietnam. President Eisenhower began sending money, supplies, and military advisers to the South Vietnamese. This continued with President Kennedy. The South Vietnamese were weak with an ineffective leader. In 1963, President Kennedy sent in sixteen thousand military advisers to form a capitalist government.

At the time of Kennedy's assassination, the United States involvement in the Vietnam War remained fairly limited. But that changed in August 1964. The US Navy was attacked by the communist North Vietnamese in the Gulf of Tonkin. This gave the US Congress permission to grant expansive war powers to the newly installed president, Lyndon B. Johnson. Congressional Republican isolationists were opposed to the war.

On March 8, 1965, 3,500 United States Marines came ashore at Da Nang as the first wave of US combat troops into South Vietnam, adding to the 25,000 US military advisers already in place. The deployment of ground forces to Da Nang had not been discussed with the South Vietnamese government. The United States entered Vietnam with the principal purpose of preventing a communist takeover of the region. In that respect, it failed: the two Vietnams were united under a communist banner in July 1976. Neighboring Laos and Cambodia similarly fell to communists.

Throughout the 1960s, there was a tremendous amount of dissent against the Vietnam War. Sit-ins in Washington, DC, and cities throughout the United States were also causing political issues.

In 1968, Richard M. Nixon ran on a campaign that promised to restore law and order to the nation's cities and provide new leadership during the Vietnam War. Nixon's victory marked the start of a period of Republican dominance in presidential elections, as Republicans won four of the next five elections.

President Johnson also ran against Richard M. Nixon in 1968 on the platform of ending the Vietnam War with peace talks. However, Nixon used collusion in South Vietnam for leverage and to guarantee that Nixon would end the war. He used Anna Chennault, an Asian who helped Nixon win the presidency by commanding Vietnam peace talks on the eve of the 1968 election.

President Richard Nixon ordered the withdrawal of US forces from Vietnam in 1973. Communist forces ended the war by seizing control of South Vietnam in 1975, and the country was unified as the Socialist Republic of Vietnam the following year.

The Vietnam War was a long, costly, and divisive conflict that pitted the communist government of North Vietnam against South Vietnam. The conflict was intensified by the ongoing Cold War between the United States and the Soviet Union. This Cold War issue ended with President Reagan.

Nixon's campaign was the obvious beginning of corruption, collusion, and mental health issues in the Republican Party. He had this war on crimes in the cities, when he was himself a criminal. He had an obvious paranoid personality disorder. He had the Oval Office rigged with voice-activated recorders. He held a fear of intellectuals, Ivy League universities, and Jewish people. He was also a conspiracy theorist, conspiring against the Pentagon and others. His paranoia led him to send people to obtain records from the Democratic headquarters in the Watergate office complex. This occurred in 1974 and eventually led to Nixon's resignation. The US Supreme Court ruled that Nixon must release the Oval Office tapes to government investigators. Gerald Ford, who was Nixon's vice president, took over the presidency and pardoned Nixon. Nixon's vice president, Spiro Agnew, was equally if not more corrupt than Nixon.

The *Roe v. Wade* decision of 1973 that upheld the right for an abortion dominated the Republican Party until 1989. Also, during this period of time, the Republicans pushed for decreased government spending and regulation. At the end of the twentieth century, the dominance of the Republicans was in the South, Midwest, Southwest, and rural areas throughout the United States.

The pardon of President Nixon caused the Democrats to become more powerful. This led to the election of Jimmy Carter in 1976.

The Hollywood star and former governor of California, Ronald Reagan, was elected in 1980. His career as an actor made him the star of the Republican Party.

President Reagan launched the so-called Reagan Republican Conservative Revolution of making America great. His conservatism has continued to the present. President Reagan used catchy phrases like "Peace through Strength." This strength meant spending large sums of money on defense. This was a political move to deter communism. In addition, he cut taxes in half to generate more revenue. He felt this would stimulate the economy, but it brought America deeper into debt. This cut in taxes and the promotion of unrestricted free market activity was called Reaganomics. The Republicans never cared about balancing the budget. They became angry when money was spent on helping Americans, as with Social Security.

President Reagan was victorious in the 1980 and 1984 elections because Democrats as well as Republicans voted for him. The Democrats who voted for him were white, blue-collar, middle-class workers who Reagan appealed to with his rhetoric. Republicans supported him on his war on drugs and antiabortion policies. Reagan Democrats were opposed to the Democratic support of African Americans and Democratic liberals. At the time, the American middle class was more conservative, and Reagan appealed to those people.

Ronald Reagan was again victorious in the 1984 election with the slogan "It's morning again in America." He proceeded to stimulate the economy by cutting taxes 25 percent and abolishing the upper tax rates. Reagan's powerful win in 1984 also gained more Republican conservative seats in the Senate.

President Regan's policy in Central America was hard-line and grandiose. He thought he could eradicate communism in Central America. He supported the contra guerillas (anticommunist) against the Sandinista (Sandinista National Liberation Front) government of Nicaragua. He provided support to the dictatorial governments of Guatemala, Honduras, and El Salvador against communist guerrilla movements. The Reagan Doctrine called for providing military support to movements opposing Soviet-supported communist governments.

The Central America anticommunism policy was also connected to Iran. The Reagan administration subsequently rewarded Iran for its participation in the plot by secretly and illegally supplying Iran with weapons through Israel and by unblocking Iranian government monetary assets in US banks. Also, part of the Iranian deal was the release of Americans held hostage by terrorists in Lebanon. Money obtained from the arms deal to Iran was used to back military support against communism in Central America. This became known as the Iran-contra arms-for-hostages scandal.

Oliver North, a veteran of the Vietnam War, was a National Security Council staff member during the Iran-Contra affair. He was involved in the scandal in which he claimed partial responsibility for the sale of weapons through intermediaries to Iran, with the profits being channeled to the Contras in Nicaragua. He was sentenced by US District Judge Gerhard Gesell on July 5, 1989, to a three-year suspended prison term, two-year probation, $150,000 in fines, and 1,200 hours of community service. North performed some of his community service within Potomac Gardens, a public housing project in southeast Washington, DC.

President Reagan also took a hard line against the Soviet Union, alarming Democrats who wanted a nuclear freeze. Instead, he increased the defense budget and increased military power. He organized a Strategic Defense Initiative called "Star Wars" by his opponents. The intent was to make America's defense so strong the Soviets or any other country would be unable to match it. When Mikhail Gorbachev rose to power in Moscow, President Reagan began to develop a friendship with him. This caused growing concern among conservative Republicans. Essentially, this relationship caused Gorbachev to deescalate the arms race and gradually release the Eastern European empire from his control.

During Reagan's eight years in office, the deficit tripled. This was the result of exorbitant defense spending and tremendous tax cuts. The Republicans' tax cuts have long been their main focus. As long as taxes are low, they have no concern about Americans in debt. Republican conservatism and cutting taxes are synonymous.

The 1960s–1980s Introduced the Neoconservatives (Neocons)

Neoconservatism is a political movement born in the United States during the 1960s among liberal hawks who became disenchanted with the increasingly pacifist foreign policy of the Democratic Party and the growing New Left and counterculture, in particular the Vietnam protests.

Those who were Democrats essentially became Republicans, possibly without changing parties. Many of these neoconservatives held major appointments during the presidential terms of Reagan, George H.W. Bush, and George W. Bush, in a total of five different presidencies. The neocons were hawkish. They participated in and helped plan the Iraq war in 2003. President George W. Bush and Vice President Dick Cheney were die-hard Republicans. However, Dick Cheney and Secretary of Defense Donald Rumsfeld consulted the neocons about the Iraq war. Some of the neocons were Jews who were active in foreign policy, especially regarding the Middle East and Israel. They are considered high proponents of democracy in the Middle East by a large military presence.

Much of this promotion was through the American Jewish Committee. Neoconservatives faded somewhat during President Obama's terms. However, neoconservatism has seen a resurgence through the Tea Party and the Trump administration. The focus has changed from democracy to fascism.

George H.W. Bush was the Republican president who succeeded President Reagan, during a time when Reagan was friendly with the Soviets. During President Bush's tenure, he continued Reagan's policy that led to the fall of the Berlin Wall in November 1991. This all started with President Reagan when on June 12, 1987, he gave a speech at the Brandenburg Gate in Berlin and said those famous words: "Mr. Gorbachev, tear down this wall." He also led an international coalition of countries that forced Iraq to withdraw from Kuwait in the Gulf War and undertook a US military invasion of Panama. He also passed the Americans with Disabilities Act.

Although a little arrogant, "Read My Lips" person, President Bush was a respectable human being with good moral values. He and John McCain were much alike.

The Self-Promoting Ego of Republican Newt Gingrich

Newt Gingrich entered the House of Representatives as a Republican from Georgia in November 1978. He had a background in history, earning his BA from Emory University in Atlanta, Georgia, in 1965. He went on to graduate school at Tulane University, earning an MA in 1968 and a PhD in European history in 1971. He was a college professor at West Georgia College from 1970 to 1978 before entering the US Congress.

Bill Clinton focused on the economy in 1992 due to the recession and ran on school choice, balancing the budget, opposition to illegal immigration, and support for the North American Free Trade Agreement (NAFTA) that President George H.W. Bush initiated.

Representative Gingrich drafted his "Contract with America" in 1994. These were essentially Democratic policies already, but he made it seem like these were all Republican ideas. This was not done in conjunction with President Clinton's policies but made it appear like these were their ideas for America. The contract had ten policies that included welfare reform, balanced budget, criminal reform, and term limits. This was also a trick to obtain more Republican seats in the House and Senate.

In 1995, Newt Gingrich became Speaker of the House. Several bills were passed that were part of the Contract for America. He also increased the ties between Christian conservatism and the Republican Party.

With his Speaker of the House power, Gingrich started his childish political polarization and undermined any Democratic policies. He began undermining democracy with a combative approach that represented the Republican Party. He called the Democrats corrupt and compared them to fascists. Of course, when one is calling someone else a fascist, the name-caller is usually the one practicing fascist policies. This is a form of psychological transference. Speaker Gingrich undermined the principles and norms of democracy with many of his tactics and policies.

His oppositional defiant disorder blossomed while Speaker of the House. He would bully the Democrats with words like traitors, bizarre, destroy, devour, sick, liars, and so on. For a person with a PhD, he had no class.

Several bills were passed for welfare reform, tax relief, and a balanced budget between 1996 and 1999 under Gingrich's leadership in the House. But these bills had to be passed by a Democratic president, President Clinton.

Gingrich tried to break up National Public Radio and the Public Broadcasting Service because they receive some funding from the federal government. He also shut down the highly regarded Office of Technology Assessment. By making this move, he allowed more money to go into the Republican pockets through increasing lobbying.

Gingrich and other Republicans promised to slow the rate of government spending, which conflicted with President Clinton's agenda for Medicare, education, the environment, and public health. As a result of the clash, Gingrich proceeded with two temporary government shutdowns for a total of twenty-eight days. This behavior reminds us of a two-year-old having a temper tantrum. Gingrich argued that the shutdowns made a difference.

The United States federal government shutdowns of 1995 and 1995–96 were the result of conflicts between Democratic President Bill Clinton and the Republican Congress over funding for education, the environment, and public health in the 1996 federal budget.

Gingrich conducted a fraudulent tax exemption. This led to the House Ethics Committee discovering that inaccurate information supplied to investigators represented intentional disregard of House rules. The Ethics Committee's special counsel concluded that Gingrich had violated federal tax law and had lied to the ethics panel in an effort to force the committee to dismiss the complaint against him.

Republican John Boehner of Ohio and other Republicans gave Gingrich an ultimatum to resign as Speaker of the House. However, Gingrich manipulated some of the Republicans into allowing him to keep his seat while President Clinton was going through the Clinton-Lewinsky scandal. Nevertheless, Gingrich was behaving similarly unethically. He was also having an affair with a very young woman.

Gingrich was reelected despite his behavior. However, he had other violations, including an unpopular book deal. A Republican caucus pressured him to resign. In January 1999, he resigned his seat. His bully behavior assured the Republicans that he no longer wanted to lead corrupt Republicans.

After Gingrich left office, he promoted his right-wing conservatism and himself. He was involved with conservative think tanks, commissions, not-for-profit organizations, Fox News, Gingrich Productions, Gingrich Communications, lucrative speaking engagements, and book deals. In 2012, he entered the bid for the presidency. However, he didn't do well in the primaries, and Mitt Romney emerged as the eventual Republican candidate.

George W. Bush, the son of the forty-first president, George H.W. Bush, won the 2000 election against Al Gore. Also in 2000, the

Republican Party gained control of the presidency and both houses of Congress for the first time since 1952.

The September 11, 2001, terrorist attack on the United States initiated President Bush's War on Terror. This led to the invasion of Iraq and Afghanistan. In Afghanistan, the mission was to kill Osama bin Laden, who many believe had masterminded the attacks.

President Bush began to lose popularity as Americans were killed in the wars without an exit strategy. Vice President Dick Cheney was also corrupted by his previous association with Halliburton, a multinational engineering and oil-field service corporation. This appeared to be a conflict of interest. Was the war a result of terrorism, or did America want oil from Iraq?

President Bush also lost popularity as the economy moved into a recession as a result of financing the expensive wars.

He succeeded in selecting competent semiconservatives to head four of the most important agencies: Condoleezza Rice as secretary of state, Alberto Gonzales as attorney general, John Roberts as chief justice of the Supreme Court, and Ben Bernanke as chairman of the Federal Reserve. He also added Samuel Alito to the Supreme Court.

Somewhat arrogant like his father, George W. Bush maintained moral values while in office. However, in Congress, Republican scandals occurred that prompted the resignations of House Majority Leader Tom DeLay, Duke Cunningham, Mark Foley, and Bob Ney.

These four congressmen were engaged in criminal activity. DeLay was indicted on criminal charges of conspiracy to violate election law by campaign money laundering in 2002. Duke Cunningham resigned from the House on November 28, 2005, after pleading guilty to accepting at least $2.4 million in bribes and underreporting his taxable income for 2004. Mark Foley resigned from Congress on September 29, 2006, acting on a request by the Republican leadership after allegations surfaced that he had sent suggestive emails and sexually explicit instant messages to teenage boys who had served and were serving as congressional pages. Bob Ney's resignation took place after he pled guilty to charges of conspiracy and making false statements in relation to the Jack Abramoff

Indian lobbying scandal. Before he pled guilty, Ney was identified in the guilty pleas of Jack Abramoff, former Tom DeLay deputy chief of staff Tony Rudy, former DeLay press secretary Michael Scanlon, and former Ney chief of staff Neil Volz for receiving lavish gifts in exchange for political favors.

In chapter 4, I defined sociopathy as having at least three of the characteristics of a sociopath. One criterion is a person who commits white-collar crimes, which is what these four embraced.

Two Good Republican Men: John McCain and Mitt Romney

Arizona Senator John McCain was the 2008 Republican nominee for president, and his running mate was Sarah Palin, the first female vice presidential candidate from the Republican Party. The Tea Party was an upcoming faction of the Republican Party, and the sentiment was that a woman would be appealing to voters and to those who identified with the Tea Party's policies. However, her intelligence or the lack thereof caused many blunders that McCain had to deal with. John McCain lost to Barack Obama but retained his seat in the Senate.

In the 2012 presidential campaign, Governor Mitt Romney was the first Mormon to ever run for president. He ran against Barack Obama, who was running for a second term. He looked good in the first debate but struggled in the rest of the debates. Also, his religion may have played a role in his loss because people feared Mormonism.

Both of these candidates were intelligent and ran on American values and principles.

The Republican Party from 2008 to 2020

Barack Obama won the presidential election in 2008. He was the first Black American to become president of the United States. His campaign addressed the economy, women's rights, immigration, and more.

President Obama inherited the financial recession of 2007–2008. He put together a stimulus package and health care reform to add twenty-plus million Americans to the health care system. Naturally, the Republicans in Congress objected to his policies. In addition, the Tea Party formed in the US as an ultraconservative prejudiced grassroots organization that objected to everything President Obama was attempting to do to improve the lives of the American people.

In 2009, with the formation of the Tea Party, the Republican Party moved further toward attracting white Americans in the South and Midwest and away from the East and West Coasts. In fact, these areas were hated and reviled. The Republican Party also shied away from Hispanics and Black Americans. The voter base was almost entirely white. The fact that the East and West Coasts and some in between put an intelligent, compassionate Black man in the White House was divisive. The rising Hispanic population as well as African Americans created fear among many white Americans that they were losing their country.

During the presidencies of Reagan and both Bushes and the Republican control in Congress during Obama, big business became bigger and commensurate with government through lobbying. America was becoming an oligarchy.

The November 2012 election instituted Republican control of the House of Representatives, and the Democrats regained control of the Senate. As a result, on January 3, 2011, John Boehner became Speaker of the House, while Mitch McConnell remained as the Senate minority leader. This all fell into place, because in 2006, Republicans chose John Boehner of Ohio for House minority leader. Senators chose whip Mitch McConnell of Kentucky for Senate minority leader.

After Mitt Romney lost to President Obama in 2012, the Republicans had to reassess their message and policies. The Republican National Committee chairman, Reince Priebus, set up reform policies. Priebus proposed a marketing campaign to reach women, minorities, and gays. The evangelicals stepped in and interfered with his proposal. Key opponents were Rick Santorum and Mike Huckabee, who opposed same-sex marriage and warned that evangelicals would desert the GOP if these policies were endorsed.

The Democrats pushed for immigration reform, and many Republicans wanted to also pass a bill in Congress. However, there was so much disagreement within the Republicans in Congress that nothing was passed.

The Senate declined to pass the health care bill with measures to delay the Affordable Care Act, and the two legislative houses did not develop a compromise bill by the end of September 30, 2013, causing the federal government to shut down due to a lack of appropriated funds at the start of the new 2014 federal fiscal year. President Obama wanted to include funding for women's health, and Speaker Boehner and the Republicans disagreed, so their solution was to shut down the government. Another expression of oppositional defiant disorder with tantrums. "You don't give me what I want! I'll just shut down the government." Nothing like making government workers take the brunt of their childishness.

The Tea Party started gaining support in the US beginning in 2012 and built strength in 2014. In the 2014 midterms, they managed to place some of their ultraconservative candidates in Congress. These were persons who were opposed to all of President Obama's policies. They were pro-life, Second Amendment, antisocialism policy people. A few of these senators had alliances to the Tea Party movement, such as Ted Cruz, Rand Paul, and Marco Rubio, who in particular was the focus of their attention.

The Tea Party movement increased Republican majorities in the House to the highest total since 1929. They took control of governorships, state legislatures, and Senate seats in nearly all southern states, except Florida and Virginia.

The Tea Party congresspeople were far-right-wing nationalists who created significant division. They wanted to diminish big government, yet they were part of government. Even though Speaker of the House John Boehner was adversarial to President Obama's policies, this was not good enough for the Tea Party. Due to the division, Boehner announced in September 2015 that he would step down as Speaker of the House. This left the speakership open, and who would take over? Next in line was Kevin McCarthy.

Majority Leader Kevin McCarthy didn't have the support from the Republicans that he wanted. House Ways and Means chair Paul Ryan announced that he would run, with the support of the Freedom Caucus. Ryan was elected Speaker on October 29, 2015.

The Decline of Democracy

Donald J. Trump won the presidency in 2016 against Hillary Clinton. This was the beginning of "The Axis of Evil."

The primaries for the 2016 presidency saw a dozen Republicans running. Each debate was like a circus, because Donald J. Trump also ran. His language was deplorable (unfit for children). He kept talking about "Draining the Swamp in Washington," which appealed to many Republicans. Many Republicans disliked President Obama and all the gridlock in Congress. Donald Trump spoke to this problem and promised to fix it. His rhetoric was aimed at white voters. He hates Black Americans, especially President Obama. Evangelicals did not mind his curse words and lies, because he promised them pro-life policies. He declared zero tolerance for immigrants. Republican agricultural owners supported this, yet they hired cheap labor from Mexico to harvest and sort fruits and vegetables, to milk cows, and to pack meat. I believe this is called heresy. Republicans also loved the fact that Trump is a businessman, however unsuccessful. He is nothing like George H.W. Bush, who was a very successful businessman.

Donald Trump won the 2016 Republican primaries, representing a dramatic policy shift from traditional conservatism to an aggressively populist nationalist ideology. Many people in his base were ethnonationalist alt-right. In addition to electing Donald Trump, Republicans maintained a majority in the Senate, in the House of Representatives, and among state governorships in the 2016 elections.

The Republicans controlled numerous state legislatures as well. This was a backlash to having a Black, progressive president in the White House.

The force of the Tea Party caused partisanship driven by disagreements about the size of government, national security, and moral issues. Trump forced his way into this divide.

In office, he held true to his campaign promises. He called adversarial government agencies the "deep state." His draining the swamp resulted in the total destruction of all of the most-needed agencies, such as the CIA, Justice Department, Department of Agriculture, Environment Protection Agency, and just about every branch of government. He fired anyone who didn't agree with him or who he perceived as disloyal. He fired or eliminated hundreds of government leaders and employees.

He also held true to his zero-tolerance policy on immigration. He started in with Muslims and moved on to Hispanics and Latinos. The number of immigrants from the southern border were much less during the Obama administration, and more poured through the border during Trump's time in office. He attempted to halt this by building a wall, which never happened. He broke up families, locking children in cages away from their parents and imprisoning adults in camps. Also, he ran on building a wall along the US-Mexico border to prevent Hispanics and Latinos from entering the United States. This was totally ludicrous and never came to pass.

The United States federal government shutdown of 2018–2019 occurred from December 22, 2018, until January 25, 2019 (thirty-five days). The main issue was placing the cost of building a wall along the US-Mexico border because President Trump believed it would prevent illegal border crossings. It was the longest US government shutdown in history. This is another example of oppositional defiant disorder by the Republicans and a Trump temper tantrum.

Fox News guided President Trump though many of his policies. The conservative media strongly supported him, and his approval rating among self-identified Republican voters was extraordinarily high. Trump exposed an American psychological sickness that was previously in the closet.

Traditional Republicans always supported free trade. Trump's isolationist policies destroyed this norm. Tariffs were instigated on almost everything from other countries: wine and cheese from France and almost everything from China. He attempted to place tariffs on cars from Germany. However, the Republicans were advocates of tariffs in the nineteenth century. His love for Russia imported more vodka, and it's amazing that he didn't import more products from Russia.

His foreign policies were terrible. He tried to break up NATO for Russian president Putin. His love affair with autocratic foreign leaders was evident. He handed Syria to Turkey and the Russians.

The ultraconservative right-wing senators from the Tea Party provided a support mechanism for Trump's policies. Republican legislation and policies during the Trump administration continued to reflect the traditional priorities of Republican donors, such as the Koch brothers and Mercers.

President Trump totally ignored the Constitution. To begin with, he disregarded the Emoluments Clause. The Foreign Emoluments Clause is a provision in Article I, Section 9, Clause 8 of the United States Constitution that prohibits the federal government from granting titles of nobility and restricts members of the federal government from receiving gifts, emoluments, offices, or titles from foreign states and monarchies. Trump received money from his Trump Hotels around the world. He received money from Saudi Arabia; foreign dignitaries who stayed at the Trump Hotel in Washington, DC; and who knows where all the money came from?

His regard for American laws was nonexistent. He chose William Barr as attorney general, so as to have his own private protector as he continued to abuse the laws of the nation. Those who supported him became advocates of fascism.

His behavior caused many to question his mental state. Despite his chronic lying, narcissism, cursing, disregard for laws, lack of empathy, and manipulation, the evangelicals thought he was a good man and continued to follow him.

President Trump was a huge conspiracy theorist throughout his presidency. It got progressively worse as he gained support from other Republican followers. It started with President Obama's birth certificate to his following of QAnon. He built a platform for white supremacists throughout the United States, including more than 140 congresspeople. The dismissal of Joseph Biden's clear election win was a big lie told by President Trump, as well as another conspiracy theory. This lie created acts of violence by white nationalist supremacists. The Republican Party has become the party of white supremacists and fascists. Many of these Republicans are a combination of sociopaths and psychopaths, because they promoted hatred and violence. It reached the point of an attempted coup on the US Capitol on January 6, 2021, causing deaths in which Republicans show no remorse or consequential accountability. Senators Ted Cruz and Josh Hawley faced no immediate accountability.

The crowd psychology theories in play are convergent theory, contagion theory, and mass delusional theory with nefariousism as the preeminent loss of morality and consequences. Religion and the faith-based religious right remain silent to all of the hatred and violence promoted by the Republicans.

Faith-Based Republican Agenda Supported by the Religious (Christian) Right

The religious right (Christian right) is a Christian political faction of the Republican Party. The *religious right* is the most extreme Far Right conservative term. The more formal term is *socially conservative evangelicals*. Jerry Falwell introduced the term New Christian Right. It doesn't matter what they call themselves; they all have the same political interference with their Far Right Christian agendas.

They fight for very conservative social issues with a forceful indoctrination and propagation. They are fundamental Christians, mostly evangelical. They seek to influence politics and public policy with their interpretation of the teachings of Christ, which conservative Republicans naturally support and incorporate into their caucus.

They support prayer in public schools, and since that could not be enforced, they promoted vouchers, homeschooling, and private schools. They pushed for support by the federal government.

The religious right are pro-life, opposed to abortions, and against embryonic stem cell research.

They endorse strong family values. These include no sex until marriage and no birth control. Sex education is not discussed. They are opposed to pornography, homosexuality, and lesbian and gay marriages. They consider marriage to be between a man and a woman. In addition, they don't drink alcohol or use tobacco. And they are opposed to marijuana.

The Republicans have always identified with fundamental Christian pietism. It goes back to the 1860s when several denominations formed the National Reform Association to politically amend the US Constitution to establish an American Christian state.

Between 1945 and 1960, communism in Russia and the ascension of atheism presented the biggest threat to American conservative religion. Radio evangelists were preaching their fear of communism. Communism was perceived as non-Christian. As noted, isolated pockets of religious right conservatism existed throughout the twentieth century.

The religious right did not gain traction in politics until the Supreme Court passed *Roe v. Wade* in 1973, legalizing abortion.

The religious right have been associated with different institutions and leaders. These include Jerry Falwell / Moral Majority, Pat Robertson / The Christian Coalition, James Dobson / Focus on the Family, and James Dobson's Family Research Council (an extreme fundamentalist lobbying and activist organization).

Paul Weyrich connected the Republican Party with conservative religious politicians in 1977 by starting his Free Congress Foundation. This is a misnomer, because there is nothing free about it since it had a religious political agenda as well as other conservative ideas. He then went on to found the Heritage Foundation, a conservative Washington think tank.

In 1978, Dr. Robert Grant, who had already founded the American Service Council, Inc., established American Voices to advocate Christian teachings and ideology but also to organize Christians to vote for conservative political candidates. Also in 1979, Jerry Falwell Sr. formed the Moral Majority, a very strong conservative religious group who represent a faction of the Republican Party. They have a significant influence in supporting conservative evangelical religious politicians and congressional agendas. Jerry Falwell Jr. has now become their leader.

Marion Gordon "Pat" Robertson is a religious broadcaster (*The 700 Club*) and political commentator who ran for the presidency and lost in 1988. A year later, he took the money he had raised for his run and started a 501(c) 4 organization called the Christian Coalition of America, composed of 50 percent Baptists and the rest Pentecostals, Catholics, and other Protestants. Their agenda is to place a Christian conservative in the Oval Office. They have encouraged the convergence of conservative Christian ideology with political issues, such as health care, the economy, education vouchers, abortion, and crime.

The Christian religious right promotes conservative interpretations of the Bible as the basis for moral values and enforcing such values by legislation. This is equating religion (church) with government.

The First Amendment to the Constitution reads: "Congress shall make no law respecting an establishment of religion, or prohibiting the free exercise thereof …"

In the early 1800s, the Danbury Baptist Association in Connecticut was concerned with their freedom of religion. Thomas Jefferson wrote a letter to the Baptist Association in 1802, reassuring them that preventing state (government) interference would allow them the freedom to enjoy their religious faith. He stated the First Amendment built a "wall of separation of church and state."

The Christian right believes that separation of church and state is not explicit in the American Constitution, believing instead that such separation is a creation of what it claims are activist judges in the judicial system. This is an intentionally distorted interpretation of the First Amendment. Thomas Jefferson made that clear to the Baptists in 1802.

The religious right's interpretation of the First Amendment is that the government cannot form a religion like the Church of England. However, the Republicans are forming a religion of evangelicals. Is that not incorporating a religious group into the government? There is no separation when lobbying occurs between religious organizations such as the Christian Coalition. They use every excuse possible to promote their agenda in government, especially religious freedom. And anything or anyone opposing their agenda is interfering with their religious freedom. They must be reminded that Mennonites, Amish, Agnostics, Unitarians, and others have religious freedom, but they are not pushing their agenda in the government. Suppose the Amish formed the Amish Coalition. In their agenda to the government, everyone must dress in black and drive horses and buggies to protect the environment and get closer to God.

The religious/Christian right have a huge influence on the outcome of Republican presidential candidates. For example, George W. Bush's election resulted in his overwhelming support from white evangelical voters comprising 68 percent of the votes in 2000 and 78 percent in 2004. Donald J. Trump won 82 percent of these same votes in 2016. This is an example of herd behavior.

Herd behavior in humans is defined as the phenomenon of large numbers of people acting in the same way at the same time. A simple animal example can be seen on a farm with milking cows. They are usually out in the pasture all day eating grass. At night, when they are milked, one can call them to the barn for milking. They all get up at the same time and head for the barn. It appears that humans are no different. The brain responds without thinking.

This phenomenon can be very dangerous. It is the form of behavior that follows autocratic leaders and fascism. Hitler's Germany is an example, and in the United States, we had a president supported by Christians who don't realize the direction of fascism and evil behavior. The fact that President Trump has no religion and no morals has no bearing on the evangelicals (Jerry Falwell Jr. association and others) as long as President Trump promotes their agenda.

The evangelical movement has its roots in American politics going back as far as the 1940s and has been especially influential since the 1970s. Its influence draws from grassroots activism as well as from a focus on social issues and the ability to motivate the electorate around those issues.

European governments were strongly connected with Catholicism before 1517. Evangelicals could learn from the European Reformation that lasted from 1517 to the early 1700s. Luther declared his intolerance for the Roman Church's corruption in 1517 by nailing his Ninety-Five Theses of Contention to the Wittenberg church door. The pope as the antichrist was so ingrained in the Reformation era. The Reformation became the basis for the founding of Protestantism, one of the three major branches of Christianity (Eastern Orthodox, Roman Catholicism, and Protestantism). The Reformation led to the reformulation of certain basic tenets of Christian belief and resulted in the division of Western Christendom between Roman Catholicism and the new Protestant traditions. However, the Reformation led to European religious wars that also involved governments. The series of wars occurred during the sixteenth, seventeenth, and early eighteenth centuries. This led to both religious and political disruption. After the Thirty Years' War, which lasted from 1618 to 1648, Catholic France became allied with the Protestant forces against the Catholic Habsburg monarchy.

It is apparent that religion should separate itself from government unless history wants to repeat itself in the United States. But is it too late? Is religion already ingrained into the fabric of our democracy?

Blame Behavior

Blame is the act of making negative statements about an individual or group and claiming their actions are unacceptable to the blamer's belief system.

Blame occurs in two neurobiological areas of the brain: the temporoparietal junction and the amygdala. The amygdala is responsible for emotion, especially negative emotion and fear. There is a connection between the two areas because they both show increased brain activity.

We place blame behavior into two categories as it applies to politics and especially the Republicans. The first is what we call *incompetent-emotional-deceptive blame*. The second is *propaganda blame*.

Incompetent-emotional-deceptive blaming is used as a defense system, where behaviors such as projection or displacement are used. It is used as destructive conflict resolution. The person doing the blaming is unable to logically understand the belief or behavior of the reasonable person they are blaming. The blamer uses illogical judgment to discern the outcome of the blaming. The main traits of the person blaming consist of their own incompetence, logic, and understanding. They are unable to accept responsibility for their own failure, so it is easier to blame, and that makes them feel good. Lastly, telling lies is a large part of the blame behavior. It is easy to lie and blame at the same time.

Blame is a negative judgmental behavior that often creates a sense of winning and grandiosity. The person being blamed in the process feels defensive and devalued, while the blamer feels superior.

The person or group being blamed develops feelings that include a pervasive sense of helplessness, passivity, loss of control, pessimism, negative thinking, strong feelings of guilt, self-blame, and depression. This way of thinking can lead to hopelessness and despair.

Republicans are masters of the blame game. It has really heated up in the past few decades. According to Republicans, Democrats are bad and wrong for everything that transpires in politics. It grew worse when President Obama was in office.

Bill Maher, political comedian and activist, keeps asking why Democrats don't fight back. Let us also be clear that there is a difference between blame and transparency, facts and truth. The Democrats don't use blame but present facts and truth. They thrive on transparency.

When the blamer is at fault (which is most of the time with Republicans), there are a couple of formidable responses. Return their blame accusations with facts and do not reattack. Don't display anger; be calm and emotionless. This is exactly the right behavior the Democrats use in response, and it drives the Republicans crazy, because they want a fight.

Another method is to disengage from the blamer and stay away from them. Unfortunately, this cannot be done in the United States Congress. Another technique is to completely ignore the blamer's blame.

Blame can be politically motivated. The intention is to deceitfully find the opposing person or group with quasi-threat or nonexistent opposing variable or psychological trait(s) causing them to instigate irrational blame for their own gain. There are several in Republican presidencies. Probably the best example is the Iraq war that Dick Cheney pushed for without real cause.

More recently, President Trump, "The Blame King," has blamed NATO, the World Health Organization, and China for the COVID-19 pandemic. He blames the Democrats for everything. Republicans will go to great lengths to instill fear through blame.

This blame game not only occurs between political parties in a country, it occurs between countries. Unfortunately, both historically and today, governments have used blaming to instill fear and to demoralize other countries. Blame is used to influence public perceptions of various other governments to induce feelings of nationalism in the public. This became especially prevalent during the Trump administration. Behind the scenes, Stephen Miller pushed for propaganda and blame, as did Steve Bannon. It is obvious that these types of people display sociopathic tendencies.

Psychoanalysis of Republicans

Examples of obvious psychological disorders in the Republican Party. This is noted by observation of behavior.

- President Richard M. Nixon
- Vice President Spiro Agnew
- Newt Gingrich
- Fox News, Rush Limbaugh, and Glenn Beck
- Mitch McConnell
- President Donald J. Trump
- Senator Ted Cruz
- Senator Josh Hawley
- Representative Marjorie Taylor Greene

Much of this discussion will address Republicans with oppositional defiant disorder, paranoia, sociopathy, psychopathy, narcissism, and con artist tendencies.

Republican Oppositional Defiant Disorder

Over the past four decades, many Republicans pointed fingers, had tantrums, and bullied Democrats. They lack negotiation skills. It is easier to blame than take responsibility. When they don't get their way, they do something destructive to show they are in control. The government shutdowns are a perfect example. This began with Speaker of the House Newt Gingrich, who acted like an entitled teenager many times. Of course, he will defend his behavior like he did in a recent NPR interview.

This behavior is called oppositional defiant disorder. It begins in many two-year-olds and may carry over into the teenage years. Most of the right-wing Republicans have not outgrown this behavior. Jim Jordan in the House really displays this behavior. Senate Minority Leader Mitch McConnell is probably worse. It is obvious that all of those in the Tea Party exhibit this childish behavior. Part of this behavior is blame.

The Republicans like to fight when there are differences of opinion. They especially like to fight with Democrats, but they also direct their defiance toward the media, with the exception of Fox News. The only senator who doesn't demonstrate behavior consistent with oppositional defiant disorder is Mitt Romney.

Another aspect of oppositional defiant disorder is when they talk about religion, God, or female reproductive rights and they get all defiant in the face of opposing idea or issues that others have. But they are the first to say how they respect others and how much they believe in freedom; this is a lie. They are quick to call peaceful protests anarchy, which they don't truly understand (see chapter 1). This is only one recent example of many. With their oppositional defiant disorder, Republicans have no tolerance for anyone except those who share their beliefs. Acceptance is not in their belief system, and as a result, they express themselves with oppositional defiant behavior.

Hypervigilance is a good trait because it keeps a person on the alert for danger in possibly dangerous situations. It is a protective mechanism.

Hypervigilance versus Paranoia

Presidents have been hypervigilant about protecting the United States. However, a few have shown paranoid behavior. What is the difference between the two? Paranoid people have a delusional belief that someone or something is trying to harm them. With hypervigilance, people are on guard in anticipation of something bad happening. Hypervigilance can occur with post-traumatic stress disorder (PTSD) and anxiety. John F. Kennedy was hypervigilant because of his war experience and thus protected the United States during the Cuban Missile Crisis standoff. I believe John McCain was hypervigilant with some of his policies in Congress as a result of his experience as a prisoner of war for five and a half years in North Vietnam.

Paranoia is a mental disorder that falls under the umbrella of personality disorders (DMS-5 and chapter 4). Paranoid persons have a fear of others, commitment, loyalty, or trustworthiness. They believe other people exploit or deceive them. A paranoid person is reluctant to confide in others or reveal personal information because they are afraid the information will be used against them.

This simplified definition explains the Republican Party. Almost all Republicans are paranoid about socialism. They call the Democrats socialists, but they don't even know the definition of socialism. We will define socialism.

Socialism is a political and economic theory of social organization that advocates that the means of production, distribution, and exchange should be owned or regulated by the community as a whole.

Prime examples of socialism are religious groups and organizations. As an example, people tithe or give money to their church, which is owned by the community (tax-free), independent of government. The church produces, organizes, and distributes its material and belief system. Religious socialism has been designed to prevent people from doing abominable, harmful, and immoral things to one another. Unfortunately, harm and evil have not been eliminated when religious groups fight and kill one another. Many wars are religious wars.

Capitalism represents the private ownership of business. However, each business is socialist. By definition, each company is a social organization that advocates that people produce something (production), persons in the company provide product distribution, and exchange by workers and ownership regulated by the stockholder community as a whole. The loyal buyer could be considered part of the whole. However, with capitalism, one has choices in products and free trade. This leads to competition, which is at the heart of American business. However, socialist theory is present throughout the United States, but the Republicans misrepresent it to instill fear in Americans, as if the US will become a totalitarian socialist state.

Democrats believe in utilitarianism, which in essence is the greatest good for the greatest number of people. The meaning of utilitarianism is the doctrine that actions are right if they are useful or if they benefit the majority. This is not socialism. Over the years in America, socialized programs have been established, such as Social Security, Medicare, the Veterans Administration, and VA hospitals. If you want to call this socialism, so be it, but it is *good* socialism. The Republicans want to dissolve these programs and privatize them. As a physician, I would rather see Medicare patients than those with private insurance. I would rather see insurance answer to Congress than to stockholders.

Republicans are paranoid concerning the Far Left, whom they call communists. By definition, communism is a theory or system of social organization in which all property is owned by the community and each person contributes and receives according to their ability and needs.

The theory of communism has been used in the United States and to some degree continues to be used. This shows that the theory can be benevolent. Milton S. Hershey, who started Hershey's chocolate, essentially built the town of Hershey, Pennsylvania, to house his workers. Houses were built for employees. Churches, cemeteries, cultural centers, theaters, museums, and the famous amusement park, Hershey's Park, were all constructed. The Hershey Hotel and Hershey rose gardens were also established. At one time, houses were leased for ninety-nine years to the inhabitants in the town. For all practical purposes, this meets the definition of communism. But it is not totalitarian because trusts and such were involved, including the Hershey Trust Company and Hershey Property Management.

The two presidents who were most paranoid were Richard M. Nixon and Donald J. Trump. Nixon was pathologically fearful of what people would say about him. So much so that he set up voice-activated recording in the White House. He was paranoid specifically about academics and intellectuals.

President Trump was pathologically fearful of being poisoned by White House staff preparing food. He fears people from other countries, making him xenophobic. He is afraid of African Americans and feels that if they are given power, there will no longer be supreme whites. He is afraid of germs, except, apparently, COVID-19.

Republican Sociopaths

We should again return to the discussion from chapter 3. We made the distinction between sociopathy, sociopathoid, and psychopathy. This serves as an introduction and short summary of the differences between all three. We have listed ten traits that distinguish between sociopaths and psychopaths, and from the list of traits with sociopaths, we also defined a subtype we called sociopathoid.

Signs and Symptoms	Sociopath	Psychopath
1. Narcissism	Grandiose, self-possessed	Not prominent
2. Lies	Pathological liar	Less apparent but pathological
3. Manipulation	Mild to moderate	Severe, extensive
4. Empathy	Very little; some	None

5. Cognition	Weak conscience	No conscience
6. Criminal activity	More risk—white collar	Minimize risk—serial killers
7. Regard for laws	Erratic	Disregard
8. Behavior	Impulsive, erratic, rage-prone	Appears levelheaded
9. Emotions	Anger	Lack emotions and guilt
10. Social interaction	Like-minded person interaction	Unattached but charming
Etiology	Childhood trauma and/or genetic	Genetic

We would propose the term *sociopathoid* when a person meets five out of the ten criteria. Or only one if they committed a white-collar crime.

We can start with an ideal example of a sociopath in Mitch McConnell. He has grandiose ideas for the Republicans. He is a chronic liar; he does as much as he can to manipulate others; he lacks empathy; and he has primitive cognitive abilities with a weak conscience. Many times, he appears angry when he addresses issues. He is erratic and impulsive in dealing with issues in Congress. And he is like-minded with many of his Republican colleagues. He meets eight out of the ten criteria, because we don't really know about his childhood. Should you not agree, at least compare Mitch's observable behavior to the normal behavior of Mitt Romney, who has none of these traits.

Another Republican who meets these criteria is Attorney General William Barr. This is most disturbing because he is America's legal protection. Most of those connected with President Donald J. Trump are sociopaths, including Paul Manafort, Rick Gates, and Michael Flynn.

Another example of a sociopathoid Republican is Mark Meadows. He is a chronic liar, has a weak conscience, and is manipulative, erratic, and possibly without empathy. Much of President Trump's cabinet were sociopathoids.

Over the past four years, psychopath Republicans have become more obvious. The psychology of President Trump described in chapter 9 goes into more detail regarding his psychopathy. He is extremely narcissistic, which is one of the traits of a psychopath. However, he does not have a narcissistic personality disorder in and of itself. Narcissism is one component for psychopaths, but in order to meet the criteria of a psychopath, all ten criteria must be met. In his case, all ten—plus more—are evident. In addition to his strong narcissistic personality, Donald Trump has no regard for human life. Under his leadership, a number of deaths were his responsibility. There was a mass shooting at a high school in Parkland, Florida; a woman was killed by a white supremacist at a rally in Charlottesville, Virginia; there was a shooting at a synagogue in Pittsburgh, Pennsylvania; there were shootings in Gilroy, California, and El Paso, Texas. The list goes on. There are more, but to top it off, the COVID-19 pandemic killed more than six hundred thousand Americans, and Trump does not care.

The coronavirus (COVID-19) pandemic has certainly shown us the psychopathology of many Republicans. By definition, serial killers are psychopaths. Those Republican governors who failed to prevent the deaths of their constituents can therefore be considered psychopaths. The governors of Florida, Georgia, Alabama, Texas, Arizona, Iowa, and South Dakota are all culpable.

Presidents with Narcissism

As an introduction to the presidents with narcissism, we will provide a discussion of narcissism, grandiosity, and finally the presidents throughout history who have been diagnosed with grandiose narcissism and narcissistic personality disorder.

Narcissism: 1. Excessive interest in or admiration of oneself and one's physical appearance. 2. Selfishness, involving a sense of entitlement, a lack of empathy, and a need for admiration, as characterizing a personality type.

Narcissism can appear in many degrees or severity. It can be fairly innocuous or very pathologic. The more benign form can be exaggerated ego, unregulated and exaggerated self-esteem, superiority, and self-absorption.

Narcissists overindulge in their physical appearance. Not only do they have high expectations of their own physical appearance, but they also express intellectual superiority.

Narcissists have admiration and entitlement and preoccupation with fantasies about success, power, brilliance, beauty, or the perfect mate.

Their interaction with others is an expression of inferiority. They enjoy having equals as associates. They demand excellence from others.

Although psychologists would describe the above features as grandiose, which is a description of high expectations with dissonance between expectations and reality, along with the impact this has on relationships, narcissists don't realize how their behavior affects others, especially those who feel insecure.

Narcissism can come in four different degrees and types. The least apparent is leadership and authority. Superiority and arrogance are more obnoxious. Self-admiration is also obnoxious, but it is the fourth one that is very exploitative.

Grandiose behavior includes descriptions such as impressive and imposing in appearance, especially pretentious, grand, overambitious, exuberant, and stately. Grandiosity is part of narcissism, but it is also found in other mental health disorders. Grandiosity and narcissism are interrelated, which makes it difficult to separate the two.

The term *grandiose narcissism* in psychology refers to an unrealistic sense of superiority, characterized by a sustained view of one's self as better than others. Narcissists believe that few other people have anything in common with them and that their communication with others is restricted to those of equal stature.

Grandiose narcissists are entrepreneurs, successful scientists, businesspeople, and even presidents. Take, for example, Elon Musk. He is a narcissist and has grandiose ideas. In the 1990s, would anyone say that by 2020 Americans would be driving around in electric cars that can go hundreds of miles before recharging? In 1990, one would have thought he was crazy, but here we are with a grandiose idea come true. Although psychologists label this as pathologic, it is less severe, and I would submit there are more extreme forms of grandiosity associated with psychopathology.

The more severe forms of narcissism and grandiosity found in personality disorders include antisocial personality disorder (sociopaths and psychopaths) and mania. The difference between narcissism grandiosity and sociopaths and psychopaths is that psychological personality disorders have additional characteristics.

Narcissist personality disorder has eight additional features other than grandiosity. These signs and symptoms include:

- The most severe form of grandiosity with delusions.
- Their fantasies support their delusions.
- They have a constant request for attention/admiration.
- They require entitlements.
- They exploit others.
- They lack empathy.
- They are highly manipulative of others and monopolize conversations.
- They exploit others without guilt.
- They intimidate and demean others (i.e., bullies).

Grandiosity also appears in sociopaths and psychopaths, but as we have previously outlined above and in chapter 4, at least nine other signs and symptoms must be associated with grandiosity.

Grandiosity is also present in mania. Grandiosity in mania is more aggressive than in the personality disorders of narcissism and antisocialism (e.g., sociopathy and psychopathy). People with manic grandiosity boast of present and future achievements. They exaggerate their personal qualities. They have a delusional, expressive exaggeration of self. They may also begin unrealistically ambitious undertakings.

In *Psychological Science* published in October 2013, a group of psychology researchers and prominent historians rated presidents on grandiose narcissism. Narcissistic leadership was evaluated positively and negatively in forty-two US presidents. Multiparameters were used to include (1) expert-derived narcissism estimates, (2) independent historical surveys of presidential performance, and (3) largely or entirely objective indicators of presidential performance. It was found that grandiose narcissism provided overall presidential greatness that also matched persuasiveness and positive public opinion. Fortunately, the positives outweighed the negatives. The negatives included impeachment proceedings by Congress and unethical behavior. The presidents were ranked as follows:

1. Lyndon B. Johnson
2. Theodore Roosevelt
3. Andrew Jackson
4. Franklin D. Roosevelt
5. John F. Kennedy
6. Richard M. Nixon
7. Bill Clinton
8. Chester A. Arthur
9. Andrew Johnson
10. Woodrow Wilson
11. George W. Bush

If you want to see the rest of the presidents, a web search for "US presidents with narcissism" will retrieve the results.

It is obvious that none of these presidents have narcissistic personality disorders or any of the other pathologic personality disorders. Compare these presidents with President Donald J. Trump, who has both narcissism and psychopathy. See chapter 9.

Tea Party Psychology

The Tea Party is a conservative right populist US Republican political movement that arose in 2009 in opposition to government regulation and intervention in the private sector and in favor of strong immigration control and limited taxation.

The Tea Party originated during the first Obama administration. Racism was also a strong factor in their formation. Economic hardship is usually blamed for populist movements; this movement was about much more than the economy. If the Republicans were concerned about President Obama raising taxes during the recession he inherited from the prior Republican president, this was perceived as paranoia.

This paranoia became more evident when on February 19, 2009, Rick Santelli, a commentator on the business-news network CNBC, referenced the Boston Tea Party (1773) in his response to President Barack Obama's mortgage relief plan. Again, President Obama inherited this problem from President George W. Bush. This mortgage abuse was also addressed when banks and mortgage companies were sued by then Attorney General of California Kamala Harris and Beau Biden of Delaware, along with congresspeople who addressed the real problem.

It didn't matter to Rick Santelli that President Reagan bailed out Chrysler in the 1980s and the Republicans bailed out the savings and loans of 1989, or the collapse of Bear Stearns, an investment bank and brokerage firm and American International Group (AIG), an insurance colossus with global reach.

Nevertheless, within weeks of Rick Santelli's Tea Party analogy, Tea Party chapters began to appear around the United States using social media. The types of people who joined this movement were conservatives, Far Right, and antigovernment members of the paramilitary militia movement. This movement was also promoted by Fox News and those Far Right pundits Glenn Beck and Rush Limbaugh. The movement was fueled by Donald J. Trump's "birthers," who claimed that Obama had been born outside the United States and was therefore not eligible to serve as president. They also proclaimed that President Obama was a Muslim, ergo not Christian, which led to the birth of rampant conspiracy theories. This is more evidence of paranoia, expressed by a rejection of authoritative accounts and generally accepted beliefs. Conspiracy theories are expressed by mentally challenged people, such as Donald J. Trump, who is a psychopath. As outlined in chapter 2, the people who follow conspiracy theories have poor cognitive function. They lack the capability to sort facts from nonfacts. This is apparent in the Tea Party following.

Their initial movement sent a message on April 15, the deadline for paying taxes. The Tea Party movement's first major action was a nationwide series of rallies on April 15, 2009, that drew more than 250,000 people.

They were very savvy by claiming that "Tea" was an acronym for "Taxed Enough Already." The movement continued to grow, appearing at congressional town hall meetings to protest President Obama's proposed reforms to the American health care system.

One of the persons in government to grab hold of the Tea Party was Sarah Palin. She resigned as governor of Alaska in July 2009 to become an unofficial spokesperson for the party, and in February 2010, she delivered the keynote address at the first National Tea Party Convention. In addition, talk radio and right-wing conservative TV commentator Glenn Beck joined and promoted the Tea Party.

The Tea Party movement needed more than Sarah Palin's looks and speech to move forward as a real political movement. It needed real political power. Republican House Majority Leader Dick Armey provided logistical support for large Tea Party gatherings, and Senator Jim DeMint of South Carolina supported Tea Party candidates from within the Republican establishment. The Republican Party was infiltrated with the Tea Party movement, part of whom was also Donald J. Trump with his conspiracy theories.

The Tea Party began obtaining political strength in the Republican Party when Ted Kennedy died and the Republican Tea Party supported Scott Brown, who defeated Kennedy's presumptive successor in Massachusetts. In the midterms, the Tea Party supported Rand Paul for the US Senate, and he won in a repudiation of the Republican establishment. Not only is Paul antiestablishment, but he promotes conspiracy theories, which indicates a potential mental health issue.

The midterm election of 2010 resulted in the elections of Marco Rubio from Florida and Rand Paul from Kentucky. The Tea Party started to become part of the mainstream Republican Party rather than a fringe sector or faction. The movement developed caucuses, and by 2013, it had thirty-five million American followers.

The conservative Koch brothers attempted to get rid of the name Tea Party by forming the conservative group Americans for Prosperity (AFP). The idea of a Tea Party Caucus was initiated by Senator Rand Paul. The leader of the Tea Party Caucus, Michele Bachmann, served from 2010 to 2015. Members of the caucus included conservatives, right-wing nationalists, libertarians, members of the religious and social right, and right-wing populists within the Republican Party.

The Tea Party Caucus was approved as an official congressional member organization by the House Administration Committee and recognized by the Senate on January 27, 2011. By 2016, the Tea Party Caucus no longer existed, and as a result, all of its members moved over to either the Freedom Caucus or the Liberty Caucus. However, the Tea Party remains strong in social media and in behavior.

The Tea Party members and the Freedom Caucus have leaders who promote conspiracy theories and direct much of their anger toward others outside their group. There is paranoia, oppositional defiant disorder, and personality disorders among the leadership. The followers have a very high belief system and low cognitive function. They have few critical thinking skills, which is why they readily believe conspiracy theories.

Summary

The Republicans have gone from a mature, progressive party at the end of the nineteenth century and early twentieth century to a regressive, immature party at the end of the twentieth century and early twenty-first century. During this latter period, there has been more corruption in the Republican Party than in the Democratic Party. The Democratic Party has become the party of facts, morality, integrity, science, and normal religion and faith. Two Democrats won Nobel Prizes, President Obama and Vice President Al Gore. Republicans work off of emotions, opinions, and nonfacts.

President Trump clearly followed all of the Tea Party issues. He gutted the government and placed loyalty, incompetence, negligence, and ignorance in charge. He created a swamp of criminals and persons with pathological personality disorders. He took the party from a normal, free-trade party to a party of nationalistic Far Right ideals that allowed him to become an autocratic fascist.

This chapter outlined evolving behavior of the Republicans. President Trump is not a symptom but rather the epitome of where the Republican Party has gone.

For the past five decades, the Republican Party has been the party of corruption. Over the past decade, it has become the party of obstructionism, blame, and defiance. And in the past five years, it has become a nefarious, deceitful, fascist, and autocratic party.

CHAPTER 8

PSYCHOLOGY OF PRESIDENT DONALD TRUMP

Based on science and medical knowledge, the author is able to formulate observations. In addition, according to the *Diagnostic and Statistical Manual of Mental Disorders* (the book that contains the diagnostic criteria for mental illnesses), President Trump fits into several personality disorders with the evaluation of several psychiatrists. A published book of his mental health is not required, because his behavior is so transparent. It does not even require a history, physical, or psychiatric evaluation, because observations, facts, and science speak for themselves.

There are those who say President Trump is a symptom of the Republican Party. No! President Trump is the extreme epitome of the Republican Party of the twenty-first century. We shall further explore this in the following chapter, "Summation of the Psychosocial Dysfunction of the Republican Party."

We provide here an observational comment on the personality disorder of President Donald J. Trump. We recognize others have offered their opinions, and we offer another. As mentioned in the chapter regarding fact versus fiction, observations are extremely important in formulating hypotheses. Observations lead to analysis and documentation. Concerning President Trump, there are years of behavioral observations that can be used to formulate and analyze his mental condition that can lead to a diagnosis or diagnoses. The disclaimer that disallows any medical or legal issues is his own behavior in public.

Mental Health and Other Brain Dysfunctions

Introduction

Psychopath short definition: narcissistic, liar, lacks empathy, uses other people for self-gain, and twists the law. I met Donald Trump in 2015 and felt at that time that he met this brief definition. This was before he was serious about running for president of the United States.

Over the years of Donald Trump's presidency, I witnessed additional observational behavior that confirms the diagnosis of psychopath and other complex behavioral patterns.

In 2018, I made the following observation about his behavior:
Manic. He stays up all night and tweets.
Psychopath (using short version):

1. Chronic liar. He told over four thousand lies in one year (2018).
2. Lacks empathy. Throws paper towels to devastated Puerto Ricans; does not care about Las Vegas and Florida school shootings.
3. Manipulative. Uses other people. "If you are not loyal *to me*, you are fired."
4. Disregards and twists the law. Congress passes sanctions on Russia that he never signs. Ignores security clearances!
5. Lack of deep emotional attachments. Pervasive cheater.

Paranoid: Afraid of all African Americans, Muslims, Hispanics, and White House cooks poisoning him. Also, he is clearly xenophobic.

Delusional: He claimed Obama was not an American citizen and that Obama wiretapped Trump Tower. Like President Nixon, he is paranoid about intellect, science, and facts. This may be considered insecurity, but when he talks about the deep state, he demonstrates true paranoia. Part of the deep state is competency and intelligence. Some of this could be insecurity, because he isn't very intelligent and may want to dominate others with other forms of power.

Repetitive compulsive language: "There has been no collusion! I want to tell you there has been no collusion with the Russians! Okay, folks, there has not been any collusion with the Russians. I have obligated no collusion with the Russians! I don't know how anyone can say there has been collusion with the Russians? This is fake news to say that I colluded with the Russians; there has not been any collusion with the Russians! I would never be involved with collusion with the Russians!"

Psychological diagnostic observations: Manic psychopath with paranoid, delusional, repetitive compulsive and impulsive behavior.

To put things in perspective, he has not had extensive neuropsychological testing by a neuropsychologist or psychiatrist. But President Trump is so obvious in his behavior, one can readily make a diagnosis without testing.

Yale forensic psychiatrist Dr. Bandy Lee, an assistant professor in forensic psychiatry (the interface of law and mental health) at the Yale School of Medicine, provided her opinion of Trump's mental health. She was most concerned with the violence he promotes with all the shootings surrounding white supremacists, law enforcement killings, and militia enforcement. She invited twenty-seven prominent psychologists and psychiatrists to provide chapters for a book titled *The Dangerous Case of Donald Trump*. Their concerns were presented to the US Congress, but since the Republicans controlled the power, their concerns were ignored. These concerns should have been grounds for removal from office.

President Trump's Psychopath Personality Disorder

As a child, Donald J. Trump had a conduct disorder. In chapter 3, I described conduct disorder in which children under the age of fifteen display the early features of a psychopath. This is supported by Mary Trump's book as well as other sources. Donald Trump spent five years at New York Military Academy (NYMA), starting in the fall of 1959, after his father—having concluded that his son, then in seventh grade, needed a more discipline-focused setting—removed him from his Queens private school and sent him upstate.

A childhood acquaintance stated that he would lash out, often physically, against peers, other family members, even one of his teachers. Unfortunately, even the military school didn't fix him, because he probably found a way to cheat the system even at that age. Of course Trump's father was a liar, a cheat, a con artist, and a sociopath. So we can see where Donald gets it. The apple never falls far from the tree.

These are all of the characteristics of conduct disorder that often lead to psychopathy.

There are various degrees of narcissism. The most severe form is narcissistic personality disorder. In her book, Dr. Mary Trump describes Donald Trump as a narcissist because he meets all nine of the characteristics of narcissistic personality disorder. These are:

- The most severe form of grandiosity with delusions.
- Their fantasies support their delusions.
- They have a constant request for attention/admiration.
- They require entitlements.
- They exploit others.
- They lack empathy.
- They are highly manipulative of others and monopolize conversations.
- They exploit others without guilt.
- They intimidate and demean others (i.e., bullies).

However, the issue was raised that he could have antisocial personality disorder, whereby, psychopathy is considered.

Researchers used magnetic resonance imaging to scan the brains of thirty-four people, including seventeen individuals who suffer from narcissistic personality disorder, and found that pathological narcissists have less gray matter in a part of the cerebral cortex called the left anterior insula.

We have made a distinction between sociopathy and psychopathy in previous chapters with the following. Narcissism is part of both disorders.

Signs and Symptoms	Sociopath	Psychopath
1. Narcissism	Grandiose, self-possessed	Not prominent
2. Lies	Pathological liar	Less apparent but pathological
3. Manipulation	Mild to moderate	Severe, extensive
4. Empathy	Very little; some	None
5. Cognition	Weak conscience	No conscience
6. Criminal activity	More risk—white collar	Minimize risk—serial killers
7. Regard for laws	Erratic	Disregard
8. Behavior	Impulsive, erratic, rage-prone	Appears levelheaded
9. Emotions	Anger	Lack emotions and guilt
10. Social interaction	Like-minded person interaction	Unattached but charming
Etiology	Childhood trauma and/or genetic	Genetic

President Donald J. Trump meets all of the ten signs and symptoms. He not only meets the characteristics of narcissistic personality disorder, he meets the criteria for a psychopath. One could then surmise that he is a malignant narcissistic psychopath.

In chapter 4, we also describe the genetics and brain function of a psychopath. MRI functional scans show poor function of the prefrontal and frontal cortex, the executive cognitive function of the brain missing in psychopaths. Genetically, a variant of the MAO-A gene is associated with psychopaths.

Mary Trump's book, *Too Much and Never Enough*, describes her grandfather (President Trump's father) Fred Trump. Her grandfather's actions and behavior are consistent with characteristics of a sociopath/psychopath. Donald Trump Jr. certainly exhibits the same behavior traits/characteristics as his father. It is apparent from descriptive and observable behavior that there is a genetic predilection for sociopathy/psychopathy.

A difference of opinion is found in Bandy Lee's book *The Dangerous Case of Donald Trump*. A notable psychiatrist, Lance Dodes, describes Mr. Trump as a sociopath. No one in the psychiatric literature has made a distinction between sociopath and psychopath as we have. His description of President Trump very much appears to be the same as psychopath. Another characteristic that we describe is the presence of killing or serial killing. President Trump has essentially been a serial killer with all of the violence and killings carried out by his base and all of the deaths resulting from his disregard of COVID-19.

Criminal psychologist Dr. Hare developed the Hare Psychopathy Checklist (PCL-Revised), used to assess cases of psychopathy. A score of between 30 and 40 denotes psychopathy.

1. Glib and superficial charm—smooth talker, great storyteller, insincere, and shallow words.
2. Grandiose self-worth—huge egos, confident, arrogant, feelings of superiority and entitlement; huge braggart about things they have done (and not actually done).
3. Seek stimulation or prone to boredom—risk-takers, sensation seekers.
4. Pathological lying—skilled liars, unafraid of being caught; lie to manipulate.
5. Conning and manipulativeness—"callous ruthlessness"—deceive, cheat, con, and defraud others for personal gain.
6. Lack of remorse or guilt—they feel pain for themselves but not others; coldhearted with no empathy for their victims—only disdain for their victims.

7. Shallow affect—friendly and charming with no feelings for others.
8. Callousness and lack of empathy—callous, heartless, contemptuous, indifferent, and tactless.
9. Parasitic lifestyle—they live off others with no sense of responsibility or accountability; will manipulate and exploit others for their own gain.
10. Poor behavioral controls—aggression, verbal abuse, outbursts of anger and temper tantrums.
11. Promiscuous sexual behavior—sex encounters are often viewed as conquests and they boast about them; attempts to coerce people into sexual relationships.
12. Early behavior problems—antisocial behavior before age thirteen—lying, stealing, cheating, vandalism, bullying, and cruelty to animals or siblings.
13. Lack of realistic, long-term goals—lack real direction but talk about big plans; sometimes a drifter.
14. Impulsivity—reckless and unpredictable, cannot control impulses, cannot resist temptation; seek instant gratification.
15. Irresponsibility—repeatedly fail to honor commitments or obligations—legally, morally, and financially.
16. Failure to accept responsibility for own actions—no sense of duty or conscientiousness, deny their responsibility and even play victim.
17. Many short-term marital relationships—inability to maintain a long-term relationship.
18. Juvenile delinquency—crimes that are manipulative, aggressive, violent, or callous between the ages of ten and eighteen.
19. Revocation of condition release—probation may have been revoked due to lack of responsibility and accountability—failing to appear.
20. Criminal versatility—often involved in diverse criminal activities, boasting about getting away with crimes.

Each of these traits is worth two points. The total score is 40. A score of 40 is a true psychopath. Observing President Trump, I get a score of 38, because number 19 does not yet fit.

Twenty-five to 30 percent of criminals in prison are psychopaths. Donald J. Trump has committed numerous crimes and has never been imprisoned. But one can see the crimes on his face.

Mug shot of a criminal

Before running for president in 2015, Donald J. Trump was already recognized as a psychopath, which had been documented in social media. Comments he made in interviews regarding birtherism, as well as repetitive impulsive behavior surrounding the Clintons and President Obama made this fact clear. He was also known for sexually predatory activities. He had obvious narcissistic traits. However, there are some who want to attribute his current behavior to a neurological problem such as dementia. The TV reality show *The Apprentice* also showed signs of his personality disorder. Those who stroked his ego and played into his narcissism by demonstrating loyalty won. There has been no change in this man's conduct since childhood.

Psychopaths who gain power can become observable evil leaders. Germany's Adolf Hitler became progressively more evil. In his early political journey, the signs and symptoms of his psychopathy were not as obvious as when he gained power. Presently, leaders like Vladimir Putin of Russia and Kim Jong-un of North Korea have displayed obvious psychopathic behavior. President Trump has shown increasing signs of psychopathic behavior as he has gained more power and support by the Republicans.

What is most concerning is that not only does he possess all of the features of a psychopath, but many in his administration and in the Republican Party fit the behavior pattern. There is a figure that 1 percent of the general American population are psychopaths, as well as 25 percent of the males in our prisons. I may add that it appears that 25 percent were in President Trump's administration.

Language Skills

As mentioned earlier, there is a repetitive compulsive issue with Donald Trump's language skills, vocabulary, and articulation. This may have initially seemed intentional, but as time passed, it has become evident that there is a problem with his brain. He repeats words excessively. We call this repetitive compulsive language, and it occurs most all the time. If it was used to make a point, it would be done infrequently and only when something was really important.

His vocabulary is extremely limited. In fact, two- to three-year-olds can say between two hundred and 1,500 words. In chapter 3, we stated that two-year-olds have a vocabulary of around two hundred words. President Trump fits into this category because of his limited vocabulary.

He used short simple sentences: "This is all a hoax." "This is nothing more than a witch hunt." "The economy is great. Just look at the stock market." And so forth.

He also repeats short sentences. "This is nothing but fake news." "You know that it's fake news." "The media loves to distribute fake news." He repeats words and thoughts all the time. Consider the example from the Bob Woodward tapes. Trump is talking about the "China Virus," and he says, "You don't get it from the touch, the touch, it's not from the touch. You get it from the air. The virus is in the air. You get it from the air." Michael Cohen believes Trump does this to make a point, but one does not ramble over and over again to make a point. This is obviously pathological.

Studies show that verbal repetition is most critically mediated by cortical regions in the left posterior temporoparietal cortex. This area could be dysfunctional genetically or developmentally, or he may have an auditory-verbal short-term memory deficit related to overlapping networks, or aphasia. Nevertheless, this observation is pathologic. It would be interesting to study this with a functional MRI.

Intelligence

It is apparent that with his lack of reading skills, poor mathematics, and limited vocabulary, President Trump most likely has an IQ of 75 to 85. What is the basis for this estimate? George W. Bush is said to have an IQ of 95, and his vocabulary was far greater than that of President Trump. We would also submit that Bush ran successful legitimate businesses. President Trump didn't start any business on his own and has lost millions.

To place IQ into perspective, President Clinton is said to have an IQ of 180. Maybe that is why President Trump and the Republicans hate the Clintons. It's called jealousy.

President Trump may also have attention deficit hyperactivity disorder (ADHD), which would also explain his learning disability and mania. This would require intensive specialized testing.

Voters voted for him in the 2016 election largely because he is a businessman. Had any of the voters supporting him done their research as I proposed in chapter 2, they would have found that he is not a successful businessman at all. He is a failed businessman who has filed for bankruptcy four times. He had to depend on foreign money (probably from the Russian mafia and Saudi Arabia) to maintain his businesses. His father gave him money; banks in America gave him money until they were duped; foreigners gave him money; and now American taxpayers give him money.

It was not long after Donald J. Trump's inauguration that leaders and people around the world saw him as unintelligent. They used words such as "stupid" and "crazy."

Stupid—Глупый, Dum, Dummkopf, persona estúpida, personne stupide, and thirty-one Chinese words/symbols for idiot.

Crazy—gal, псих. Verrückt, loca, fou, pazzo, 疯狂的疯狂

What part of the brain is involved in the formation of intelligence? Neuroimaging or functional MRIs have shown that intelligence arises from a network mostly located in the frontal and parietal lobes.

President Trump and the Evangelical Religious Right

These two belong together. None of them practice what they preach. Neither are religious when they fail to follow the Ten Commandments, King James Version (KJV) by Relevance, Exodus 20:3–1.

The Ten Commandments are as follows:

1. I am the Lord thy God! Thou shalt have no other Gods but me!
2. Thou shalt not take the Name of the Lord thy God in vain!
3. Thou shalt keep the Sabbath Day holy!
4. Thou shalt honor thy father and mother!
5. Thou shalt not kill!
6. Thou shalt not commit adultery!
7. Thou shalt not steal!
8. Thou shalt not bear false witness against thy neighbor!
9. Do not let thyself lust after thy neighbor's wife!
10. Thou shalt not covet thy neighbor's house, nor his farm, nor his cattle, nor anything that is his!

President Trump has failed every single one of the Ten Commandments. It is beyond comprehension how any moral and ethical person of religious faith can follow him. These people are like wolves in sheep clothing or *Little Red Riding Hood*. Leaders can do anything as long as they follow the religious right and the right-wing conservative agenda.

Businessman

When the author talks to Trump supporters (Trumpsters), I ask them why they support President Trump. The single most common answer is that he is a businessman. I am in awe at this response. How can anyone believe he is a good businessman when he's had four bankruptcies? He reneged on his multimillion-dollar loans from American banks and lenders. It was only a matter of time before his inability to borrow money in the US would cause him to look elsewhere. Obviously, he would turn to a wealthy, corrupt oligarchy like Russia. Apparently, the Trumpsters approve of corrupt businessmen. There are those who believe President Trump is in love with Russia because of autocrats like President Putin. Why only Russia? It's about the money.

Building an overpriced casino in Atlantic City that could not be supported by locals was a poor business decision. And what about all the contractors and builders he never paid?

Trump judges the economy on how well the stock market is performing. All the huge investors like President Trump, like telling them things like a vaccine is right around the corner. The stock market works best for those who have inside knowledge, like the Republicans in Congress. The stock market also operates on emotion and is not the best way to judge the health of the economy in a vacuum.

Trumpism

The definition of Trumpism: An insane autocratic leader of a nationalistic and Far Right oppressive, ignorant.

How does that compare with fascism? The *Oxford* definition of fascism is similar: 1. An authoritarian and nationalistic right-wing system of government and social organization. 2. (In general use) extreme authoritarian, oppressive, or intolerant views or practices.

It should be apparent to logical, intelligent, and reasonable people that this is the path of the president and the Republicans who support President Trump. The followers are the Trumpism herd.

Fascism can easily progress in a democracy. Excellent examples are twentieth-century Italy with Mussolini, followed by Hitler in Germany. These are the most extreme examples, but one should observe the four-year origins of the same political system. When there is an attorney general like William Barr, the leader of law enforcement supporting this type of political system, Americans should not be complacent like the Germans of the 1930s. We must evaluate this movement not with paranoia but with hypervigilance.

Heil Trump (Hitler)

President Trump has followed the examples Mussolini and Hitler in that his participation with fascism is almost identical with his white supremacist following. He led the Proud Boys and fascist groups to form an attempted coup on the US Capital in Washington, DC, on January 6, 2021. In 1923, Hitler and his fascist Nazis led a coup d'état in Munich for the Nazis to take over the local government. There is no difference between the two. President Trump has unleashed a following that tries their best to undermine democracy.

The obsessive dishonesty is also a part of Trumpism. Telling thousands of lies by a leader of the free world is, I suppose, a First Amendment right, but it is certainly unethical, immoral, and misleading. When I propose the dishonesty issue to Republicans, the answer is that all politicians lie! This is not a fact. One of the few Republicans who doesn't lie is Mitt Romney. And Democrats morally and ethically seek truths and facts.

Trumpism promulgates conspiracy theories. These are a malignant form of nonfacts. It too is unethical, immoral, destructive, and malicious. It is an act of evil. But it too is becoming the norm.

Trumpism promotes ignorance. However, ignorance runs rampant in the Republican Party. Republicans don't want Americans to be educated. It feeds into their insecurity and paranoia when Americans are smart, intelligent, and educated. Uneducated Americans are more likely to follow Republicans than Democrats who promoted facts and education. Republicans perceived education as liberal and progressive. Trump has become their leader of regressive education principles. The evangelicals want to have their own school so they can brainwash the children with regressive education.

White supremacy has been evident in the Trump family beginning with Donald Trump's father, who refused housing to African Americans in their housing projects in New York City.

Trump plays both sides, making it look like he likes Black people, if it benefits him. The woman on *The Apprentice* reality show who later became a White House aide, Omarosa Manigault Newman, was a token Black person whom Trump thought provided him with cover to act despicably toward Black people. Nevertheless, he hates Black people, especially intelligent people who are smarter than he is. The whole birtherism conspiracy theory about President Obama was straight racism.

Trump has also expressed hatred toward Muslims. During the 2008 presidential election, Trump repeatedly accused Barack Obama of secretly being a Muslim. In a March 2016 interview, he stated, "I think Islam hates us." Trump also called for a blanket travel ban on

Muslims in the Middle East entering the country, while promising to help the Christian Syrians, a minority in their country, safely enter the United States.

Summary

As a child, Donald J. Trump displayed evidence of conduct disorder that in and of itself precludes psychopathy. That observation is verifiable.

Mr. Trump has a very complex, minimal functional, pathological brain. His executive portion of the brain, prefrontal cortex, and frontal lobe are dysfunctional. Functional MRIs of the brain show dysfunction of these two areas in psychopaths. The intelligence portions of the brain are the frontal and parietal lobes. The left side is specific to mathematics and language. This is obviously not functioning normally in Mr. Trump. The right side is attributed to creativity, which he lacks. His fear, insecurity, and paranoia originate from an overactive amygdala. And in fact his whole limbic system may be overactive. Verbal repetition is most critically mediated by the cortical regions in the left posterior temporoparietal cortex. This also appears to be dysfunctional. Loss of volume in the hippocampus may be the cause of mania and lack of sleep.

It is clear that many areas of his brain are dysfunctional. The neural pathways and circuitry are misfiring. This leads to chaos in the brain, reflected in Mr. Trump's behavior.

References:

Lee, Bandy. 2017. *The Dangerous Case of Donald Trump*. New York: Thomas Dunne Books, St. Martin's Press.
Trump, Mary. 2020. *Too Much and Never Enough*. New York: Simon & Schuster.

CHAPTER 9

SUMMATION OF THE PSYCHOSOCIAL DYSFUNCTION OF THE REPUBLICAN PARTY

This book has thus far addressed many issues, including facts versus fiction (nonfacts). The reason we use nonfact is because fiction only applies to written and certain media, whereas nonfact applies to all forms of information and language that are untrue. This is so important in today's setting, because lying has become a norm along with nonfactual information and unintelligent conspiracy theories. Americans must be educated regarding facts and information that is not factual. Republicans operate on misinformation and lies. Over the years, Rand Paul has said that there are two sides to every story. The key word is *story*. The factual part of a story is the part that really happened—the rest gets more outlandish every time someone tells it. Stories can also be nonfactual. The issue is facts. Facts are not disputable. This belief that there are two sides to every story is typical of congressional Republicans. When presented with facts, they want to call out liberals.

There should be courses in middle and high school that address critical thinking and discerning facts from nonfacts. This would hopefully prevent conspiracy theories, untruths, and herd psychology.

It would create independent thinkers, which would be more democratic than following political leaders who have bad and nefarious intentions.

Child development and the psychology of children aged two to five years old was presented to provide a summary of normal development, such as language skills and behavior with normal brain development. The language development is important in communication skills with President Trump and other Republicans.

The psychology involved in this age group distinguishes normal psychological development from psychological disorders that progress into adulthood. This is important background information for analyzing the behavior of Republicans in Congress. The observation of abnormal child behavior establishes understanding of the Republican Party.

The two childhood behavioral disorders that have persisted into adulthood are oppositional defiant disorder and conduct disorder. After observing how Republicans in Congress behave, it is clear that these two behaviors are prevalent. Examples of defiance include shutting down the government when Republicans don't get what they want. They also engage in hostile verbal antagonism toward the Democrats. They are parsimonious to the point of causing harm. They reject and block bills in the Senate out of spite. The malicious, cruel, dishonest rhetoric indicates another example of oppositional defiant disorder. It started with Newt Gingrich and has persisted up to Jim Jordan. Within four days of President Biden taking office, Newt Gingrich told the media that Biden was out to destroy the Republican Party. How malicious and nonfactual was that? I think President Trump and half the members of the Republicans in Congress are out to destroy the Republican Party. The psychoanalysis of the Republican Party indicates they need a lot of treatment and therapy to address pathology and mental health.

Oppositional defiant disorder has been the behavior of the Republicans for five decades. It started with Newt Gingrich and has continued throughout the decades. Jim Jordan has shown this behavior with his speeches to Congress. Almost all of the Republicans suffer from this fixed behavior from childhood.

Extreme oppositional defiant disorder and conduct disorder are found in right-wing conservatives and nationalists. This behavior can only lead to a dangerous breach in our democracy. This is nothing new in terms of history. Italy and Germany were socialist and democratic countries before Mussolini and Hitler turned both political systems fascist. We are going in the same direction if the Republican Party persists with their pathological behavior. The observable conduct disorder (psychopathy) of President Trump and the Tea Party and Libertarian Caucus have generated principles of fascism. Whether they realize the truth of this statement or not, it cannot be denied. They want to instill fear in Americans by yelling about socialism, but their behavior is fascist in nature. It is a violent, hateful group in the Republican Party, not the Democrats. The fact that Republicans project their hate and violence toward the liberal Antifa is misguided, because Antifa is not a violent terrorist group. The radical liberal left is not as large or organized as the Far Right.

Antisocial behavior is frequently associated with corruption. We associated sociopathic behavior with white-collar crime and psychopathic behavior with killing people. Many Republicans have committed sociopathic white-collar crimes. It has become prominent, from ex-President Richard Nixon and Vice President Spiro Agnew to the numerous present-day criminals, including Steve Bannon, Michael Flynn, and Paul Manafort, as well as Republican Congressmen Duncan Hunter of California and Chris Collins of New York. It goes as far as Republican state representative Phil Lyman of Utah, who led an ATV protest through restricted Native lands. In a clear demonstration of white supremacy, Lyman protested the fact that the US Bureau of Land Management closed Native American land to ATVs. It's not egregious enough that white supremacists killed off Native Americans in their quest to own North America, but they also have to desecrate their sacred protected land? White supremacists in the 1700s and 1800s slaughtered North American Natives and stole their land. This is psychopathic behavior.

We explained socialism in an attempt to get readers to understand that socialism is not as bad as the Republicans claim. They yell about socialism as a scare tactic. Republican congresspeople associate *liberal* with Democrats, but Republicans and independents can also be liberal. This is another attack on Democrats. Ignorant Americans buy into this fear. Do Sweden and Norway as well as other democratic socialist countries appear dangerous? The United States will never become socialist because capitalism is ingrained into the fabric of our economy and politics. However, fascism, which doesn't include the economy, can infiltrate democracy, because it is a hateful, violent political progression.

The religious right and conservative Republicans who fear socialism must realize that whatever organized religion they belong to is socialist. Socialism is a political and economic theory of social organization that advocates that the means of production, distribution, and exchange should be owned or regulated by the community as a whole. There is a financial contribution to the church required for the production of buildings, sometimes schools or colleges, and information written or media produced, all of which is distributed and owned by the membership as a whole. As an example, the Catholic Church functions as a hierarchical government with the pope at the top. It then moves down to bishop, archbishop, cardinal, priest, and deacon. All Christian religions have some sort of hierarchy like a government and have attempted to form their own political parties, like the Christian Democratic Union of Germany. Europe has allowed religions incorporation into their governments. Historically, this has been a problem, such as causing wars and associating with evil, as the Catholic Church did with Mussolini and Hitler in the early stages of fascism. It is for this reason that our American founders attempted to separate church and state. However, that separation has not been complete.

The Republicans have been unable to differentiate between socialism and social democracy in a capitalist system. We have Social Security, Medicare, the Americans with Disabilities Act, the Veterans Administration, the bank bailout of 2008, COVID-19 economic stimulus, and on and on. Why do Republicans fear these programs, especially when some programs have been their own? And why do Republicans instill fear in Americans when they cry about socialism when it comes time for elections? It's a lie.

Moral humanism must be based on utilitarianism, a form of social democracy that creates the greater good for the greatest number of people. The Democrats have been following this humanitarian concept for some time, with Republicans battling them all the way. This fighting and bickering with the Democrats prevents progress and utilitarian benefits. The current status of the Republican Party is nefariousism. Nefariousism was created to oppose utilitarianism. Nefariousism states in brief that the greatest bad is created for the greatest number of people. It is the black swan of evil and death.

Crowd psychology and herd behavior or psychology are synonymous, but herd behavior is also addressed with animals. The many theories of crowd psychology are useful in understanding the behavior of the Republican Party. The most useful theories describing crowd behavior of Republicans are convergence, contagion, mass delusional, autocratic leader, monetary, and mimetic crowd behavior.

Convergence theory states that people who want to act in a certain way come together to form crowds. The contagion theory states that crowds cause people to act with a hypnotic influence over their members. They express anonymity, and large numbers of people abandon personal responsibility and surrender to the contagious emotions of the crowd. A crowd thus assumes a life of its own, stirring up emotions and driving people toward irrational, even violent actions.

We see that when Republicans converge with and elect someone with the same beliefs, (e.g., a Far Right conservative), this theory holds. Over the past four years, mass delusional theory has gone into effect. All the conspiracy theorists have created delusional Republicans in Congress, because the congressmen believe this group of people will keep them in office. The monetary crowd theory is seen with Republicans when groups like the National Rifle Association stuff money into the pockets of Republicans so gun manufacturers make money on gun sales. Again, nefariousism comes into play when thousands of innocent Americans are killed in shootings.

Political leaders like President Trump, the Republicans, Far Right evangelicals, con artists, evangelists, William Barr (former attorney general), and Senate Majority Leader McConnell have fit into the power leadership and monetary theories.

Herd psychology also comes into play. A herd is a large group of animals, especially hoofed mammals, that live together. A herd can also describe a large group. The term is used in herd psychology and herd immunity. Herd immunity should be expressed as population immunity.

Herd psychology is present in many mammals. This means there is a leader and a group of animals or humans who are followers. Herd psychology is the same as herd behavior or mentality. It is also included in crowd psychology. But we should be clear about the herd phenomenon.

Confusion occurs when discussing herd disease and immunity. Should the entire herd acquire a disease or infection, the herd will either survive or die. In terms of an infection, one animal can get the infection and spread it, or the entire herd can get the disease. In terms of immunity from an infectious disease, human and animal immunity are similar. Immunity can be natural in which the animal/human acquires the disease and later becomes immune. The risk is that some animals/humans can die from the infection before obtaining immunity. Natural immunity can also be unpredictable. As we stated previously, in the example of foot-and-mouth disease in animals, only about 30 percent developed natural immunity in the herd. The alternative to herd immunity is vaccination.

The purpose of vaccinations is to introduce animals/humans to noninfective parts of the virus or bacteria, usually through injections. The immune system then recognizes and remembers the virus/bacteria when exposed, and that prevents infection and, in many cases, death.

Vaccinations can totally eliminate an infectious disease in a population. An example is smallpox. However, the majority of the population must be vaccinated for this to occur. Another important issue is mutations. Viruses are composed of either DNA or RNA genetic material. When the virus infects humans or animals, the genetic material of the virus infects cells in the human/animal and is then incorporated into the DNA and RNA of cells. This replication process incorporates human/animal DNA or RNA of the virus, hence a mutation. Mutations can be prevented by early vaccinations of the population. It is for this reason that with any viral/bacterial infection, it is extremely important to have the population immunized. This was the method that President Biden advocated after his election.

With President Trump's chaotic brain, he got confused between herd mentality (his followers) and herd immunity. Natural herd immunity was a disaster for COVID-19. For example, we had no idea what the immunity consisted of in COVID-19, because all of the testing was haphazard. Prevention was haphazard due to the negligence of President Trump and the Republican Party. They kept pushing natural herd immunity, but there was no prediction as to who would live and who would die with natural herd immunity. Republican Senator Rand Paul was one of the promoters of natural herd immunity, but as a physician, he should have known better.

Crowd psychology also considers the worst of behavior as well as normal behavior of a crowd. Examples of nefarious crowd behavior result from conspiracy theories and propaganda.

Conspiracy theories are covert, illusory lies about someone or something. The person who initiates the theory is usually a person of authority or someone who claims to be in the know. He/she has an antisocial personality disorder incorporating fear, paranoia, illusions, distrust, and dishonesty and is nonempathetic. The followers are weak, lazy, precarious thinkers and emulators. They obsess about the theory and through social media mimetically indoctrinate others. The very dark side of these nefarious theories/beliefs is hatred and violence against those who are the victim(s). The latest example is QAnon, which shows how a person of authority started the irrational, crazed, illusory conspiracy theories.

QAnon got started in October 2017 when an anonymous user put a series of posts on the message board 4chan. The user signed off as "Q" and claimed to have a level of US security approval known as "Q clearance." This is something someone like Steve Bannon or Stephen Miller would start. Why and how would President Trump know these people? It is incomprehensible how anyone with any rational, critical thinking can involve themselves in these nonfactual, illusory beliefs. But the Republicans have topped the list of idiocy, especially with Representative Marjorie Taylor Greene.

Propaganda is communication that is intended to sway a crowd of people by persuading then with one-sided arguments that are usually untrue. Propaganda has been used to great effect by evil autocrats such as Mussolini and Hitler.

Propaganda was obvious with Donald J. Trump. Symbolism such as red baseball caps, slogans like "Make America Great Again," and repetitive, dishonest rhetoric against Democrats were everywhere.

Crowd psychology has been applied to fascism, because almost every crowd theory and crowd psychological description can be applied to fascism. With the Republican Party becoming a Far Right conservative nationalist party, crowd psychology of fascism can be used as an example to explain the direction of the Republican Party.

Fascism is an authoritarian and nationalistic right-wing system of government or social organization. Its members believe in oppression and intolerance.

Fascist ideology is racist to two extremes: they feel superior to all other people, and they have hatred for certain other people (i.e., Blacks, Asians, Muslims, and Jewish people). They have many fears (to the extent of paranoia) and phobias, such as homophobia, xenophobia, and misogyny. They attempt to suppress their opposition, often with denigrated rhetoric and frequently with violence.

Fascist behavior has become prominent in the Republican Party. There is so much hatred directed toward the Democrats regardless of any action by the Democrats.

The Republicans have a real fear of the Democrats' competency. They show their superiority and supremacy with verbal attacks against those on the Democratic side. These are the same behaviors of fascist white supremacists.

Donald J. Trump has promoted all of the fascist characteristics and behaviors to the extreme. It nearly reached a level of Hitler's fascism. These are autocratic, Far Right conservative policies and hatred toward

Democrats as well as xenophobia, racism, propaganda, coups, and violence. Trump fits the definition of a fascist, and many Republicans followed.

The psychosocial behavior of the Republican Party has transcended from an ideology of natural rights, freedom, and a pluralistic society to one of racism and obstructionism. How did this take place? History offers an analysis of the present-day Republican Party.

The Republican Party originated in 1854 and was opposed to slavery, especially the expansion of slavery from the South to the West. The Republicans opposed the Kansas-Nebraska Act, which promoted slavery in the West. The party supported English philosopher John Locke's classical liberalism. The ideology is a driving force of well-being for all. The political ideology advocates civil liberties under the rule of law with an emphasis on economic freedom. It believes in individualism and equal rights. This is the reason the early Republicans supported the abolition of slavery and opposed slavery's expansion.

This classical liberalism of the nineteenth century lasted in the early Republican Party from 1854 until 1912, when the party was becoming too liberal during Theodore Roosevelt's presidency. He vigorously promoted the conservation movement, emphasizing efficient use of natural resources. He dramatically expanded the system of national parks and national forests. He later attacked big business, proposing a welfare state, and supporting labor unions. From 1912 to the present, the party has moved to the right, becoming more conservative as classical liberalism took hold in the Democratic Party. Conservatism became stronger with President Franklin D. Roosevelt's policies, especially after the New Deal.

Republicans held the White House throughout the 1920s. The largest corruption scandal, called the Teapot Dome scandal, took place under President Harding. It involved bribery for oil drilling.

The Republican base shifted to the southern states after the Civil Rights Act of 1964 and after the Voting Rights Act of 1965.

The end of the twentieth century and beginning of the twenty-first century accelerated conservatism to the Far Right. It began with President

Reagan's economic policies and social values. The GOP supported lower taxes, free market capitalism, restrictions on immigration, increased military spending, deregulation, elimination of abortions, and restrictions on labor unions.

The repressive agenda of the Republican Party was growing, but the coercive reactionary behavior by Newt Gingrich initiated the process, starting in the 1970s and climaxing when he was Speaker of the House of Representatives. From the 1990s, the Republicans engaged in constitutional perversion. Speaker Gingrich undermined House procedures and norms. He polarized the parties with hateful partisan prejudice. Speaker Gingrich frequently questioned the patriotism of Democrats, called them corrupt, compared them to fascists, and accused them of wanting to destroy the United States. Did he confuse fascism with socialism? Nevertheless, his behavior was and still is reprehensible and heretical for a conservative Christian.

The reactionary insolence of the democratic norms also persisted through the Senate in the early twenty-first century with Mitch McConnell. As Mitch McConnell rose to power from Senate minority leader to Senate majority leader during the Obama presidency, his abuse of the filibuster and abuse of power using obstructionism reached an all-time high during President Obama's two terms. McConnell's abusive obstructionism went so far as to slow the Senate's ability to process even routine measures and limited the sheer volume of liberal bills that could be adopted.

Constitutional abuse of norms progressed to even greater levels when McConnell refused to hold hearings on Supreme Court nominee Merrick Garland during the final year of Obama's presidency.

McConnell then became a staunch supporter of President Trump's abuse of power throughout Trump's presidency. He supported all of Trump's policies. As the second most powerful Republican, McConnell accelerated the Republican Party to a hateful Far Right nationalist party that accepted lies, corruption, conspiracy theories, and, finally, violence.

The past five decades of the Republican Party have been repressive, defiant, slanderous, demeaning, dishonest, nonfactual, and obstructive to progress. All of these descriptions and more are symptoms of the Republican Party over the years. As Donald Trump came into power, these symptoms were accentuated. A cancer may present itself as bleeding from the colon for colon cancer, but it may progress to the liver or lungs to cause metastasis, which is much more difficult to treat and may lead to death. Donald Trump has become the metastasis cancer to the Republican Party. Unfortunately, he is not alone. Almost half the Senate and House have been the targets of the metastasis.

The psychoanalysis of Donald J. Trump is unquestionably and undeniably psychopathologic. He fits all of the criteria. Narcissism is a component of psychopathy, and with Trump's mental profile, narcissism is rampant. The three other components are pathological lying, total absence of empathy, and disregard for laws. The very few feelings he has surround power (autocracy), monetary greed, hatred, and suffering to others. He has been directly and indirectly responsible for hundreds of thousands of American deaths and has shown no remorse. In fact, when he learned more African Americans and Hispanics were dying from COVID-19, he did even less to control the virus. He has blood on his hands from many deaths caused by white supremacists, from Pittsburgh to El Paso. He shows no remorse.

As president, he challenged the US Constitution like no other president in history. He challenged it in opportunistic, nefarious modalities that created a fragile democracy. His modus operandi is comparable to Adolf Hitler, and perhaps given a chance, he could have annihilated Hispanics and African Americans. It is irrefutable that Donald J. Trump is nefarious to the extreme of evil.

Christians, Evangelicals, and the Religious Right

The Republican Party has always been a party of Christian religions. It has been comprised of fundamentalist religions such as Lutherans, Presbyterians, conservative Catholics, and more. Evangelists such as the Reverend Billy Graham traveled throughout the United States and held large meetings with stadiums full of followers, mostly Republican.

Religious leaders such as Norman Vincent Peale and Robert Schuller had large followings of Republicans. TV evangelists such as Oral Roberts and Jim and Tammy Bakker had a large Republican base.

Robert G. Grant, a Republican, is a political activist who has been the leader of several American Christian right groups in the US. He has led the advocacy group Christian Voice. He is considered the father of the religious right. Jerry Falwell Sr. formed the Moral Majority, another Far Right Republican group with religious orientation. In addition to these two leaders, others also became prominent in the religious right, including Ed McAteer's Religious Roundtable Council, James Dobson's Focus on the Family, Paul Weyrich's Free Congress Foundation and the Heritage Foundation, and Pat Robertson's Christian Broadcasting Network.

Conspiracy theories and fearmongering have been the backbone of evangelicals since the post–World War II era. Communism was the main threat to religion in the US during the 1950s and 1960s, according to radio evangelists. America would lose its religious freedom as communism infiltrated American politics. This paranoia became evident in Senator Barry Goldwater's anti-red (communism) behavior.

As evangelism ramped up after the 1950s, the 1970s saw a development of a faction of evangelicals, the religious right. They created the narrative that the American family was falling apart as a result of the liberal Democrats.

The next big fear was morality in America. Jerry Falwell Sr. saw the nation as fallen and secular forces as the enemy of Christianity. His Christian beliefs and political views were pitched as a battle for America's soul. Some also saw their religious pursuit as a battle between secular humanism and Christianity. It is difficult with polling to determine the number of Americans comprising the religious right, but some estimates are fifty million. Obviously, Southern Baptist evangelicals also include African Americans, but the religious right is said to be 80 percent white.

Religious right leaders promoted conspiracy theories that the civil rights movement and protests were instigated by liberals and communist forces.

Jerry Falwell Sr. claimed that America was being led by the wicked (liberals) and religion had to lead America back to religious values in order to be great. The evangelicals viewed the government with fear, and ministers like Pat Robertson felt that evangelicals had to infiltrate the government to instill their values.

Fear and guilt are part of Christian fundamentalist religions. They are instilled in children and last throughout life. These beliefs are fundamental to conservatism. There is an argument to be made that these beliefs form the matrix of the Republican Party.

The Republicans will continue their obstructionist, dishonest, and conspiratorial behavior. They will continue to call Democrats socialists, and then the religious right will seek redemption to win back the White House.

Businesspeople and Big Business

The Republican Party has traditionally been a pro-business party, mostly increasing alliances beginning in the 1920s. About 50 to 60 percent of Republicans are self-employed small business owners. Wall Street is largely Republican. Business owners are also employers. The cost of employees is about 40 percent due to salaries, payroll taxes, unemployment, workers' compensation insurance, disability insurance, human resources, and other regulations, depending on the business.

The policies and platform of the Democrat Party include higher taxes and more regulation, both of which could hinder a company from realizing a profit. The Republicans seem to favor fair taxes and commonsense regulations. Hence, businesspeople support Republicans. As a result, businesspeople will vote Republican regardless of the candidate. Businesspeople voted for Donald J. Trump because he is a businessman, ergo, a president who would help businesses. They failed to recognize that Trump failed in business four times. He is a corrupt businessman who paid no taxes, yet all business owners voting for him paid taxes. His deregulations caused failures for farmers and businesses.

The United States Chamber of Commerce helps small businesses. Over the last twenty-plus years, the Chamber invested $250 million a year into the Republican Party—one that held legendary sway over public policy. As an example, in 2003, the Chamber led the passage of a business-backed scheme to create a prescription drug benefit for Medicare, the public health insurance for the elderly. The bill, backed by the Bush administration, was widely seen as a giveaway to the insurance and pharmaceutical industries. Also, the Chamber funneled $86 million to Republicans to battle the Affordable Care Act.

Big money and big business have always been associated with the Republican Party. Robert Mercer and the Koch brothers have donated mega-money to Republicans and the party. The Freedom Partners Chamber of Commerce is part of the network established by the billionaire Koch brothers, who contributed $5.5 million to the Republicans between 2012 and 2015. The Mercers contributed a large amount to Trump when he ran against Hillary Clinton, because Mercer viewed Clinton as a socialist.

Farmers and Rural Conservative America

There are multiple reasons that farmers are associated with Republicans. Farmers have historically been white Americans. By nature, they are bound to the land and want to protect it fiercely. They are multidenominational fundamentalist Christians. Their profit margin is minimal on small farms but much larger on mega-farms. They must manage money very conservatively. Their investments are in the land and growing products, which are almost totally dependent on the weather.

Another issue is family, which is considered to be a Republican concept. A century ago, large families were common, and the children helped on the farm.

As opposed to urbanites, a farm community is often isolated from progressive thinking and diversity. This creates fear when these concepts are introduced. Many people feel safe with their conservatism.

They fear big government. Republicans have always been opposed to regulations. Farmers are exposed to many regulations and want the Republicans to do more to deregulate, thus making their jobs easier. Farmers are intensely regulated by government agencies, including the United States Department of Agriculture (USDA), the Food and Drug Administration (FDA), the Environmental Protection Agency (EPA), the National Oceanic and Atmospheric Administration (NOAA), and the Occupational Safety and Health Administration (OSHA).

The EPA regulates anything from auto emissions to banning the use of pesticides such as mirex and DDT; from cleaning up toxic waste to protecting the ozone layer; from increasing recycling to revitalizing inner-city brownfields. The EPA's achievements have resulted in cleaner air, purer water, and better protected land. For the farmer, pesticides are regulated.

In 1986, an umbrella act allowed the EPA to work with other government agencies, such as NOAA.

Farmers have caused water pollution with fertilizers and toxic chemical release; however, the EPA set the first national standards limiting industrial water pollution, launching a program that today prevents one billion pounds of toxins from reaching our rivers, lakes, and streams each year. I grew up on a small farm in southeastern Pennsylvania. A large pond was dammed along Indian Creek. Trout could be caught, and in the wintertime, the pond froze, and we played ice hockey. Sixty years later, the pond was filled in with bushes and grasses, and the creek was almost gone. This occurred as a result of overfertilization by farmers.

It would seem reasonable that the Farm Bureau would help the farmers find solutions. However, the Farm Bureau is part of the problem. It is a not-for-profit organization that is totally Republican based. The US Department of Agriculture appears to be finding solutions.

Republicans and the Tea Party have been opposed to regulations. Without federal regulation, pollution would be out of control. Having national rules from the EPA is critically important. But there is still much more to be done. I have had patients exposed to toxic chemicals who have died prematurely from liver and lung cancer.

The other problem with Republican farmers is the estate tax. This tax is worrisome for the agriculture community: farmers, much more than other industry, tend to pass down land and assets through generations and have long been concerned about the cost of taking over a parent's farm. Hillary Clinton, who ran for president in 2016, wanted to increase the estate tax by 65 percent. The farmers were adamantly opposed to this, and she lost their vote.

Another issue is big business that turns farms into big businesses. Farms purchased for $200 an acre fifty years ago have now gone up to as high as $12,000 an acre. This has been especially prominent in areas of urban sprawl where farmers make huge profits and no longer need to sweat on their farms to make a meager living. The developers are Republican, and the mega-farms are Republican.

Two other areas in which the government cuts into the costs of the farmers' production are the Affordable Care Act and the fifteen-dollar minimum wage that is slowly becoming a national law. Both of these governmental regulations force workers to have health insurance and be paid a higher minimum wage. Republicans have opposed both of these laws. The hypocrisy of Republican farmers, especially in California and the Southwest, is their opposition to immigration, but they are highly dependent on Hispanics to pick their fruit and vegetables in a timely manner before it rots.

Die-hard, Relentless Republicans

These individuals are born into a Republican family, taught Republican ideology, and register to vote Republican for the rest of their lives. My family have been stalwart Republicans. Admittedly, I voted for President Nixon, but that was a disaster, and after his crimes, I took a much more critical approach to choosing a candidate. It became apparent to me that one must do his/her homework before voting.

My sister has voted Republican all her life and voted for Trump in 2016. His behavior was finally too crazy for her, and for the first time in her life, she voted Democrat in 2020.

This is a perfect example of why people are stuck in a political rut. This example supports the contagion theory. My sister lives in a Republican town where she was born, and she has Republican friends. It is natural to vote Republican with all of one's Republican friends. There is an acceptance of flaws or corruption in candidates.

Nixon crossed the line with me. It was like "lessons learned are like bridges burned; you only cross them but once." From that time, only candidates who were qualified and ethical were given my vote.

The problem with Trump as president has been the support from extreme stalwart Republicans.

Conservatives

Conservatism is a political philosophy that states that if changes need to be made in a society, they should be made gradually.

Conservatism was first described in a political context by François-René de Chateaubriand in 1818 after the French Revolution. In many countries, the term is associated with right-wing politics. In America, conservatism has been associated mostly with the Republican Party. It has had many descriptions over time. With Republicans, the conservative ideology advocates for the preservation of personal wealth and private ownership (capitalism), limited government, free markets, individual liberty, traditional American values, and a strong national defense, and it emphasizes self-reliance and individualism.

They maintain the existing or traditional order and oppose the attempt to achieve social change though legislation or publicly funded programs. However, they believe social change can only be controlled through religion. They are opposed to liberalism and change and reject the optimistic view that human beings can be morally improved through political and social change. Conservatism is as much a matter of temperament as of doctrine.

Conservatism is often inherited. There is a very slow evolutionary pattern of change lacking abstract and ideal thinking.

While the Democrats have a few conservatives, it is largely the purview of Republicans. There is overlap in views, beliefs, and policies among all of these factions, which makes it difficult to label personal association.

There are several conservative factions or caucuses within the Republican Party. It is like a smorgasbord of conservatism. Most all major conservative factions are listed here:

Traditional conservatives: These conservatives are opposed to change, especially social institutions. They are opposed to big government institutions. They are opposed to any rapid evolutionary process.

Social conservatives: Social conservatives are Christians who usually support traditional norms and Christian fundamentalists. They are paramilitary and support police enforcement. They oppose marches, such as antiwar and Black Lives Matter. They tend to strongly identify with American nationalism and patriotism.

Fiscal conservatives: This faction of conservatism supports economic and political policy that advocates for low taxes, a balanced budget, limited government spending (especially on social issues and welfare), and minimizing the size of government and government interference in the economy.

Neoconservatism: This group originated in the early and midtwentieth century as foreign policy interventionists. They promote democracy in foreign countries.

Neoconservatives are considered interventionists. Interventionists were present in Congress during World War I and World War II, but the name identifying this group was not used until the 1960s to offset the paleoconservative faction who are isolationists. During the Vietnam War, neocons felt the Democrats were pacifists. They were opposed to the Great Society of President Lyndon Johnson. They became critical of the New Left and counterculture and antiwar demonstrators of the sixties. They promoted the installation of democracy around the world, with military force if necessary. They are opposed to any political radicalism, especially communism. However, their origins were in liberalism, especially the short-lived Socialist Party and Social Democrats. They eventually opposed the New Left. It gradually grew from George McGovern to Ronald Reagan.

Neoconservatism peaked with President George W. Bush with their promotion of war in Iraq and Afghanistan. When George W. Bush first ran for president, the neoconservatives believed he was too weak on evil countries opposing democracy. After September 11, 2001, and his invasion of Iraq, they perceived President Bush and Vice President Cheney to be neoconservatives.

The military intervention of neoconservatives has always been at the forefront of this group's policies. Even though George H.W. Bush started the Gulf War (1991) in Iraq, they wanted President Bush to remain in Iraq and eliminate Saddam Hussein. They pushed President Bill Clinton to invade Iraq.

Politicians who have been considered neoconservatives have been President George W. Bush, former Senator John McCain, Senator Tom Cotton, Senator Lindsey Graham, and Mitch McConnell.

Paleoconservatism: This group is a rebirth of the Old Right and isolationists. They arose in opposition to the neoconservatives. They believe that multiracial, multiethnic, and egalitarian states are unstable. Foreign intervention creates suspicion.

The ideology of paleoconservatives is restriction of immigration, decentralization, trade tariffs, economic protectionism, and return to conservative ethics. A group that branched off from the paleoconservatives is the alt-right, who are white nationalists.

The noted paleoconservatives are Pat Buchanan and Tucker Carlson (Fox News).

Libertarian conservatives: This group of conservatives has a strict interpretation of the US Constitution with respect to federal power. They are pro-business, social moderates and want a rigid enforcement of states' rights, individual liberty, limited federal spending, and limited government size. They don't oppose the use of marijuana, because of their belief in individual liberty. Senator Rand Paul claims to be a libertarian.

Constitutional conservatives: This group interprets the United States Constitution their own way and attempts to preserve its principles. They defend liberty and the First and Second Amendments. US Constitution Amendments can be interpreted and manipulated. The Tea Party conservatives associate with this group. Senators Ted Cruz and Josh Hawley also claim to be constitutional scholars.

Christian conservatives: This group of conservatives believes the United States was formed as a Christian nation. They believe in strong, strict family values and prayer in the schools (and all public gatherings), and they oppose abortion and same-sex marriages. They prefer homeschooling so their children are not exposed to the sins of the world. They attack sex and profanity in movies and media. They fight against anyone who opposes their beliefs. They love that President Trump installed two Catholic antiabortionists on the Supreme Court and fought to prevent Sandra Day O'Connor from being appointed to the Supreme Court in the 1980s because she was pro–women's rights. An example of their power was Proposition 8 in California in 2008, which tried to ban same-sex marriage. There were rallies around the state, especially in the Republican stronghold of California, the San Joaquin Valley. Proponents held signs that read "YES on 8." These groups are more radical and make up the religious right.

Nationalist conservatives: This group represents the extreme Far Right conservative nationalists. They originated during the Cold War with conspiracy theories of communism infiltration of the United States. They are opposed to any interaction with allied countries. There is opposition to all form of immigration, civil rights, women's rights, and other races such as Jews and Muslims. They are white and believe they are superior to nonwhites. They promote isolationism and limitation of a global economic exchange. This has become a populist movement among conservatives. President Donald J. Trump has been a leader of their group of conservatives. This faction has become the most chaotic and regressive form of conservatism.

When a person states they are a conservative, what do they mean? Do they believe in the ideals of the conservative described above, or do they say that to acknowledge they are opposed to change? That supposes that they are opposed to any form of progress, such as medical research or science. It also suggests an opposition to competition, where progress is absolutely essential.

All of these different factions in the Republican Party create disorganization, confusion, and conflict. However, in the past four years, national conservatism and white nationalism have been winning. This explains why, over time, they have moved in the direction of national conservatism. President Trump bought it to fruition. Crowd psychology has been applied to the behavior of the Republican Party, which perceives itself to be a white nationalistic party.

History of Conservatism

Edmund Burke (1729–1797) was a British statesman and philosopher who has been widely regarded as the philosophical founder of modern conservatism. John Adams has been regarded as the original conservative in America. The father of twentieth-century conservatism is Russell Kirk, a philosophical and literary genealogist to emergent political conservatism. Russell Kirk had a huge influence on William Frank Buckley Jr. (1925–2008), who was an American public intellectual and conservative author and commentator.

William F. Buckley Jr. is known as the intellectual father of conservatism. He started the *National Review* and attempted to bring various conservative ideas together with his magazine that he started in the mid-1950s. In the magazine, he expressed his views. Initially a traditional conservative, his views were a mix of ideas we recognize today as conservatism, including free market capitalism, support for American military actions, libertarianism, opposition to civil rights, and social conservatism. Today, he was what we call a neoconservative, a social conservative, and a libertarian. He did draw a line against the John Birch Society, the anti-Semites, and other radical right-wing groups.

He started the PBS TV show *Firing Line* in 1966, where he interviewed notable persons from religion, politics, and academia. He would interview liberals and conservatives, challenging their views in a polite atmosphere with his leg crossed and holding a clipboard and pen, speaking with quiet dignity. He attempted to intellectualize conservatism, but over the past three decades, his conservatism has moved far right along with the Republican Party.

White Supremacy—White Nationalism, White Identity, and Radical White Supremacy

The author's definition of white supremacy is as a spectrum of white (Caucasians) people who have a superior identity over racial and ethnic groups, consistent with anything from quiet prejudice to name-calling, to institutional racism, to radical/violent white supremacy, although radical white supremacy is designated separately.

White supremacy (*Oxford Dictionary*): The belief that white people constitute a superior and therefore dominate race and should therefore dominate society, typically to the exclusion or detriment of racial and ethnic groups, especially Black or Jewish people.

Our definition is more general because white supremacists feel superior to Hispanics, Latinos, and Muslims, and just about everyone who is not white.

White Identity: White Nationalism and White Supremacy

White identity should not be misconstrued as radical white identity in this section. The discussion is about nonradical white identity/supremacy. This includes whites who are not obviously prejudiced, but their actions are subtle. For example, eastern universities in the past have been all white. The Ivy League schools such as Harvard and Yale were predominantly white. Harvard started taking Jewish students because they were smarter than American whites. Businesses have only hired whites in the past. African Americans were only able to get work picking cotton and doing hard labor, while Hispanics traditionally worked in the fields in the Southwest and on the West Coast, while whites owned the land. Until the midtwentieth century, only whites were allowed to play professional sports.

White identity in politics is backward. Southern white democrats in the early to midtwentieth century were conservative racists and segregationists. This flipped to conservative Republicans in the latter half of the twentieth century and into the twenty-first century. They have gradually moved from white identity to radical white identity.

In the *Merriam-Webster Dictionary*, the first documented use of the term *white nationalist* occurred in 1925, to refer to a member of a militant group that espoused white supremacy. However, the term is used instead of white supremacy to appear more credible while also avoiding negative stereotypes about white supremacists. For example, the Ku Klux Klan view themselves as white nationalists. However, the violence they engage in is a part of white supremacy.

White nationalists are the group who ideologically believe that white people are a race who seek to develop and maintain a white racial and national identity. Scholars describe white nationalism as overlapping with white superior norms and white separatism. White nationalists believe that through natural selection, the entire state should be white. Although they are extremists, they do not approve of the term *white supremacy* because of the negative connotation. They believe white people must maintain their dominance in a majority white country; they are opposed to immigration and hateful toward other races. This white-only dominance takes the form of politics, economy, businesses, and institutions.

There are several different radical white nationalist groups who use several different names. There are the Proud Boys and Oath Keepers, to name a couple. Proud Boys was chosen to establish white pride, which exists solely to provide a sanitized public face for white supremacy. Most white nationalist groups promote racial violence. Those who promote violence fulfill the criteria of antisocial personality disorders, particularly psychopaths.

In terms of identity, white nationalism and radical white supremacy are similar; they overlap in their beliefs and the extremism they display. Some analysts consider them to be different, but white nationalists, radical white supremacists, and white separatists all share the common idea that white people are superior to all other races. Therefore, they seek to preserve, protect, and maintain whiteness, even at the expense of violence.

Radical white supremacy has its roots in a past century of now-debunked scientific claims. For example, it was believed that Blacks had bigger hearts and muscles, allowing them to labor more easily in harsh conditions and for longer periods of time. These myths were applied and led to a belief that Black people were inferior and animalistic. The radical white supremacists of the South were vigilantes. It has been estimated that between 1882 and 1968, 3,446 Black people were lynched.

When American media and texts discuss white supremacy, they usually focus on African Americans and anti-Semitism. White supremacy has its origins in Europe during the time of monarchies, aristocracy, class hierarchies, and wealthy landowners. This carried over into America and Columbus. It also continued with colonialization in many countries, for example in Africa, Canada, and Australia.

Radical and violent white supremacy in the United States began long before it was concentrated on Black slaves in the South. Genocide of indigenous North Americans occurred from 1492 to the 1800s.

Scholarly work by Russel Thornton claims that the estimated population of indigenous Native Americans in the contiguous United States before 1492 was around forty million, and by the beginning of 1900, it was down to 250,000—the biggest genocide in recorded history. There are many reasons for this, including disease, war, genocidal violence, enslavement, forced relocations, the destruction of food sources, and the devastation of ways of life. This is shameful white supremacy and is the height of evil. The contiguous United States belonged to the Native Americans—it still does—and everyone else is a guest. But they are denied respect. Instead we have beaten them into submission, given them the worst land on which to live and grow food, and assuage our guilt by allowing them to build casinos. Americans voted a Black man into the presidency in 2008, and the Republican white supremacists had problems approving Deb Haaland, a Native American, for secretary of the interior in 2021.

Radical white supremacy originally focused on Natives and Blacks, and although this has not changed, there have been demographic changes in the US. An influx of immigrants from Asian, Hispanic, Latino, and

Muslim backgrounds have created white anxiety and paranoia. White nationalists see this change as declining education and Christian values. They believe the only approved immigration is from Europe.

Sociology of White Nationalism / White Supremacy

White identity theory was described by psychologist Janet Helms. It is a racial theory regarding white people and their role in creating and maintaining a racist society. It also addresses the need for them to act responsibly by dismantling systemic racism through a framework of power and privilege.

Systemic racism is also known as institutional racism. It is a form of racism embedded into the fabric of societal norms, businesses, organizations, and institutions. It is not overtly radical but more subtle and often less perceptible. Systemic racism is not easily recognizable because it receives far less public condemnation than individual or radical racism.

The sociopathic phases of white identity begin with a child's conscious identity of whiteness and privilege. This distinction changes as they are introduced to other races or ethnic persons.

When a white person meets a person of a different race, they then realize their power and privilege with the other person they encounter. This forces them to focus on their own race and the role they play as a white person. This forms one's identity within their own race.

The person reaches emergence in identifying with their group in the form of beliefs and symbolism. This phase has multiple factors; individuals feel pressured to choose one racial or ethnic group identity over another. This is a phase of choices that is influenced by status of the group, parental influence, cultural knowledge, and appearance. They now receive support from parents, peers, and group members. The person becomes secure in their own sense of white identity. They internalize their feelings and beliefs.

Lastly, the white person reaches a phase where they find ways of translating their personal sense of the opposing race into a plan of action or general sense of commitment to concerns about the other race as a group (racial prejudice/bias). This is sustained over time as comfort with their own race and those around them grows.

At any one stage, except the initial one, the person has a choice between integration and disintegration. This is an evolutionary process from their nonracial identity to one of racial bias.

The author's initial encounter with other races was as a child between five and twelve years of age. Growing up on a farm in Lancaster County, Pennsylvania, everyone was white. My mother belonged to the Farm Women's Society and had a program called Fresh Air Children where children from the Bronx and Brooklyn would spend two to eight weeks on the farm in the summer. Over the years, I was introduced to Black, Chinese, and Puerto Rican children. We played together, did chores together, ate together, and slept together. They got to learn how food grows and is harvested and experienced the rich culture of farming. I learned that they were no different from me other than their race and where they were from. At this age and with this background, I felt no privilege other than I grew up on a farm and they grew up in a big city. Unfortunately, this program no longer exists, but these types of integrative childhood programs would teach us not to hate.

History of White Nationalism in the United States

The citizenship laws in America have gone through an evolutionary process beginning in 1790 with the Naturalization Act. This law was directed at free white persons of good moral character. This was unchanged until after the US Civil War of 1868. This led to the Fourteenth Amendment of the US Constitution, which granted citizenship to Black people born in the US, but it specifically excluded untaxed Native Americans, because they were considered separate nations.

The first insurgent group after the defeat of the Confederate States of America was the Ku Klux Klan (KKK). Their intent was to maintain whiteness in the southern racial system throughout the Reconstruction Era. They sought to maintain the Confederate States and instill fear in African Americans through violence.

The second chapter of the KKK was founded in Atlanta, Georgia, in 1915 and, beginning in 1921, it adopted a modern business plan of recruiting white racists around the nation. There were violent sectors within the KKK. During its first decade, the KKK had about four million members. This faded as insurrection and criminal activity occurred. However, starting in the 1960s, white nationalism grew in the United States as the conservative movement developed and became more mainstream.

The resurgence of white nationalism in the 1960s was likely a result of the Immigration and Nationality Act of 1965. White Americans feared losing their white Protestant, English-speaking, and European superior identity.

White nationalism developed into several subcultures during the 1980s. Some of these subgroups instituted radical ethnocentric characterizations incorporating mystical, religious, occult approaches in a defensive affirmation of white identity. These subgroups vary from reactive white politics to neofascists and neo-Nazis. Some have gone on to the national stage. Also included are conservative revolutionary groups, such as the European New Right. The religious right is also considered one of the subgroups.

Alt-right US conservatism originated in 2010; it developed as a Far Right incorporation of all nationalist groups and subgroups opposing traditional conservatism.

The second decade of the twenty-first century created a new resurgence of white supremacy when Donald J. Trump ran for president. It was very obvious that Trump was their leader. He was endorsed by various white nationalist and white supremacist movements and leaders. The former grand dragon of the KKK, David Duke, endorsed Trump in February 2016. Stephen Bannon's alt-right Breitbart News Network also supported Trump.

Leaders of the white nationalist alt-right, such as the National Policy Institute's Richard Spencer, editor of the neo-Nazi website the Daily Stormer, and Rocky Suhayda, chairman of the American Nazi Party, all had a platform to promote their racist agendas. President Trump supported all of these racist movements.

Other Republicans

This section encompasses modern or liberal Republicans. This Republican group is bicoastal. The Northeastern group is known as Rockefeller Republicans. Moderate Republicans have also been labeled Main Street Republicans or Business Conservatives or, by their conservative Republican critics, Republican in Name Only or RINOs.

Moderate Republicans believe in fiscal responsibility/conservatism and support social issues, such as affirmative action and civil/women's rights. Colin Powell, who served as secretary of state during the George W. Bush administration, was a moderate Republican who left the Republican Party in January 2021 after the insurrection at the US Capitol by white supremacists.

Center-right Republicans include South Park and Log Cabin Republicans who have slightly different policies.

After the second impeachment of President Donald J. Trump, those moderate Republicans who voted for impeachment were derogatorily called RINOs and were threatened with damage to their political careers.

Republican Hypocrisy and Heresy

Republicans have difficulty staying on their Christian path of moral ideology and values despite constantly promoting them. They are unable to follow the most rudimentary principles of the Ten Commandments and are guilty of lying, dishonesty, cheating, and then some.

Republicans claim fiscal responsibility, but President Regan cut taxes and spent huge sums of money on defense. The Iraq War placed us trillions of dollars in debt. But when the Democrats want to do something good for Americans, like the Biden-Harris 2021 Recovery Plan, the Republicans obstinately refute the cost.

Republicans proclaim to promote business. What they support is big business, but they do nothing for small business owners.

Republicans have been opposed to socialism (i.e., social issues) and slur the Democrats as socialists, yet social programs have been popular in the US.

Republicans are opposed to big government or the deep state. During the Trump administration and in the Tea Party faction, President Trump created the "shallow state," which was the most irresponsible and incompetent government in modern times.

Republicans are opposed to regulations, and with deregulations over the Trump era, there has been more damage to humans and the environment.

President Donald J. Trump's Followers

Trump's followers can best be described as sharing in mass delusional crowd theory as well as sheeple. Sheeple is a term that combines *people* with *sheep*. In simple terms, it means people that follow the herd (the majority).

The *Merriam-Webster Dictionary* defines the term as people who are docile, compliant, or easily influenced: people likened to sheep. It is a derogatory term describing the passive herd behavior of people easily controlled by a governing power of market fads. Sheeple can also voluntarily acquiesce to a suggestion or proclamation without any significant critical analysis or research.

The *Oxford Dictionary* claims the word originated in the 1940s. It was used by W.R. Anderson in his London newspaper column of the *Musical Times* in 1945. In his column, he wrote: "The simple truth is that you can get away with anything, in government. That covers almost all the evils of the time. Once in, nobody, apparently, can turn you out. The People, as ever (I spell it 'Sheeple'), will stand anything."

The term became more popular in the 1980s and '90s, especial on several radio programs, such as *Coast to Coast AM* by Art Bell. It became misused as antigovernment and conspiracy theories, not realizing sheeple was referring to them. The commentators failed to realize that sheeple meant that Americans had become complacent, tolerating or following bad policies. They failed to understand the sheeple follow the herd without thinking. It is another example of contagion crowd behavior theory.

Two hundred thirty-nine million people were eligible to vote in the 2020 presidential election, and roughly 66.1 percent of them submitted ballots, totaling about 158 million. Joe Biden received about eighty-one million votes, Trump about seventy-four million votes. The seventy-four million sheeple voting for Trump are a huge concern to the Republican Party, because without doing an analysis, they don't know the distribution of factions. If all were white nationalists, not only would the Republican Party have a problem, but the United States would need to address this problem. The Republican Party are sheeple who follow Donald Trump.

The means of overcoming sheeple is critical thinking. Critical thinking can be learned, but it can be difficult in some situations and at certain ages. Critical thinking is learned through a specific process of self-improvement called deliberate practice, and it can take a long time to master it. Obviously, presenting facts from nonfacts encourages critical thinking. It would be useful to have specialized classes in schools designed specifically to teach critical thinking at a young age. Educational institutions that don't want students to learn critical thinking are military and Christian schools. They want to maintain their doctrine without question. The other aspect of Trump followers can be explained by mass delusional crowd theory.

CHAPTER 10

RECOMMENDATIONS TO REFORM THE REPUBLICAN PARTY

The Republican Party would best serve its members by returning to classical liberalism and building the moderate Republican base. Over the past five decades, the Republicans in Congress have become progressively more corrupt, unethical, opinionated, and obstructionist. It reached the level of a frenzy when a crazed crowd of white nationalists stormed the US Capitol in an attempted insurrection. The Republican Party has become enamored with Trump and Trumpism. However, just because the seventy-four million sheeple (followers) voted for him does not mean they would not vote for a moderate, classical, liberal Republican.

Republican leaders need to grow up and develop healthy mental health. Obstructionism, opposition defiance, and antisocial behavior are all very negative and interfere with progress. Their childishness is not admirable and should be considered taboo.

Republicans should relinquish most of the conservative factions, except fiscal conservatism. But they should not be hypocritical on this one. Do something good like balance the budget each year and start figuring out ways the government can make money beside taxes.

Conservatism is a backward belief system of regressive and retrogressive beliefs. It lacks compassion and progress. America must get competitive, and that can only be done through progress. China began to lead in technology, finances, construction, and manufacturing. The Chinese are in Africa, holding Africa hostage, and in Southeast Asia. We need to be competitive, and the Republicans are obstructing progress. It would be wonderful to see Republicans agree with Democrats on progressive bills.

Facts: Republicans must start utilizing facts and denounce nonfactual disinformation, fiction, opinions, and conspiracy theories. This drama is a waste of time. It is nonfunctional, ignorant, dishonest, and addictive. This nonfactual information is rampant in conservative media and in right-wing misinformation on social media. It is also apparent in the Republican Congress. It is a dangerous business, but mega-money can be made despite a lack of responsibility and ethics.

Conspiracy theories and theorists should be denounced by the Republican Party. These theories are intentionally harmful to other persons. It is a form of nefariousism considered evil. To allow a conspiracy theorist in Congress is wrong. Proponents cite the First Amendment and the right to free speech, but what they fail to understand is that while people can say what they want, they are not protected from the consequences of their words.

Nature and the planet must be respected. Everyone should be a steward of the planet, because this is what God created. By trashing the planet, we are trashing God. This is God's experimental creation, starting with dinosaurs and winding up with humans.

Fossil fuels from oil drilling have caused significant global warming due to the greenhouse effect trapping heat close to the earth. Do Republicans believe oil is going to last forever? The oil companies are going to destroy the planet to get their last barrel of oil. It is already starting with oil companies drilling anywhere they please. This is one of the reasons the Republicans have been opposed to a Native American as secretary of interior. She will not allow them to drill anywhere they please.

How will we travel around the planet when there are no more fossil fuels? What about jet fuel? Has Boeing thought about building jets with alternative fuel, or is it more of the same jet planes? Greed doesn't care about the future; it only cares about the present.

The author created a rhyme for this purpose: ring around the rosie, a pocket full of cash, boo to the Republicans, for the earth they want to trash.

Presidents Abraham Lincoln and Theodore Roosevelt, both Republicans, were the two most conservationist presidents in history. What happened to the Republicans? Big business, greed, and disrespect for our planet are a few reasons. It is becoming apparent that global warming is in progress. Republicans would do good to once again align with these two presidents. Even President Nixon, who was corrupt, passed good laws to save the planet.

Republicans championed civil rights with and after President Lincoln. As the party became more conservative with whiter privilege, prejudice, and bias, everything changed. It reversed that which the Republican Party stood for in the beginning. African Americans have been protesting, seeking political offices, and preaching for their rights. This is ongoing and needs to continue. However, there is another group that has been left far behind: the indigenous Native Americans. They need to do the same protesting as African Americans. They also want to live without being oppressed. Like African Americans, they need better education and a better standard of living. They should be farming; after all, they were the first farmers of American soil. They need to have more representation in politics.

Although Trump's chaotic presidency is over, his white nationalism lives on, not only in white America but specifically in the Republican Party. The Republican forces that propelled his misinformation crisis to surge in white nationalism to a crackdown on voting rights remains a clear and present danger and threat to American democracy. The whiteness has become an addiction.

White nationalism, white supremacy, and Far Right fascism are evident in a radical, militant, and violent faction of the Republican

Party. None of these are found on the Democrat side, nor are they a part of liberalism. Republicans call Antifa radical and violent. They are ignorant to the fact that Antifa stands for antifascism. What civilized human being would not be opposed to fascism? Antifa groups show up at white supremacy rallies to bring attention to fascism. The violence that occurs at these rallies is caused by the white supremacists. An example is Charlottesville, where a white supremacist drove his car through a crowd, killing a young woman who was protesting fascism. President Trump's moral ineptitude failed to differentiate right from wrong.

The white supremacist insurrection at the US Capitol caused no Republican denouncement or shared responsibility. Instead, they once again played the blame game. They blamed it all on Antifa! The right objective for the Republican Party is to denounce these groups and take legal action against them.

Republicans acknowledge their faith in God as Christians. That being said, God created tremendous forms of diversity. Since God created Blacks, Asians, Indians, Jews, Persians, and so forth, why is it so difficult to accept people as humans and not hate? Reasoning suggests the only answer is there is no God, because humans have not followed God's program.

Republicans should discontinue their criticism of regulation and their promotion of deregulation. Their own president, Richard M. Nixon, established the Environmental Protection Agency. Their support of toxic chemical companies has created a deterioration in human health by *super fund* toxic sites. Companies like Kerr-McGee produced six toxic chemical super fund sites, without any oversight or regulations. And in Kerr-McGee's uranium plant, employees were not provided with protective gear. They were exposed to high levels of radiation, which is a death sentence. Karen Silkwood, a chemical engineer who raised concerns about the safety of these sites, was killed as a whistleblower.

If all American businesses used good moral and ethical practices to prevent harm to their employees and citizens, regulations would not be necessary. But greed at the expense of human health and well-being rules. Certain Americans do not understand that laws, recommendations, and regulations are initiated to prevent harm to *all* people. Ignorance and greed place Americans at risk for their health and safety. A recent example is wearing a mask to prevent transmitting the infection of COVID-19. The Republicans and libertarians tell us that wearing a mask invades their freedom. No, not wearing a mask is an invasion of everyone else's freedom. Using their argument, no one needs to wear a seat belt when one drives a car/vehicle. It's called regulation for one's self and others, and it has gone so far as the car manufacturers force us to wear seat belts. Has the seat belt not prevented their freedom? Since some people refuse to wear a mask, OSHA will require employees to wear masks in businesses. This shows how regulations originate.

The Republicans (the Tea Party group) love deregulation, because they can then abuse and destroy the planet and cause injury to employees. But they don't care since it is all about money.

Republicans should learn moral universalism. This is an ethical system of universality. It applies to all similarly situated individuals regardless of race, culture, sex, religion, nationality, sexual orientation, or ethnicity. Moral universal obligations are independent of feelings and beliefs. Moral obligation incorporates cognizant thinking. It incorporates moral realism, which is the view that there are facts about which actions are right and wrong and about which things are good and bad. Moral universalism incorporates ethical values, which are more factual. There is some overlap between moral and ethical values. Universal ethical values are honesty, integrity, trust, promise keeping, fairness, concern for others, respect for others, law abiding, commitment, accountability, courage, not stealing, not cheating, nonjudgmental, forgiveness, tolerance, and treating others as you want to be treated. Also included is social justice.

Do Donald J. Trump and his followers follow ethical universalism? No! Many of the Republican congresspeople also fail to apply these values.

Republicans need significant therapy. We lost some good ones like Abraham Lincoln, Theodore Roosevelt, Dwight D. Eisenhower, George H. W. Bush, John McCain, Mitt Romney, and other good Republicans to current nefariousism. When they want to claim they are the party of Lincoln, they should act like Abraham Lincoln. Lincoln was known as "Honest Abe," but current Republicans are no longer the party of honesty, facts, and moral obligations.

Recommendations to Improve American Democracy

Voting in America: For many, many years, gerrymandering has been a technique used to obtain votes for both parties. But the Republicans have abused it. The Republicans have used every corrupt means possible to win elections, including but not limited to voter suppression, fraud, limited ballot boxes, and restricted mail-in ballots, to name a few. But as soon as a Democrat wins fairly, they cry fraud. As a result of Trump's second-term loss, they have sworn revenge. They passed the most restrictive voter suppression laws in Republican-dominated states. Americans want fair elections. H.R. 1 is the first step to legitimate and legalized voting.

H.R. 1, also known as House Resolution 1 or the For the People Act, is a bill in the United States Congress aimed at expanding voting rights, changing campaign finance laws to reduce the influence of money in politics, limiting partisan gerrymandering, and creating new ethics rules for federal officeholders. This bill eliminates dark money donations to candidates, such as Citizens United and large PAC money, and allows American citizens to contribute, much like they did with the presidential campaign for Joe Biden.

The bill originated in the House in 2019 and finally passed on March 3, 2021. The obstructionist Senate will block this bill because of conservatism and a lack of factual, logical thinking.

Opponents of the bill are Republican conservatives. Anytime a bill is logical, reasonable, anticorruption, utilitarian, and good for Americans, they oppose it. One of their arguments opposing the bill contends that it was "designed to auto-enroll likely Democratic voters, enhance Democratic turnout, with no concern for ballot integrity." That is a lie, because voter integrity and prevention of corruption is written into the bill. The bill allows as many Republicans as Democrats to register and vote. Another opposition to the bill calls it a "radical assault on American democracy, federalism, and free speech." This represents opinion and not facts. That which they hate the most is that the bill subverts states from manipulating voter laws, and it would finally prevent states from making up their own rules for voter suppression. The Republicans have manipulated voting for years. Since Donald Trump lost in 2020, all Republican states are designing laws to favor their white Republican voters.

The Republican conservatives, such as the Heritage Foundation, argue that the bill is preventing the First Amendment right to free speech. The other argument is that it is unconstitutional to deny states their own rights and the power to oversee and regulate elections. Again, this is an unwarranted opinion. This argument is unsupported by facts. Their opinion is refuted by the Elections Clause in Article I, Section 4, of the Constitution, which gives the Congress the power "at any time" to "make or alter" state election regulations.

The most logical and convenient method of voting would be mail-in ballots, uniformly throughout each state. States like Colorado have proven this method to be safe, convenient, secure, and least likely to experience fraud. There could be a uniform ballot used by each state for the presidency with another state ballot for state races.

The Electoral College has made two huge mistakes in favor of the Republicans: dismissing Al Gore for president and electing Donald J. Trump. There is no longer a need for the Electoral College. It is biased and unfair and disregards the importance of the popular vote. Americans doubt voting when the Electoral College elects a president.

Media ethics and social media censorship: Media ethics is a division of applied ethics. The ethical applications set the principles and ethical standards for media to follow. It applies to all forms of media. Media ethics promotes and defends values, such as a universal respect for life and the rule of law/legality. Journalism has the highest standards of ethics, and the internet / social media the lowest. Some of the core issues of media ethics in online journalism include commercial pressures, accuracy, and credibility. This include the issues dealing with verification of facts, regulation, privacy, and news gathering.

An important issue in media is integrity. This refers to the ability of a media outlet to serve the public interest and democratic process, making it resilient to institutional corruption. This is where Fox News crosses the line. Censorship is present in newspapers, TV, film, and movies. Film and movies have ratings systems and supervision by agencies. Social media lacks censorship. When Mark Zuckerberg introduced Facebook, he brought the Dalai Lama to Silicon Valley to show the world that Facebook is an ethical platform. It has now become the Darth Vader of the internet. It has turned into a hate forum and has a cancel culture. Nefariousism should be eliminated from social media. President Trump was a prime example of dark, evil communication. Twitter finally eliminated his use of Twitter, which has created a more appealing social media platform.

Section 230 is a piece of internet legislation in the United States that was passed into law as part of the Communications Decency Act (CDA) of 1996, also commonly named for Title V of the Telecommunications Act of 1996, formally codified as Section 230 of the Communications Act of 1934 at 47 § 230.

As the internet became widely available, companies were sued for censorship and others who had no responsibility for their content. The issues involved were whether the internet companies were considered publishers (more responsibility and liability) or distributors. Section 230 arose to settle and prevent litigation. It provided internet service providers with safe harbors to operate as intermediaries of content without fear of being liable for that content as long as they took reasonable steps to delete or prevent access to that content.

Section 230, as passed, has two primary parts, both listed under §230(c) as the "Good Samaritan" portion of the law. Section 230(c)(1), as identified above, defines that an information service provider shall not be treated as a "publisher or speaker" of information from another provider. Section 230(c)(2) provides immunity from civil liability for information service providers that remove or restrict content from their services they deem "obscene, lewd, lascivious, filthy, excessively violent, harassing, or otherwise objectionable, whether or not such material is constitutionally protected," as long as they act "in good faith"

Section 230 has been challenged. Between 2001 and 2017, social media was used for sex trafficking on such sites as Craigslist, Facebook, MySpace, and others. When discovered, groups such as the National Center for Missing and Exploited Children forced these sites to remove these posts, which they did. Backpage then entered into the sex-trafficking sites. Lawsuits were filed, but Backpage used Section 230 to win their lawsuits.

Winning their lawsuit led Congress to pass laws against internet sex trafficking. Two bills were passed in 2017: FOSTA, the Fight Online Sex Trafficking Act, and the Senate bill, SESTA, the Stop Enabling Sex Traffickers Act, have been hailed by advocates as a victory for sex-trafficking victims. The FOSTA bill was independent of Section 230. However, the Stop Enabling Sex Traffickers Act (SESTA) from the US Senate bill introduced by Rob Portman (R-OH) in August 2017 combined the FOSTA-SESTA bills, which modified Section 230 to exempt service providers from immunity when dealing with civil or criminal crimes related to sex trafficking. This removes section 230 immunity for services that knowingly facilitate or support sex trafficking. This addition and combination of a law and Section 230 offers a president the ability to modify Section 230.

Over the past decade and especially during the Trump administration, Section 230 has come under scrutiny, especially by Republicans. Two of their issues include internet bias against conservatives and political conservatives (especially by the Big Ten, such as Google, Apple, and other large internet companies) and the promotion of liberalism by the large tech companies. They cite the fact that internet providers published facts about the Russian involvement in the 2016 election. But it was acceptable for Republican congressmen and Fox News to criticize and slander Hillary Clinton and her emails as corrupt.

In December 2018, Republican representative Louie Gohmert introduced the Biased Algorithm Deterrence Act (H.R. 492), which would remove all Section 230 protections for any provider that used filters or any other type of algorithms to display user content when otherwise not directed by a user.

The Republicans want to eliminate Section 230, and they are attempting to do this in the form of internet neutrality. Internet neutrality is the principle that internet service providers (ISPs) must treat all internet communications equally and not discriminate or charge differently based on user, content, website, platform, application, type of equipment, source address, and destination addresses. This is not related to content. The discrimination part has to do with ISP discrimination of another ISP. Republicans are again confused between Section 230 and internet neutrality, or they are misusing the term *neutrality*.

To Republicans, neutrality means conservatism dominance. They fail to self-realize there is more bias by conservatives against liberals than vice versa. Freedom's Watch has attempted to use antitrust laws to break up platforms like Google, because they argue that Google is opposed to conservatism. Their definition of internet neutrality would cause more political censorship by the Republicans, more lawsuits, and a free-for-all. Republicans fail to understand the background for Section 230, which arose out of significant case law on internet publishing versus distribution of material. Thus immunity was formed, and the lawsuits stopped.

The Republicans want to control any internet carrier who is considered liberal and is seen as anticonservative. They promote internet neutrality.

Senator Ted Cruz (R-TX) argues that Section 230 should only apply to providers that are politically neutral. This suggests that a provider should be considered a liable publisher or speaker of user content if they pick and choose what gets published or spoken. This sounds more like Republican control of content (a Republican fascist move) than neutrality. It also shows us that Ted Cruz cannot discern the difference between tech neutrality and Section 230.

In June 2019, Josh Hawley (R-MO) introduced the Ending Support for Internet Censorship Act (S. 1914) that would remove Section 230 protections. It would make the Big Ten internet media companies liable for any type of bias or censorship and allow small companies to be immune from any content. There could be ten small companies to one large tech company publishing all sorts of nefarious misinformation, which would keep them immune from liability.

On May 28, 2020, Trump signed Executive Order on Preventing Online Censorship (EO 13925), an executive order directing regulatory action at Section 230. President Trump stated that internet companies have unchecked power to censor, restrict, edit, shape, hide, and alter virtually any form of communication between private citizens and large public audiences. Therefore, his goal was to remove the Section 230 protections from such platforms. This would leave them open for censorship and monitoring. Any bias would be monitored by the Federal Communications Commission. In addition, he named about a half dozen other federal government agencies as additional mediators, including the US Department of Justice. The executive order would prompt numerous lawsuits.

One of the first lawsuits against the EO started with the Center for Democracy and Technology filed in June 2020 in the United States District Court for the District of Columbia. Meanwhile, Trump tweeted more abusive language and misinformation, which Twitter flagged, causing outbursts of anger from President Trump.

After the November 2020 election, which Joe Biden won, Trump profusely tweeted on Twitter and other social media that the election was rigged and fraudulent. Social media companies marked these posts as potentially misleading, similar to previous posts Trump had made. As a result, Trump threatened to veto the defense spending bill for 2021 if it did not contain language to repeal Section 230.

On January 6, 2021, President Trump led the insurgence on the US Capitol by radical white nationalist groups to try to overturn the election Biden had won fairly. He used social media to perpetrate the attempted coup. As a result, Twitter, Facebook, and other social media services blocked or banned Trump's accounts, claiming his speech during and after the riot incited further violence. Due to Section 230 immunity, Trump was unable to bring lawsuits against these companies. Although the actions of the social media companies were supported by many politicians, Section 230 was reviewed for other reasons.

Section 230 came under scrutiny for the communication of hate and incitement of the insurrection. The alternative issue was that politicians who were targeted in the riot wanted to reconsider Section 230, as these politicians believed that Section 230 led the companies to fail to take any preemptive action against the people who had planned and executed the Capitol riots.

Facts versus nonfacts or misinformation are a problem on the internet. This should be moderated, especially when the nonfactual information is harmful to individuals or the general population. Two main ethical and legal issues are hateful or nefarious language and the promotion of domestic violence.

There were several postings on the internet from the white supremacist killers associated with the shootings in a Pittsburgh synagogue, Christchurch, New Zealand, El Paso, Texas, and Gilroy, California, that created impact on Section 230 and liability toward online hate speech has been raised. These perpetrators posted hate speech manifestos to internet platforms such as 8chan and others, including image boards known to be favorable for the posting of hatred and extreme views. Does any logical and ethical person think this activity is responsible as a First Amendment "right"? The answer is that hate speech is generally protected speech under the First Amendment. Are there not ethical issues with the First Amendment that allows death to innocent American citizens? As a moral and ethical society, this type of speech crosses the line.

Hate speech, false accusations, and slanderous speech were moderated by Twitter regarding President Trump's harmful tweets about mail-in voter fraud. This enraged President Trump and caused him to complain that social media was biased against conservatives, and he wanted to eliminate Section 230 and regulate computer companies, creating company liability. This led him to write an executive order. This rhetoric is synonymous with an autocrat.

Trump's account was deactivated, which caused outrage. He was angry that his litigious greed could not be used against Twitter due to Section 230. This prompted an executive order to eliminate Section 230, which failed.

Domestic terrorism speech on the internet has also presented a problem for internet carriers, American citizens, the US Justice Department, and politicians.

Section 230 should not be eliminated but rather modified by adding new laws. There is a proceeding law to set precedent. The women sex-trafficking laws (combined FOSTA-SESTA) are an example of combining laws with Section 230. This can be done for nefarious and false content. For example, social media is providing misinformation about COVID-19 vaccinations, which prevents people from getting vaccinated. As a result, population (herd) immunity cannot be achieved. This delays eradication of the virus and allows more mutations. It prevents society from engaging in normal pre–COVID-19 activities.

Hate language, intentional character assassinations, conspiracy theories, excessive violence, harassing/bullying, or otherwise objectionable content should be monitored and removed. The outcry will be about First Amendment rights. There are censorship laws already established. Section 230(c)(2) already provides a law for monitoring nefarious internet content. For this reason, President Trump was unable to form his usual and customary lawsuits against Twitter and Facebook for removing his accounts.

A step further would be to monitor domestic violent groups and file charges for their activity. There must be a line drawn regarding First Amendment rights, since the constitutional creators never foresaw the power of the internet.

Internet carriers could also become responsible, using algorithms, artificial intelligence, and ethics committees made up of sociologists, ethicists, attorneys, religious leaders, and professors to decide on a monitoring process. There must be self-regulation and work with Congress to sort out all the hatred, harmful conspiracy theories, and violence on the internet.

The Federal Bureau of Investigation should troll the internet for domestic violence activity and act on it. Case law has made it difficult to hold social media companies accountable for allowing violence on their platforms. In the case *Force v. Facebook, Inc.*, 934 F.3d 53 (2nd Cir. 2019), the court ruled in favor of Facebook. While previous rules at the federal district and circuit court level have generally ruled against such cases, this decision in the second circuit was first to assert that Section 230 does apply even to acts related to terrorism that may be posted by users of service providers, thus dismissing the suit against Facebook. The Supreme Court refused the case. As a result, it has become apparent that Congress must pass reasonable laws.

It is time for censorship on social media. Section 230 could remain, but regulations are needed for social media and the internet. It is significant to digital censorship because it prevents anyone under eighteen from viewing information that is inappropriate or offensive. If someone under eighteen uploads anything inappropriate or offensive, they can be punished by law. It is interesting that adults care about children seeing things but ignore those who post the objectionable material.

Racism: White supremacy for the purposes of this book is defined as all forms of behavior oppressive to other races or ethnic groups, including hostile speech or action. Radical white supremacy is inclusive of white supremacy but differentiated due to inciting violence or force against a race. A prototype is the Ku Klux Klan.

Do we as a society need to pass more laws to stop this terrible injustice? White supremacy must come to an end after six hundred years in North America. African Americans have done well in their fight and battle against racism with previous civil rights leaders in the past, such as John Lewis. Although progress has been made, racial injustice remains apparent. African Americans have worked hard, but there are silent racists who, too, are concerning.

Native Americans are indigenous to North America. When European whites arrived in North America, many showed their supremacy by massive killings of Native Americans. Then they decided to give them land as reservations, to essentially provide additional control. The US gave land to the Native Americans that was similar to their original environment (homeland). The demoralization of Native Americans is shameful. White people denigrate Native Americans for alcoholism and drug use. Let's put some white folks on reservations and see how well they function!

Columbus called the indigenous people Indians because he falsely believed he was in Indonesia, which held for centuries and had a negative connotation. And white people are so proud of calling sports teams Indians! White people did their best to eradicate them from North America. The Trail of Tears is one example, as well as massacres in the West. And Hollywood made movies and TV shows that made Indians look bad.

The Trail of Tears occurred in 1838 when sixteen thousand Native Americans were forcibly marched over 1,200 miles from the southeastern US westward over rugged terrain. More than four thousand died of disease, famine, and warfare. They were moved from their homelands in the southern United States to Indian Territory in Oklahoma (an environment unlike their homeland). Indigenous peoples from the Cherokee, Muscogee, Chickasaw, Choctaw, and Seminole tribes were forced to march at gunpoint. The disgusting irony is that white people in Oklahoma named towns after the tribes. The Cherokee suffered most of their deaths as they traveled through southern Illinois.

The Trail of Tears was created by President Andrew Jackson (a Democratic Republican from Tennessee), who signed the Indian Removal Act. Jackson was a white supremacist. There were a few members of Congress, like Davy Crockett, who argued that Jackson violated the Constitution by refusing to enforce treaties that guaranteed Indian land rights.

It is never ending for Native Americans. The Republicans opposed the confirmation of Native American Deb Haaland as secretary of interior (though she was eventually confirmed). They run oil pipelines over Native lands and drill even when Native Americans oppose it.

The white southern landowners brought Africans to America to work on their farms as slaves but continue to hate their descendants. The white farm owners in California brought Hispanics to work on their farms but then show hatred toward them. What more must be done to stop this evil? Religions failed and are part of the problem. Is the answer behavior modification through regulations like wearing seat belts to form an ethical, empathetic, caring, loving society?

There has been similar treatment toward Asians in the United States. An example is the Japanese internment camps. Japanese American internment happened during World War II when the United States government forced about 110,000 Japanese Americans to leave their homes and live in internment camps, which were essentially prisons. Many of the people who were sent to internment camps had been born in the United States and were American citizens.

Missionaries and diplomats brought Chinese to America in the mid-1800s. The diplomats brought them to perform labor. They migrated to the US and helped build the first transcontinental railroad. After they helped build the railroad, anti-Chinese sentiment began. This led the federal government to pass the Chinese Exclusion Act of 1882. This banned any future immigration from China and prevented naturalization, another white supremacist act.

One of the main causes for hatred was that Chinese were hard workers and laborers. The hatred was strong, and it led to massacres and murders. The same proclamation made against Black men raping white women was used against Chinese men.

The slanderous term *yellow peril* was popularized by William Randolph Hearst in his *San Francisco Chronicle* newspaper. Chinese racism continues. Some of the hatred is due to China becoming an economic world power. More recently in 2020 with the COVID-19 pandemic, more hatred has developed against Asians because President Trump fueled this hatred by referring to COVID-19 as the "China virus."

Both Blacks and Chinese did not migrate willingly to the US. They were brought to America through labor trafficking by white people and by their churches. Labor trafficking continues today, especially in the Southwest and California. Hispanics are brought in to do all sorts of labor that white people do not want to do. When will white Americans stop their xenophobic hatred and learn acceptance?

Preservation of democracy: President Trump and his administration breached the boundaries of the Constitution. He bribed Ukraine, ignored subpoenas, misappropriated funds, illegally spent taxpayers' money, ignored laws, supported white nationalists, levied inappropriate pardons, and so forth. This insurrection at the Capitol resulted in a slew of bills to limit presidential power. For every bad action, there can be a good result. In September 2020, House Democrats introduced the Protecting Our Democracy Act—a landmark reforms package that will prevent future presidential abuses, restore our system of checks and balances, strengthen accountability and transparency, and protect our elections.

Included in these reforms is the Congressional Power of the Purse Act, introduced by House Budget Committee chairman John Yarmuth, which will reassert Congress's Article I spending authorities and safeguard our nation's separation of powers.

One of the most blatant abuses was cabinet members wasting taxpayer money on lavish, expensive trips, overpriced office furniture, soundproofing offices, and other abuses—and there was no criticism by the fiscal conservative Republicans.

The most devious action was the pardons of all of the Republican criminals in prisons. When Trump issued these pardons, it became evident that laws should be passed for presidents to provide a list of names to the House Judiciary Committee for a vote that would then go to the attorney general. The Protecting Our Democracy Act addresses this abuse of the presidential pardon similarly. Any presidential pardons must be submitted to the US Justice Department for evaluation. Therefore, legal opinion decides, not the president. Naturally, the Republicans oppose this, because when a Republican president is in office, they can no longer release their corrupt cronies from prison.

In order to make democracy fair and transparent, there should be no exchange of money by lobbyists to legislators. It should be a criminal offense for lobbyists to pass bills in their favor. This cronyism is in part the reason Republicans block good utilitarian bills that would help Americans.

First Amendment rights: The First Amendment to the US Constitution protects the freedom of speech, religion, and the press. It also protects the right to peaceful protest and to petition the government. These are important rights, because totalitarian governments prevent these human principles. President Trump tried to intervene in some of these human rights. Supporters have been blind to his attempts.

The meaning of the First Amendment has been the subject of continuing interpretation and dispute over the years. Not all speech is protected. The United States Free Speech Exceptions by the Supreme Court ruled on categories of speech that are given lesser or no protection by the First Amendment. Speech that is considered restricted includes fraud, child pornography, speech integral to illegal conduct, speech that incites imminent lawless action, speech that violates intellectual property law, true threats, sedition, words of violence, classified information, copyright violation, trade secrets, and food labeling.

Other restrictions to free speech are laws against libel, slander, and defamation, including statements that harm the reputation of another. Therefore, the First Amendment does not promise anyone the right to say whatever one wants. The issue with social media relates to establishing monitoring and protection of others' rights.

Censorship is the suppression of speech, public communication, or other information. This may be done on the basis that such material is considered objectionable, harmful, sensitive, hateful, violent, or unlawful. Censorship can be conducted by governments, private institutions, and other controlling bodies.

All of these issues concern social media. It would seem logical for them to self-regulate to prevent censorship laws or government intervention. This could be done through the user agreement, not in fine print but in bold lettering. They could create an organization that self-regulates. Medical groups often self-regulate. This prevents government interference and ensures a higher quality of medical care. Something must be done. Otherwise countries like Australia eliminate Facebook, because of its dark side. This is not difficult; it's called ethical standards.

Second Amendment rights and gun control: The Second Amendment was part of the Bill of Rights that was added to the Constitution on December 15, 1791. This amendment protects the rights of citizens to bear arms or own weapons such as guns. Back then, all that was available were single-shot muskets, not semiautomatic human-killing machine guns. This was obviously a bad amendment but good at the time! Since the adoption of the Constitution and the Bill of Rights, it has been amended seventeen times to reflect changes to our society over the past 230 years. This translates into a new amendment every thirteen years. Republicans, please tell Americans how this is a perfect right. Unfortunately, innocent Americans die each year from guns. Does anyone think the writers of this amendment intended for its citizens to be killed?

The alcohol prohibition of the 1920s produced bootlegging gangs such as Al Capone's. These gangs used short-barreled machine guns with silencers to kill anyone interfering with their business. This led Congress to pass the National Firearms Act of 1934 (NFA) that requires the registration with the federal government of fully automatic firearms (termed "machine guns"), rifles, and shotguns that have an overall length under twenty-six inches, rifles with a barrel under sixteen inches, shotguns with a barrel under eighteen inches, and firearm sound suppressors. This law is intact today, but states can modify the act. There is also no central federal repository for guns. The NFA falls under the Bureau of Alcohol, Tobacco, Firearms and Explosives founded on July 1, 1972.

Military-style guns were in development in the 1950s and '60s. Colt developed the M-16 military rifle for use by the troops in the Vietnam War. Colt also got approval from the Bureau of Alcohol, Tobacco, and Firearms to commercially sell a semiautomatic rifle they named AR-15. This rifle was patented, and Colt ramped up production. Other gunmakers produced their own automatic rifles when the Colt patent expired. They sell for $1,000 and higher.

The United States cannot produce an accurate number of automatic rifles present in the country, but estimates range from ten to fifteen million. There is a problem with registration. It might be good to start a national repository for military-style assault rifles.

Why anyone wants this type of gun is beyond comprehension. Victims have filed lawsuits against the gun manufacturers, but that possibility was halted with Protection of Lawful Commerce in Arms Act. This law grants gun manufacturers immunity from certain types of lawsuits when their weapons are used in criminal acts. This law essentially gives gun manufacturers the right to kill innocent Americans. There must be responsibility and accountability. This is another example of greed and unethical irresponsibility in the US by the Republicans. Otherwise, they would do something about it, other than block bills to limit mass murders. Background checks are a start, but these military-style rifles should go back to the military.

Most mass shootings in the US are carried out by white men, yet many Republicans refuse to call this domestic terrorism.

The Public Safety and Recreational Firearms Use Protection Act, commonly called the federal Assault Weapons Ban (AWB and AWB 1994), was signed into law by President George H.W. Bush in September 1994. The ban, including a ban on high-capacity magazines, became defunct (expired) in September 2004 per a ten-year sunset clause. Conservative Republicans failed to reinstate the law. However, current states that ban assault weapons are New Jersey, Connecticut, Hawaii, Maryland, Massachusetts, and New York. Most also prohibit magazines of more than ten rounds.

There are those who want to repeal the Second Amendment, but this would create more problems. Repealing the Second Amendment would not give government the power to amend or infringe on the rights guaranteed by the Second Amendment. It would merely remove the prohibition. Most gun control proposals could still be fought on other grounds. Scholars state most opposition to gun control measures is not based on the Second Amendment as it stands.

Additional comments:

- A proposal: The challenge in psychology, psychiatry, and neurophysiological research is to better understand antisocial personality disorders. This diagnosis is broad and too general for diagnosis and treatment purposes. We attempted to form a distinction between sociopathy/sociopathology and psychopathy. Genetic testing, neurochemistry, and functional magnetic resonance imaging should be done to make a behavioral and diagnostic

distinction. It would appear that sociopaths and sociopathoids could be rehabilitated. On the other hand, psychopaths may not.
- We need to teach facts versus nonfacts in our educational institutions. This could be a special class in primary and secondary education that explains the difference. We should teach young people critical thinking so they can make wise choices in life.
- We must teach civics beginning in middle school. We must teach American history, comprehensive history that teaches both the good and bad things Americans have done. However, we should teach that democracy is the best form of government. Children in high school should also be exposed to Russian, European, Chinese, and Southeast Asian history. They should learn about the different forms of government, such as socialism, communism, totalitarianism, fascism, and so forth. One of the best ways to teach children that democracy is the best form of government is to expose them to other forms, which helps them understand how fortunate they are to be living in a democracy. In addition, critical race theory provides an understanding of the radical racism in the history of America, including the genocide of the Native Americans.
- We could teach universal principles, such as truth, love, respect, compassion, acceptance, responsibility, honesty, mindfulness, meditation, moral aptitude, and knowledge in our school curriculum. Most all of these are found in all religions, so why must we brainwash children with a specific religion? The philosopher Immanuel Kant proposed universal laws of morality and nature. Nature should be included in the universal principle category, since we are the stewards of the planet that God created, and nature has tremendous forces greater than we can control. Kant's analysis of the common moral concepts of *duty* and *goodwill* led him to believe that we are free and autonomous as long as morality itself is not an illusion. We should study the philosophers of the sixteenth, seventeenth, eighteenth, and nineteenth centuries to learn the many intellectual struggles of morality and ethics humans were presented with during this time of history.

- Americans need a clear amendment that separates church from state. Yes, this means more laws, but perhaps that is needed to keep our democracy in order and out of harm's way. The originators of the Constitution could not see the future.
- We must become stewards of the planet Earth. Most religions do not have love for our planet. But regardless of anyone's religion, God in all its power and forces created what we have, and we cannot afford to be stupid about our planet. It is our home; it is what God or whatever forces in the universe created. Republicans will pay a significant price for their greed and disregard for what God created. One can pray, go to a house of worship, and perform all of the rituals related to religion, but if we ignore all of the forces of God's Earth, the next generations will bear the destruction we have been doing for years. It is already happening.

The greenhouse effect is caused by the atmospheric accumulation of gases such as carbon dioxide, methane, and other entrapped gases. These gases form a layer or veil around the planet. One can imagine this enclosure around the earth, similar to a greenhouse. When the sun's energy reaches the earth's atmosphere, some of the heat energy is absorbed, and some of it is reflected back to space. The reflected sun's energy that travels back to space gets trapped under the veil of gases, reheating the earth. After seventy years of research, why is this being denied? Oil, the cause of excessive carbon dioxide, prevents Republicans from doing anything because of super PACs like Citizens United.

With President Biden's infrastructure bill, the Republicans should say, "I'll raise you one, and we will propose adding two trillion dollars to get more infrastructure issues accomplished." However, fighting, obstruction, blame, oppositional defiance, and opinion are the standard operating procedure of Republicans. The argument is not money when the Republicans spent trillions on wars in the past three decades and spend on frivolous things like border walls. How many Republican recessions have the Democrats reversed?

Taxes: No one wants to pay taxes, but there is no way around it unless you're Donald Trump. There are a few issues regarding taxes. The

Republicans want them low, and the Democrats want them fair. I think the American people would not have a problem with taxes if they knew the money was used responsibly and not corruptly and irresponsibly as with the Trump administration. Also, Americans personally balance their budgets, so the US government should do the same. Billion- and trillion-dollar companies pay less than small businesses. Instead of greed, can we have responsibility and fairness?

Big government: So many Americans are paranoid about big government. That being said, these people should go live in a totalitarian country and experience fear. In our democracy, we can petition and litigate the government for wrongful actions. A democratic government should be viewed as a family. The government is the parents, and the citizens are the children. What do good parents want for their children? They want them to have shelter, food, safety, education, morality, and fun and to be successful and happy. The Republicans have not become good parents. They create fear, bully, punish, blame, lie, corrupt, indoctrinate, and harm their children. Republicans identify themselves as the moral majority, but with all the corruption in the Republican Party and very little in the Democratic Party, it's apparent that the Democrats have become the moral majority.

Job Description for a US President

Most businesses provide job descriptions for employees. People working in government have job descriptions. Why do Americans not care about a job description for our president?

The following are suggestions for responsibilities and qualities a president should display:

1. Must be intelligent and knowledgeable. Base all information on facts. He/she must be able to educate Americans with political, scientific, social, and general knowledge.
2. Moral and ethical individual. Religious background must not interfere with political practices.

3. He or she must exhibit empathy, because Americans will naturally face harmful, emotionally difficult, and life-and-death situations.
4. He/she must have at least five years of experience in government. No more Hollywood stars, TV reality stars, singers, or businesspeople (unless they have ten years of experience in government).
5. Must communicate proficiently and articulate plans and policies for the American people.
6. He or she must have humility—not the passive kind taught by fundamentalist religion but the kind whereby he/she can admit mistakes.
7. Must be connected to competent, experienced, intelligent persons who can help him or her make tough decisions.
8. Must be mentally as well as physically healthy.
9. Must have all qualities of leadership as noted below.

According to the Center for Creative Leadership, great leaders consistently possess these ten core leadership skills:

1. Integrity
2. Ability to delegate
3. Communication
4. Self-awareness
5. Gratitude
6. Learning agility
7. Influence
8. Empathy
9. Courage
10. Respect

Other leadership groups also add:

- honesty
- confidence

- inspire others
- commitment and passion
- good decision-making
- accountability
- creativity and innovation
- reliance
- emotional intelligence
- humility
- transparency
- vision and purpose

The Center for Creative Leadership also lists five qualities of effective leaders:

1. They are self-aware and prioritize personal development.
2. They focus on developing others.
3. They encourage strategic thinking, innovation, and action.
4. They are ethical and civic-minded.
5. They practice effective cross-cultural communication.

Americans must learn to think critically when electing the president and congresspeople.

Summary

There are those who will say that I am being too critical and unrelenting of the behavior and direction of the Republican Party. The intent is not to cause further polarization but to present the facts. Facts tell the truth. The main concern is that there is a cancer culture that has developed in the Republican Party that requires surgical excision. It is malignant culture that has metastasized much like a contagious infection/virus. It has all of the features of contagion, convergence, deindividuation, mimetic, and mass delusional crowd theories. Awareness of crowd behavior should help lead the change, because the Republican Party and congresspeople have become a threat to democracy. This is intended to bring about change. It is meant to create awareness of the problems. As with business culture, change can only come from the top. Leaders of the Republican Party must make these changes, and a good start is denouncing Donald J. Trump, unless the Republican Party wants to be the party of nefariousism and the Democrats the party of utilitarianism and morality.

There are many historians, civic people, and scholars who recognize the same problems. In psychotherapy, one must be made aware of the mental problem as to formulate methods to correct the problem. I have presented the problem, and it needs to be treated.

The current white conservative nationalistic direction is not healthy for democracy. It involves regressive thinking and behavior that prevents progress we need in this country for global competition. We can never have another four years like the Trump administration. It was chaotic, corrupt, misguided, reckless, shameful, and dangerous to our Constitution and to the American people.

General References

1. Google—searches and fact-finding
2. Wikipedia—general and specific information
3. Online Encyclopedia Britannica
4. Stanford Encyclopedia of Philosophy
5. Centers for Disease Control and Prevention website
6. WebMD
7. Mayo Clinic website
8. Psychology Today website
9. Oxford Dictionary and Lexico website
10. Miriam-Webster Dictionary website
11. National Medical Library, PubMed website
12. Various National Institutes of Health websites

Other specific references were made in different chapters to support specific facts.

CPSIA information can be obtained
at www.ICGtesting.com
Printed in the USA
JSHW021316030323
38403JS00001B/10

9 781665 727556